Surety Bonds

SURETY BONDS

Nature, Functions, Underwriting Requirements

By

EDWARD C. LUNT, A.M.

Vice-President and Head of the Bonding Department,
The Fidelity and Casualty Company of New York;
Member of the New York Bar

NEW YORK
THE RONALD PRESS COMPANY
1922

Copyright, 1922, by
THE RONALD PRESS COMPANY

All Rights Reserved

PREFACE

When the gentleman in one of Molière's comedies was asked whether he knew Latin, he replied, "Oh yes, I know Latin, very well; but please proceed exactly as if I didn't." In writing this book I have assumed that my readers will be like the man in the comedy—they will know all about bonds, of course, but will nevertheless not mind my proceeding precisely as if they didn't. I have not hesitated, therefore, to handle the subject in an elementary way, and to make things as plain and simple as I could.

I have tried to cover all the classes of bonds that are frequently called for and some additional kinds, that, though not common, present special points of interest or difficulty. In the case of each class treated I have tried to show, first, what purpose the bond serves in the business, legal, or political world; and secondly, in more or less detail, according to the importance of the subject, what considerations and principles control the underwriting of the given class of bonds. These two aims, indeed, are so closely related as to amount, in reality, only to different aspects of the same subject—the science of underwriting; because in order to underwrite a bond intelligently and safely, one must know first of all why the obligee desires a bond, then what the danger is in the given situation against which the bond safeguards him, and finally what the thing is all about anyway.

Students of the science of suretyship understand and sympathize with the college professor who devoted his life to a study of the Greek alphabet, and who, at the close of his long and learned career, lamented the fact

that he had not confined his researches to a single letter
of the alphabet, preferably gamma or epsilon. Similarly, surety executives, whose positions require them to
effect some sort of limited mastery of the entire vast
field of suretyship, envy the fortunate underwriters
whose narrower spheres of duty enable them to study
exhaustively a small division of the subject. The classification of surety bonds used by the companies for statistical purposes embraces about one hundred divisions of
risks, with about three hundred subdivisions. Two of
these classes, constituting a group of cognate risks, include bonds given in attachment, replevin, injunction,
supersedeas, *lis pendens*, libel, bail, mechanics' lien, and
a broad variety of other legal proceedings. Two other
classes include the bonds given by executors and administrators, guardians *ad litem*, testamentary trustees, and
similar fiduciaries. Some of the remaining ninety-or-so
classifications are equally abstruse and hard to master.

In order, for example, to underwrite court bonds with
dispatch and safety, one should be a lawyer, or in any
event must know a good deal of law. No one, likewise,
should undertake the conduct of a large fiduciary department unless he is well versed in probate law, and understands surrogate practice; because every hour in the day
questions will arise and decisions must be made that
cannot be adequately cared for without such knowledge.
In the contract-bond department wide and varied business and technical information is essential to successful
underwriting, and rare judgment, of course, as well. In
the depository-bond department a knowledge of banking,
economics, and business affairs generally is a necessary
part of an underwriter's equipment; and sound judgment is no less essential here also, in analyzing bank statements and in making final decisions upon all the known

facts. In the fidelity department professional and technical training is of less importance; but here the underwriter should be a past master in the art of reading and understanding human nature in all its manifold moods; and he must be a keen psychologist.

While surety underwriting is thus a difficult and complex business, few subjects, on the other hand, are more interesting. One of the pleasantest features of the surety calling is the fact that it touches upon life at so many points and angles; a surety man may reasonably say with the old Roman dramatist, "Everything that pertains to life is of concern to me."

I hope that the "Tabular Index" constituting the Appendix of the book will prove of value to fieldmen and others requiring ever-ready help in time of trouble. I have tried to assemble there, in convenient and understandable form, a table of references to various passages in the book containing the essential information that a fieldman should have in order to handle efficiently any bond likely to come up in the day's work.

Parts of Chapter III were originally written for *The Weekly Underwriter* and for the American School of Correspondence respectively, and part of Chapter VII first appeared in the *Insurance Age*. Some of the other matter in the book was taken, with numerous changes, from articles originally contributed to the house organ published by the Fidelity and Casualty Company. The publishers of these periodicals have kindly authorized the re-use of the material.

EDWARD C. LUNT

New York City,
   July 1, 1922

CONTENTS

CHAPTER I

PRELIMINARY AND GENERAL TOPICS

1. The Origin of Corporate Suretyship

The first attempt to organize a company to insure the fidelity of employees seems to have been made in London, in 1720, at a place known as "Devil Tavern"—an appropriate birthplace, perhaps, for such a piece of business. *The London Daily Post* made the announcement as follows:

> Whereas, notwithstanding the many excellent laws now in force for punishing hired servants for robbing their masters or mistresses, yet noblemen as well as commoners are daily sufferers; and seldom a session but great numbers are convicted, to the utter ruin of many families, as also a scandal to the Christian religion. This is to give notice that at the request of several housekeepers, books will be opened next Saturday at the Devil Tavern, Charing Cross, at ten o'clock, wherein any person may subscribe, paying 6 pence p. c. for a share called a one thousand pound stock; no more shares than 3,000 and the call for the stock not to exceed 10*s* p. c. the first year by quarterly payments. This society will insure to all masters and mistresses whatever loss they shall sustain by theft from any servant that is ticketed and registered in this society.

These ambitious promoters were a century or more ahead of their time, and it was not until 1840 that a company was organized for the writing of fidelity insurance —a company entitled the "Guarantee Society of London." At first the venture was viewed with disfavor by many people otherwise sensible, and objections were made that seem curious now. It was maintained, for example, that the business would not succeed because an employer would not engage a person who could give only

3

the security of a corporation. "The moral security is wanting," was the concrete form of the objection. This view proved to be altogether mistaken, and the business of corporate suretyship has so far expanded in England that numerous companies are now operating there.

In this country fidelity insurance was late in arriving and slow to take root. As far back as 1853 the New York legislature enacted a law authorizing the formation of fidelity insurance corporations, but no one cared to avail himself of the enabling act for twenty-two years. In 1875 the present Fidelity and Casualty Company was chartered (under another name), and began operations three years later, becoming thus the first company organized in the United States to issue fidelity bonds. A few years before that, however, the Guarantee Company of North America had been organized in Canada, and it began to write business there in 1872 and in the United States in 1881. In 1884 the American Surety Company started its successful career, the Fidelity and Deposit Company in 1890, the United States Fidelity and Guaranty Company in 1896, the National Surety Company in 1897, and so on. Since the early days of the business a large number of companies, many of them unhappily extinct, have entered the lists. Today there are about twenty-five companies engaged in active competition for fidelity and surety business in all parts or in many parts of the country, while a number of other companies do a local bonding business.

2. Parties to a Bond

There are three parties to every bond—the *principal*, the person who is primarily liable; the *surety* (also called *obligor*), who guarantees that the principal will not default upon his undertaking, whatever it may be; and the *beneficiary* (also called *obligee*), in whose favor the bond runs. The principal upon a given bond is the most important man in the world to the surety so far as that particular bond is concerned, since the surety cannot sustain any loss if the principal meets his obligations. It is desirable, of course, to deal always with trustworthy people, and sometimes a bond is more or less open to suspicion because of the character of the obligee; but a bond is sometimes commended to an underwriter on the ground that the *beneficiary* is a strong corporation, when the real point is that the *principal* is altogether too weak for the given risk.

3. Difference between Suretyship and Insurance

Most insurance agents do not at first realize the profound difference between insurance and suretyship as regards the underwriter's attitude toward risks and his reasonable expectation of loss. In the case of ordinary insurance the underwriter as a matter of course takes all the risk, while in the case of suretyship, pure and simple, the bonding company takes, theoretically, no risk whatever. That is one reason why in the case of companies transacting both surety and casualty lines the bonding departments are able to carry along their organizations so handsomely notwithstanding the grievous handicap of the casualty divisions! When surety bonds are issued, a principal, presumed to be abundantly good for the amount of liability assumed in his behalf, always stands between the bonding company and loss; and in addition, in a considerable percentage of cases, cash collateral or its equivalent further secures the company. It is easy to see why this must be so. Appeals from legal decisions, for example, are said to be lost on the average three times out of four; and in many other cases the contingency covered by the bond occurs in at least 75 per cent of the actual instances. If, therefore, these bonds were written upon the theory of insurance (the accumulation of a premium fund sufficient to pay losses and expenses and leave a small profit), it is obvious that the premium charge would need to be, not 1 per cent or so of the bond amount as now (frequently less), but 75 per cent, before even losses were cared for, not to speak of acquisition and overhead costs. In fact, what are called for convenience "premiums" upon surety bonds are really not premiums at all in the insurance sense, but are only *service fees*. Somebody needs credit badly, and a surety company, if properly secured, will provide this credit, lending to the debtor the responsibility of its seal and signature, in return for a microscopic (comparatively) service fee.

While all the foregoing applies without qualification to the more important classes of surety bonds, it has limited applicability to fidelity bonds and hardly any to many kinds of license and similar bonds. When, therefore, it is said of certain bonds that they are "written on an insurance basis," the reference is to this aspect of the matter—to the fact that underwriters expect to pay their losses from a fund saved for the purpose from the premiums collected, rather than from collateral furnished by principals when the bonds are issued, or from cash secured upon the occurrence of loss from responsible principals or indemnitors.

4. Difference between Fidelity and Surety Bonds

Some violent political partisan said that, while every horse-thief was undoubtedly a Democrat, it did not follow that every Democrat was a horse-thief. Similarly, while every fidelity bond is likewise a surety bond, the converse is not necessarily true. Any written agreement executed with certain formalities whereby one party becomes surety for another is a surety bond. Sometimes such an instrument makes the surety guarantee the fidelity of a person, and in such a case it is a fidelity bond. Sometimes the guarantee is not one of fidelity only, but is much broader, while still including fidelity; and sometimes the instrument of suretyship has little or nothing to do with fidelity, but guarantees that the person will perform a certain contract, or will pay a stated amount in the event of a given contingency, and so on. In these two latter classes of obligations the instrument is a surety bond. While fidelity bonds constitute an important part of the business written by the companies, surety bonds are more numerous, harder to underwrite as a class, and much more important generally.

Bonds of suretyship are infinite in variety and number. Hundreds of well-defined species of bonds have flourished for years, and additions to their number are created continually, with the increasing complexity and ever-improving organization and conduct of business. All these bonds serve a useful and beneficent, and frequently an extremely important, purpose, protecting public and private obligees against loss and trouble in all the affairs of life. Many situations otherwise awkward in a high degree are quickly, easily, and inexpensively cared for by means of a surety bond.

5. Indemnitors

An indemnitor is a person who executes an indemnity agreement in behalf of a certain principal upon a certain bond whereby he undertakes to reimburse the surety company for any loss sustained in connection with such bond. When a principal is quite unworthy, on his own merits, of suretyship, it is rarely advisable to bond him *merely* because outside indemnity, even of a presumably good character, is offered. That is so because experience shows that in the event of trouble the indemnitor will frequently seek to escape liability, and will sometimes find means of doing so. On the other hand, in border-line cases (that is, where the principal is *not* altogether unworthy of suretyship), good indemnity will sometimes turn the scales in favor of the bond, particularly where the indemnitor has some connection with the matter occasioning the bond that makes it advantageous to him to have the bond written. A contractor, for example, may be trying to obtain a bond, and the indemnitor may be a manufacturer of material needed by the contractor in the given work; and the situation may be such that the manufacturer, by becoming an indemnitor upon the bond, will obtain a large and profitable order. The principal, again, may be a small and close corporation, not heavily capitalized, but thought to be good for its obligations because of the high character and experience of the men connected with it; and in any such case almost all underwriters would think it highly appropriate, and from their point of view quite necessary, for these men to execute indemnity agreements in behalf of the surety company in connection with any bond that the close corporation might require.

When the proposed indemnitor is a corporation, extreme care must be exercised to make sure that the indemnity agreement executed by the corporation is legally valid. A resolution passed by the board of directors referring specifically to the given indemnity agreement may be necessary.

Surety companies are asked at times to issue a bond upon a married woman's agreement to indemnify them in case of loss. The conditions are rarely such that underwriters feel able to assume a risk in reliance upon such indemnity. It is sometimes certain, and at other times probable, that the proposed indemnity would be valueless for the purpose intended. Even if the underwriters could satisfy themselves, by laborious research, that the common law in the given state had been so far changed as to enable married women to become sureties, they would still feel reluctant to assume a liability unacceptable on its merits because of the receipt of a married woman's indemnity. It would not be pleasant, even if it might be legally practicable, to enforce collection from such an indemnitor in the event of a claim under the bond.

6. Collateral Security

In many cases surety companies are not willing to issue a given bond unless they first receive good collateral security. It is evident from the questions frequently asked in these cases, and from the nature of the collateral offered, that many agents do not understand what sort of security is requisite. When the circumstances are such as to make collateral necessary, it is clearly not in order to offer security that is either of doubtful value or is of known incommensurate value—disproportionate to the amount of the bond involved. Even if the security offered equals in value the amount of the risk, yet if it is known only to a small class of local investors, it is of doubtful acceptability, and is never of instantaneous, telegraphic acceptability.

Generally speaking, what an underwriter means by "good collateral security" is cash, savings-bank books, certificates of deposit, Liberty Bonds, or standard stocks or bonds regularly listed and quoted on the leading exchanges—instruments (these latter) whose worth would either be well known to anyone who was familiar with security values or could be readily ascertained by such a person.

Underwriters are continually asked to accept as security mortgages upon real estate; and they are continually compelled to reply that such security will not serve the purpose. Surety companies require collateral only when it is by no means unlikely that they will be called upon to pay, or when it is necessarily assumed (in the case of appeal bonds, for example) that they will surely have to pay; and in either case it is essential that they have in their possession in advance something to pay with when the fatal hour arrives. Obviously when the attorney writes that the principal has lost his case (as he did in the court below), and demands a check for the amount of the judgment and accumulated costs "immediately if not sooner," there is no time for the surety company to go out and try to find a buyer of the mortgage. Moreover, in the rare cases when in the event of loss upon the bond the underwriter has a chance to draw a breath or two before drawing his check, there are still difficulties in the way of taking real-estate mortgages as security. How is the surety company to know that the mortgage is a first one? And if that fact is established, how is it to know that the property is worth the amount of the mortgage? Obviously, again, an expert independent appraisal would always be in order in such cases, and a title-company search and certificate as well. For numerous reasons, therefore, real-estate mortgages are not acceptable as collateral security.

7. Refunds of Premium

Refunds are not nearly so common in the surety field as they are in most lines of insurance, and fieldmen should be careful not to make refunds unless they are sure that such a course is altogether in order. Frequently the Rate Manual states explicitly that a refund is, or that it is not, permissible. Sometimes the bond form itself requires the surety company to make a refund under certain conditions—this is frequently so in the case of fidelity bonds. If the bond form is silent on the point, as it usually is, and if the Manual throws no light upon it, the question should be taken up with the home-office. Occasionally not even the home-office is in a position immediately to decide the point, especially in the case of new kinds of bonds; it may be necessary to refer the question to the Rating Bureau, since a refund privilege is a vital part of the rate.

8. Procedure at "Renewal" Dates

While most policies of casualty insurance are issued for definite stated terms (ordinarily one year), many kinds of surety bonds are issued for no stated period of liability, but are so worded as to remain in force indefinitely in default of cancellation by either the surety company or the assured. Such bonds are called "continuous," because, in the absence of positive action on one side or the other, or of some automatic termination (death of the person bonded, for example), the bonds remain in force indefinitely.

Similarly, many other kinds of surety bonds are issued for definite periods, but for terms which extend more than one year and which are not endable by the surety. A bond, for example, covering a county treasurer whose term of office is to continue four years would necessarily have a term of four years, though the bond itself would in most cases contain no explicit statement to that effect; and the surety would be inescapably on the risk for the

full four years from the moment it issued the bond at
the beginning of the official's term.

Similarly, again, still other kinds of surety bonds are
issued for indefinite periods the duration of which cannot
be known, except within wide limits, when the bond is
issued. A contract bond, for example, remains in force
until the contract is completed, frequently more than a
year, and perhaps several years, after the bond is issued;
an executor's bond does not terminate until the estate is
administered, a final account rendered, and the executor
discharged; an appeal bond continues until the judgment
from which the appeal is taken is either confirmed or
vacated by the higher tribunal; and the terms of all
these bonds (and of many others like them) are obviously
indefinite and not explicitly statable in advance.

In all the cases referred to, although the premiums are
as a rule paid annually in advance, it would be quite in-
appropriate for the surety company to issue at premium-
anniversary dates a certificate "renewing" the suretyship
after the manner of casualty renewal certificates, because the suretyship remains in force anyway, regardless of anything that the company may do. All that it
is proper for the company to do at anniversary dates is
to issue a bill for the premium then due, and to give a
receipt when the bill is paid. In practice, companies
issue these receipts in advance precisely as if they were
renewal certificates, and agents speak of them as if
they were renewal certificates, and as if it were vitally
important to the obligee to have them at the anniversary
date. In fact, it makes no difference whatever to the
obligee, so far as the validity of the suretyship is concerned; whether or not he ever gets a receipt; and they
are used by the companies primarily as a convenient accounting and collecting device.

9. The Surety Association of America

Prior to November 12, 1908, when the Surety Association of America came officially into existence, and when its constitution and by-laws were adopted, each bonding company went its own devious way as to rates, commissions, brokerage fees, underwriting methods, and the like, without regard to the practices of other companies in such matters.   It is true that the executives and underwriters of the various companies sometimes held conferences concerning questions of immediate moment; and it is also true that since April 4, 1906, a group of companies interested in excise bonds in the state of New York had been writing such bonds with brilliant success through a co-operative organization; but in all other lines and in virtually all respects the surety companies of the country, up to the date mentioned, conducted their vitally important and rapidly growing business in unrestrained, more or less irresponsible, and well-nigh disastrous competition.

The result was what might have been expected, and it became increasingly evident that most of the companies in the business would ultimately go under unless something were done to stabilize rates and otherwise bring competition within reasonable bounds.   Under such conditions the Surety Association of America was organized, receiving at once the support of all the active and prominent companies; and since then, though seeming at times to be on the verge of dissolution, it has steadily gained in stability and influence.   No one familiar with the surety business need be told that the competition of the companies is always intense, and is sometimes a thing to be spoken of with bated breath; but most companies in recent years, as a condition of continued solvency if for no other reason, have tried to temper their competition with decency and fairness toward each other in the adjustment of contactual points through the medium of co-operative associations. They have seen to it, moreover, that the public welfare and a spirit of genuine service to the assured were kept well to the front in their consideration of co-operative proposals. They have realized that upon no other basis, in the final analysis, could such movements be justified and permanently maintained.

It is sometimes stated, and perhaps in a sense is true, that the surety companies were forced into their combination of 1908 by certain heads of state insurance departments, who saw that the companies were headed straight for disaster, by reason of their senseless rate-cutting. Certain it is that many state insurance departments have given consistent support to the Surety Association of America and the Towner Rating Bureau. While the broad-minded attitude of these officials is most commendable, in view of the popular feeling toward any sort of "trust," even a little reflection will show that the bonding companies are not to be classed in such a matter with ordinary mercantile and manufacturing branches of business. Surety companies have outstanding all the time millions of instruments whereby, under certain conditions, fulfilled in practice in numberless cases, they agree to pay enormous amounts of money to widows, wards, elderly people, and many other classes of beneficiaries who would be grievously affected by the inability of the sureties to make good their promise to pay. Many enlightened state officials have realized that co-operative methods are not only vitally important to the surety companies themselves, but are also equally beneficial to the insuring public. This declaration is not a paradox, and there is no inconsistency between the two stated results of competitive co-operation. On the contrary, in a business of this nature, where inefficiency and ultimate insolvency on the part of companies inevitably mean distress and loss to the public holding the obligations of such companies, whatever tends to promote sound practices and conservative courses is necessarily beneficial to the public.

While, therefore, state insurance officials may support co-operative organizations among competing companies with propriety and with no violation of, but rather in pursuance of, their primary duty to safeguard the interests of the insuring public, yet it is a correlative truth that all such organizations should be supervised by such officials.   In fact, that is done to some extent at least, in the case of bonding companies. When the Surety Association of America was last examined by the New York Insurance Department the investigation lasted several months, and was thoroughgoing as to every aspect of Association work. The accounts were minutely scrutinized. The minutes of all meetings were read, and when found to be condensed (as sometimes happens in such reports) they were developed, by inquiry and research, into complete and intelligible reports. Even the correspondence of the Association officers with member companies was examined with scrupulous care. The Insurance Department could and doubtless would have done all this in any event; but the process was facilitated by the determination of the Association officers at the outset to co-operate cordially with the Department in every way. The Association desired the Department to know everything that there was to know, in order that its practices might be changed if they proved in any case to be such as the Department could not approve.

It was gratifying to find that the Insurance Department after its thoroughgoing investigation regarded the Surety Association as a legitimate and commendable organization. The official report of the investigation concluded as follows:

> From examination of the Association records it is apparent that the following are among the objects it seeks to accomplish:
>
> (1) The adoption by all member companies of the premium rates promulgated by the Towner Rating Bureau.
>
> (2) The inclusion in its membership of all properly qualified surety companies.
>
> (3) The regulation of the payment of commissions and brokerage.
>
> (4) The elimination of rebates.
>
> (5) The limitation of the number of agencies maintained by member companies.
>
> (6) The defeat of legislation injurious to the interests of member companies, and the enactment of favorable legislation.
>
> These objects are generally considered legitimate and as inuring alike to the best interests of the surety companies and the insuring public. To the extent that the purposes, aims and activities of the Association make for uniformity of premium rates and limitation of expenses, it deserves commendation and encouragement.

10. The Towner Rating Bureau

Much that is said in the preceding section about the Surety Association applies with equal force to the Rating Bureau, since neither could function efficiently without the other, and since both are essential to the welfare of the bonding companies. The disruption of either would mean that rates, acquisition costs, and underwriting practices would all revert to the old conditions of demoralization and chaos; and any such adverse development would be regarded by all competent authorities as a deplorable check to the orderly and prudent development of the bonding business, as little less than disastrous to the surety companies, and as an ultimate misfortune and menace to the public.

People intimately concerned with the bonding business—large buyers of corporate suretyship as well as the sellers thereof—know that almost all the surety companies in the country are now, and for a considerable period have been, charging uniform rates for bonds. These rates are based upon the aggregate experience and the composite underwriting judgment of the numerous companies concerned. They are promulgated by a central bureau, to which the companies contribute their experience. This is unquestionably a proper and praiseworthy and scientific solution of a highly complicated and difficult problem; and it surely marks a vast advance over the chaotic and largely guess-work system of independent rate-making that it supplanted.

It is gratifying to know that certain states have recognized, and thus tacitly approved, the system of determining proper insurance premiums through rate-making associations. They have done this by enacting laws that lay down rules for such associations and by requiring the latter to file with the state insurance departments certain information. The surety companies do not fear, but rather do they welcome, laws of this character; because people who are doing well and in a scientific way a piece of work that is of vital importance to the public have nothing to fear from investigations and supervision by representatives of the public. Some time ago, for example, the New York Insurance Department made a complete and searching investigation of the activities of the Towner Rating Bureau, going over all the correspondence and records of the office. The result of the investigation was summarized by the examiner as follows:

2

I am of the opinion that the Bureau performs a work that is essential to the proper conduct of the surety business, since it is obvious that if each company were without any restraint in the matter of rates, competition would lead to promiscuous rate-cutting and consequent demoralization, and probably in some cases to insolvency.

It behooves the surety companies, nevertheless, to see to it that the reasonable and logical and wholly defensible theory of rate-making associations is carried out in practice, and that only such rates are promulgated by the central bureau as can be justified by experienced and competent underwriting authority. Corporate suretyship is comparatively young, and no great body of premium and loss statistics is as yet available. A good deal, however, has already been accomplished; and the Surety Association of America some years ago laid down for its members a comprehensive and detailed statistical plan that cannot fail to be of immense value to those charged with the duty of making suretyship rates sufficient to cover the risk and at the same time fair to the public.

It was Emerson, perhaps, who said that all institutions were only the lengthened shadows of some men; and certain it is that the Rating Bureau established by Mr. R. H. Towner on October 1, 1909, and conducted by him continuously since then, has always reflected the knowledge and wisdom of its founder. Fortunate, indeed, have been the surety companies in this respect. Not long ago, when an important member company threatened to withdraw from the Bureau, Mr. Towner, in a moment of emotional disturbance quite out of character, mentioned the incident in a circular letter to his subscribers, and made a touching reference to the fact that whereas all his patrons expected him to serve them with 101 per cent of efficiency and wisdom, yet none of them ever had a kind word to say about the Rating Bureau. He should harbor no such unhappy illusions, because everybody knows how deeply indebted the surety companies are and have long been to the Rating Bureau and its chief. Various factors contribute to the welfare of a rating bureau, but the very first essential of success is some outstanding figure of such attainments and character as will command the confidence and regard of all the leading men in the business. Mr. Towner has long supplied ideally this fundamental need.

CHAPTER II

THE UNDERWRITING OF FIDELITY BONDS FROM THE STANDPOINT OF THE PRINCIPAL

11. A Comprehensive Outlook upon Human Kind

Although fidelity suretyship is a modern institution, it has already attained enormous proportions, and now includes every branch of human activity and every post of duty, from messenger boy to bank president. Executives, cashiers, bookkeepers, clerks, and all other employees of financial institutions are commonly required nowadays to furnish fidelity bonds as a condition precedent to admission to the staff. The same thing is true, in varying degrees of completeness, with the officers and other employees of public-service corporations, beneficial associations, fraternal orders, labor unions, and a great variety of mercantile and manufacturing concerns. More and more, in every walk of life, are fidelity bonds coming to be regarded as a natural and essential incident of a given position.

The underwriting of these risks starts with and is primarily based upon the "application" that the person to be bonded makes when he seeks the suretyship. These applications contain comprehensive and minute information, extending to highly intimate details of the applicant's affairs. The archives of the average surety company hold hundreds of thousands—in some cases millions—of these extremely interesting documents concerning persons presently or at some time bonded. In order to keep their information up to date, some companies scan daily papers closely, and extract therefrom for their files anything of permanent interest concerning their "risks," as they call them. Sometimes these clippings make interesting additions to the prior stock of information. Not long ago, for example, a man was made president of one of the largest railroads in the country. A certain company's card index having disclosed the fact that he was one of about 500,000 persons whose authentic and detailed biographies were contained in its files, the papers were produced and this last piece of information added to them. It appeared that he was bonded twenty years before as a railroad station agent in an obscure Nevada settlement. At that time he was a young man and had only recently been promoted from the position of day laborer. His credentials even at that early day were strikingly good, everybody consulted speaking of his character in the highest terms. From a section hand in the lonely passes of the Rocky Mountains this man, in about twenty years, had risen to the presidency of a great railroad system. Where but in America could it have happened?

12. An Instrument Worse than an Income-Tax Blank

The first thing that a bonding company does when a person asks it to guarantee his honesty is to hand him one of these application blanks—a formidably long document intended (and aptly fashioned for the purpose) to develop all the salient facts in his career bearing upon his general trustworthiness.

He must give his full name, age, place of birth, present and past residences; describe his domestic conditions and relations; state his possessions in real and personal property, his income, his debts; describe his occupations for ten years back, particularized as to positions held and employers served, with exact dates; give three or more competent and trustworthy references; and so on.

Some applicants for bonds never get beyond this stage, and are not heard from again after they read the application blank and see what confronts them; they know that their careers and characters would never bear any such scrutiny as that. Occasionally even innocent and quiet bondable applicants are strangely affected by the inquisitorial document. Not long ago, for example, a young woman was asked by her employer to obtain a corporate bond. She seems to have been a most estimable lady, with a stainless past; and the bonding company handled the matter with all the delicacy and tact that such a situation obviously demanded. The application blank, however, started an unhappy current along the young woman's nerves. When the bond was issued she became absolutely panic-stricken, and gave up her position, as the only way out, evidently, of an impossible situation. It is not known what she thought was going to happen next, but it is clear that she did not regard bonding as a civilized transaction.

The foregoing case is exceptional, and usually the underwriter's experience is all the other way—he must protect himself against the wiles of rogue applicants for bonds rather than reassure worthy candidates as to their own misgivings. It continually happens, for example, that persons who have been dishonest and found out in a certain employment will try to conceal the fact by suppressing all mention of the occupation in their statement of career, and by manipulating the dates of their other employments so as to cover the period of the dishonest service. It is a common device in such cases for the applicant to account for the period of unmentionable service by citing an imaginary employment with some unscrupulous confederate, who will confirm the applicant's allegations and give him a flawless "character." Sometimes these confederates overshoot the mark, offering testimony so pat as to arouse the underwriter's suspicion.

13. Reasons for Rejections Stated

Fidelity underwriters are often asked on what grounds, or in accordance with what principles, they reject applicants for bonds. Each case is decided on its merits, and it would be rather hard to formulate a set of rules that could invariably be followed and would cover all the multitudinous cases treated. In a general way, however, it may be said that the chief reasons actuating underwriters in their rejections are the following, arranged in the order of their damaging importance:

(a) Dishonesty in a former employment.
(b) Addiction to drink, either at present or within a comparatively recent time.
(c) General dissipation, undesirable associates, and the like.
(d) Gambling in general, or race-track gambling, or speculation (stocks, grain, oil, etc.).
(e) Debts, or extravagance, or tendency to live beyond means.
(f) Inability to find references, or the receipt of adverse information from them, or their refusal to say anything.
(g) Inability to verify the applicant's statement of career or to account satisfactorily for all of his time—because he has willfully suppressed some employments, knowing that a full disclosure would be fatal; or because he has not taken the trouble to make an accurate statement.

14. Dishonesty in the Past

Some of these reasons are obviously of a highly detrimental character, while others may not seem at first blush particularly serious. Let us consider each of them. Underwriters are frequently asked to ignore former dishonesty, especially by applicants themselves, but occasionally also by employers, who believe the applicants to have reformed, and who deem themselves sufficiently protected anyway by the bond. It is noteworthy, by the way, that these employers, while protesting vehemently against the rejection by the bonding company of the person who has admittedly been guilty of dishonesty in the past, will rarely, if the bond is withheld, keep the man in their service and carry the risk themselves. They are confident that he is all right, but when the surety company declines to "hold the bag," their confidence seems to ooze away. It is not a sufficient retort to this comment to say that it is no part of the employer's business to furnish fidelity insurance, while that is the precise function of the bonding company. Not in the least is it the function of surety companies to guarantee the honesty of employees under the circumstances cited. Companies make their rates and otherwise conduct their business upon the basis of covering normal risks only. As reasonably might a fire company be charged with cowardly inconsistency for refusing to cover a building in the direct path of a conflagration raging a few doors away, or a life company for withholding its insurance from a subject suffering the last stages of a fatal disease.

Agents and employers who urge underwriters to cover subnormal cases do not realize that they are asking the companies to do in the given case something which, if adopted as a consistent practice (and other agents and employers would have exactly as much right to expect it), would invariably mean heavy losses. The fact is easily demonstrable: for assuming 100 per cent of liability, the bonding company receives a premium of, say, one-half of 1 per cent (in fact, fidelity premiums probably average much less than that). These cases almost always concern comparatively small bonds, so that half the premium, on the average, may reasonably be regarded as used up in making the investigation. Add to that half acquisition costs, and the surety company has left for losses only about one-fifth of the gross premium. Actually, therefore, in return for agreeing to assume 100 per cent of liability, it gets, for loss-paying purposes, only one-tenth of 1 per cent. In other words, if more than one risk in 1,000 goes wrong, it loses. Would anyone for a moment believe that a surety company could cover in responsible positions of trust, one after another, 1,000 principals, every one of whom had in some former service stolen his employer's money, and not have a single loss in the whole 1,000? On the contrary, would not everybody say that the company would be extraordinarily lucky, if, having accepted even 100 such dubious cases, it should have no loss on any of them?

15. Addiction to Drink, Dissipation, and Gambling

These related vices may conveniently and logically be treated together because it is rather unusual in practice for one of them to mar a man's credentials without at least sympathetic traces of the others; and oftener than not when any one of the three is present in force, the other two accompany it. While, therefore, a man would not be rejected merely because he indulges at times in a friendly game of poker, or takes a little "home-brew" on occasion, if the investigation papers make frequent mention of such practices, the fact would heavily handicap him. Enslavement to downright gambling of any kind (cards, horses, Wall Street, etc.) is highly damaging to any applicant. Few people understand how prevalent race-track gambling is, or how closely and causally it is connected with defalcations. Probably no experienced fidelity underwriter would bond a man in any capacity who was known to "play the races" habitually or even frequently. As for a confirmed speculator in stocks, cotton, oil, and the like. hardly any underwriters would knowingly bond him, because they would all feel that the man might easily carry his aleatory operations so far as to become financially involved, and perhaps seek a way out through the cash-drawer of his employer.

Bank officers and employees are almost always bonded. Many of them are necessarily in close touch with Wall Street affairs, and must often be tempted to try their fortunes there. To do so means ultimate disaster in so many instances that underwriters deem it a duty to their companies to discontinue suretyship on such a principal who is known to be speculating. Sometimes the bond is continued upon the principal's promise to renounce utterly his speculative practices—an outcome of the incident no less happy for the principal than for the surety. In the case of bank defalcations it seems safe to say that at least 75 per cent of the losses paid by the surety companies on bank bonds are due to the fact that the principal has become hopelessly involved in speculation, and has finally appropriated the bank's cash or securities in a desperate effort to extricate himself. A rule of the New York Stock Exchange prohibits members from carrying a speculative account for the clerk of a bank, trust company, or insurance company, "unless the written consent of the employer has been obtained."

It must not be supposed, of course, that fidelity underwriters adhere to unreasonable and impracticable standards or expect all their applicants to be Sunday-school superintendents. What they like to see emerging from their study of an applicant's papers is a normal, red-blooded, well-informed principal, who has been exposed to the dangers and temptations of life, and is shown by his record to have countered them successfully thus far. They have a lot of sympathy with the subject of this anecdote related in a technical paper by a distinguished civil engineer:

> I knew an experienced contractor who, when he met the engineer in charge of a piece of work on which bids had been invited would offer him a cigar. If he refused it the contractor would ask him to take a drink. If he declined, and in the course of his conversation did not use as much as one little "cuss" word the contractor would go on without bidding. He did not want any work under that fellow.

This contractor seems to have been somewhat premature in anticipating trouble—in his place most people would have looked for a little more evidence of coming unreasonable exactions before giving up the chance of good business and going home. But fidelity underwriters understand the contractor's point of view and frame of mind. They have the same sort of feeling sometimes in looking over the papers about some applicant for a fidelity bond: the man seems so incredibly good that they begin to have their doubts, and to hope that someone will charge him with beating his wife or with some similar truly human characteristic. Yet there is nothing tangible or definite to which they can take exception. They feel as Mark Twain did in his last illness when he could not forego his jest even with death. "This is such a mysterious disease," he complained. "If we only had a bill of particulars, we'd have something to swear at."

Underwriters find themselves most subject to this reprehensible disposition when they are treating applications for fidelity bonds from persons not long out of school or college. They always try to obtain in such cases information about the applicants from former professors and teachers. They attach much importance to reports from such sources, and are unwilling to issue the bond if the reports are unqualifiedly bad. They feel, however, that it would not do to reject an applicant merely because his career at school or college proved to be not altogether faultless. I knew a man once, for example, who in his Sophomore year climbed an electric-light pole in Harvard Square about 1 A.M. and tried for a long time to blow out the light; and yet that man turned out to be rather a decent sort of citizen and never caused his surety any loss—at least he has not yet.

One feels a little less depraved over this admission of underwriting weakness in being able to cite from the classic columns of the *Atlantic Monthly* this testimony in point from an able and successful educator, Robert M. Gay:

> Yet it must be admitted that every teacher who has managed to remain human is confronted by a dilemma. As a teacher he is expected to inculcate ideals of perfection, not only in studies, but in deportment; and yet when he happens to come upon a student who approaches perfection it is a mournful occasion.

I recall, too, the frank admission of the divinity-school president, who, when the parish committee called upon him in search of a minister, told them that the students fell readily into three classes—those who had talents without piety, those who had piety without talents, and those who had neither.

16. Debts and Extravagance

The justice of fidelity rejections is often doubted when they are based wholly or chiefly on this ground, but all claim examiners know how important a part this feature of a defaulter's life has often played in his undoing. There are few things that an underwriter is more pleased to find in the papers concerned with his subject than evidence of thrift and saving habits. It is astonishing how often men holding high and responsible positions are found to have made but slight financial progress. Such men are bonded, of course, if their credentials in other respects are satisfactory, but they would be bonded more confidently if they had trained themselves to save. On the other hand, a case that might not seem in all respects up to the mark will often be settled in favor of the applicant if the investigation shows that he has contrived in some way to save money. Where the latter condition is present, however, the other aspects of the risk are almost always excellent.

17. Suspicious Experience with References

When an applicant gives his surety a number of references, and letters addressed to them are all returned as undeliverable, the presumption is that he has made up fictitious addresses in default of ability to furnish genuine ones. Similarly, when references who are known to have received inquiry blanks (important second requests are frequently sent by registered mail) fail to return them at all, or send them back with non-committal information and leading questions unanswered, the presumption is that they are charitably withholding knowledge that they know would not help the applicant with the underwriter. Both these presumptions, however, are rebuttable, and applicants should not be turned down *merely* upon negative evidence of this kind, unless and until every effort has been exhausted to develop the facts. The first difficulty may be due to the ignorance or carelessness of the applicant or his failure to recognize the importance of this detail; and the second difficulty may be due to the fact that the applicant is not popular, and has made enemies who are trying to get even with him in the way indicated. Perhaps he is as unfortunate in that respect as was the man of whom Oscar Wilde said, "He has no enemies; and none of his friends like him."

Fidelity examiners must be forever on their guard against "knockers." I fear that the word is not yet in good society as to its English standing, but everybody knows what it means—a person who speaks ill of another without warrant and unjustly. Underwriters get to know knockers when they see them, and they have a hearty contempt for them. They do not judge their risks from a single witness only, nor even from two or three, but from numerous witnesses and factors and from all the various papers in the case. By reason of such thoroughgoing methods they can oftener "spot" a knocker at once; and in that event the latter has overshot his mark and defeated his own purposes, since he has caused the underwriter to feel a certain sympathy with the risk that might not otherwise be present. The Stoic philosopher, Epictetus—he would have made a fine fidelity examiner—was talking about knockers when he said, 2,000 years ago, "What another saith of thee concerneth more him that saith it than it concerneth thee."

18. Inability to Verify Alleged Career

It continually happens in the experience of fidelity underwriters that persons who, having some time in the past applied to a company for a bond and having occasion afterward to make another application, give the second time a statement of their career seriously inconsistent with the original statement. Their identity is established by the date and place of their birth as shown by the two applications, by their signatures, and the like.

If the applications are absolutely irreconcilable, and show clearly that the person is "faking" a record for the purpose of misleading the underwriter, the latter does not waste much time over him; but if the variances are such as might come from carelessness, ignorance, or forgetfulness, the underwriter will try to help out the applicant and in some way get a true line upon his past. Oftentimes these people are honest enough, but are indifferent and careless, and do not realize the importance of accuracy in such a matter. Perhaps, however, they are disciples of Emerson, and act upon this precept of the philosopher:

> Let today say what today thinks in hard words, and tomorrow say what tomorrow thinks in hard words again.
> That is the only way to make progress.

It is one certain way, however, of failing to make progress with a fidelity underwriter.

About a year ago a person, who may be called for this purpose John Grady, applied to a bonding company for a bond. After an investigation his application was rejected. Six months later "Jacob Gradsky" applied to the same company for a bond. He might have been referred to any one of twenty examiners, but as ill luck

would have it, he was referred to the particular examiner
who had handled John Grady six months before. This
examiner recognized his old friend Grady in the revised
Hebraic version, and charged him with the double
dealing. The applicant readily admitted the fact, and
explained that, since he had been unable to get a bond
under his own name, he thought he would try a fictitious
one. The examiner told him that the circumstances
required additional thought on his part. He recently
met the requirement, having the sublime assurance to
apply once more for a bond, this time under the name of
"Warshowsky." What he will call himself when he
applies again six months hence is an awful thing to
contemplate.

19. A Solomon Often Needed

Sometimes the conditions are such that an underwriter, if he would deal with entire justice to everybody
concerned, needs the wisdom of a sage. His first duty
is to the assured (the employer). He has no right, of
course, for purely sentimental reasons, to place in the
service of the assured, by issuing the bond, a person who
has been found unworthy of trust, and who may cause
the assured far greater loss than the bond would cover.

Secondly, he must consider the interests of his own
employer, the bonding company. He would not be just
to that interest, if, in order to spare a father's feelings,
or for some other reason unconnected with the real
merits of the question, he should put his company on a
risk when all the conditions indicated danger.

On the other hand, fidelity underwriters do not forget
that they are dealing with human beings, and that their
decisions may have far-reaching consequences to the
person immediately affected. They do the best they can,

keeping in mind all the interests concerned. Solomon himself in some cases would not find it easy to make a decision in which he had full confidence.

Sometimes the gravity of the situation is relieved by an amusing letter. This one, for example, recently came to hand:

> Kindly excuse me for bothering your honor with my communication. Dear Sir; you will do me a great favor, by answering my information! Why was the bonds of.........
> cancelled? which was employed with............ I am very much interested to know, as I am a father of his.
>
> Having five children and I can assure you that every one of my child is honest and upright, etc.............the oldest son is............which is employed with.........
> for the last 8 years and still now with them. I myself am employed with............for over 5 years. Please look up our records.
>
> Dear Sir; asking you again as you will only do your duty as a man, to let me know the reason why? You can be sure, that your kindness will never be forgotten. I am sure that it was some dishonest party that could not see a honest family be happy.

I should not think of publishing this letter, even with the identifying names omitted, if there were any chance of the dear old man's seeing it. But it is good enough to print.

What was done about bonding the young reprobate—for that is what he was? Ah, that's telling!

20. Demands for Explanation of Rejections

The fidelity underwriter's life is not altogether a bed of exquisite jacqueminots. After cancelling a bond because the principal has shot up a town or murdered his mother-in-law or committed some similar slight indiscretion, the underwriter is likely to be bombarded with indignant protestations from five different quarters—

3

the employer, the agent, the applicant, the applicant's friends, and the applicant's attorney. The employer objects because he shortsightedly takes the ground that the trouble to him of procuring a new employee outweighs the advantage of eliminating from his service a person found unworthy of a bond. The agent objects because on general principles he is anxious to placate the employer, whose dissatisfaction in this matter may cause the loss of other business. The applicant objects for a multitude of natural reasons, and his friends object because he objects. The attorney is paid good money for objecting.

It has happened repeatedly that applicants rejected by underwriters and retained in the service pending efforts to procure reinstatement have made off with funds of their trusting employers while the controversy was raging. In one interesting case of this kind I wrote to the employer as follows:

> In view of your evident confidence in this man we deem it our duty to put you on your guard. Our information about him is seriously adverse, and is multisourced, and we do not see how there can be any mistake about it. It is our understanding that he was found guilty of forgery a few years ago, and served a prison term.

The employer was naturally disturbed by this letter, and he started an investigation of the man's accounts; but before it was completed, the man had disappeared with $1,000 of the employer's money.

21. Disclosure of Reasons to the Applicant

Dr. Holmes's Autocrat is right in this as in so many other things—that John (that is to say, you and I and everybody) has three personalities: (a) There is the real John, as he actually exists and is known to his Maker;

(b) there is John's John, the person that John, as he looks in his mind's eye, supposes himself to be; (c) finally, there is other people's John, a composite personality that the world in general conceives to be John. From the nature of the case the fidelity underwriter's final view of John comes to be substantially (c). Underwriters have infinite trouble in their business because (b) and (c) are so widely different. John applies to them for a bond, and gives them (b), etched by him with vivid detail. They then go on in their conscienceless way and build up a (c) that could never by any chance to taken for (b).

Some people show by their letters that their moral standards are such as to make it not worth while to discuss the matter of their rejection with them at all. It is amazing that people cannot see why their applications for bonds are turned down, when their own admissions contain abundant reasons. They sometimes say substantially this: "I came in to see why I was rejected. It is true that I stole $1,000 from my last employer. I cannot imagine what you have against me." They do not put it, of course, as to words, so crudely as that; but logically and in essence that is just what they say. The absurdity is due partly to a lack of common sense (that explains so many things!) and partly to queer moral standards. These people regard as wholly negligible certain habits and traits of character that make it really out of the question for any surety company to bond them.

Some time ago, for example, I found myself unable to bond a certain applicant for a number of reasons that seemed in the aggregate to constitute a clear case of unrevokable rejection. The man himself admitted that "following the unfortunate circumstances connected with the killing of that half-breed Choctaw negro in

Oklahoma," he had "quite a little trouble." He admitted, too, that at one period in his picturesque career he had been accused of setting fire to his gin plant, and also of cow-stealing; that he had "trouble" (as he put it again) about a lease that he broke; and that there might have been "a few other little incidents likely to prejudice" his case with the bonding company. The gentleman was a good guesser: there *were* other little incidents similarly indicating the probability of "trouble" for the surety company if it should provide the suretyship requested.

This applicant's papers showed that he attended for a time a certain western university. It must have been the institution whose entire disciplinary code consisted of the following:

(a) No student shall set fire to any college building.
(b) No student shall kill any member of the faculty.

While some bonding companies rarely give rejected applicants any statement of the reasons for rejection (that is, of course, in cases where the applicant is beyond doubt unworthy), the better and more consistent practice is to state the reasons frankly, where that can be done, as it often can be, without injustice to third persons. If, for example, a man has been rejected for his notorious addiction to drink, no harm will come to anybody from telling him so, and possibly the effect upon the man himself will be salutary.

The underwriter is also able to tell the applicant why he was rejected in those numerous cases where the underwriter knows that the applicant knows as well as he knows. In one case of this kind, for example, I wrote to the applicant as follows: "In reply to your recent letter asking why we cancelled your bond, we would advise you that we did so because we learned that you had been convicted under another name of the crime of forgery and served a term of three years therefor at the state prison in Sing Sing."

The gentleman seemed to think the reason sufficient, as nothing further was heard from him.

22. Compulsory Disclosure of Cancellation Reasons

Bills have been introduced in a number of western legislatures (and perhaps have been passed in some cases) intended to force surety companies to make known to persons whose bonds have been cancelled the reasons for such action. The Senate Labor Committee, for example, of a certain western state tried to procure the enactment of a bill reading essentially as follows:

> (a) No common carrier shall accept as surety a company that does not maintain a general office within the state at which every bond of the common carrier shall be approved or cancelled, and at which all records of such bonds shall be kept.

> (b) No bond shall be cancelled except for a breach of the condition thereof. Upon such breach by an employee the surety may cancel the bond by giving the employee (1) ten days' notice in writing, setting out in full the reasons for such cancellation.

> (c) Any person or corporation or manager who shall violate this act shall be guilty of a misdemeanor and be punished by a fine of not less than $100, nor more than $1,000, and by imprisonment in the county jail for not less than 30 days nor more than 1 year.

Idiocy like that is diverting. It seems odd, by the way, that the framer of the bill did not include a fourth section as follows:

> (d) If the reasons for cancellation submitted by the surety are deemed by the employee insufficient, the salary of the em-

ployee shall be immediately doubled, and the underwriter responsible for the cancellation shall be electrocuted within five days.

It is a wise and necessary rule of law that common carriers, innkeepers, and the like, must serve all comers without discrimination. Legislative attempts have sometimes been made, especially in the West and South, to make surety companies common bonders. A bill introduced in a western legislature, for example, had some such idea at its root, and gave a rejected applicant for a bond the right to take his case to a district court, and the judge thereof, after a hearing, was authorized to "command" the surety company "to furnish or provide such bond within a time to be fixed by the judgement."

Efforts of this kind on the part of labor leaders and "reformers" are entirely understandable, and will probably be continued, and the operations of the surety companies may some time be embarrassed by the passage of such laws. All the more important is it for underwriters to do their work expertly, thoroughly, and sympathetically, so that unjust rejections or insistence upon unreasonably severe requirements may not lend weight to attacks upon the old and tested methods of investigation and bonding.

CHAPTER III

UNDERWRITING OF FIDELITY BONDS FROM THE STANDPOINT OF THE OBLIGEE

23. Defalcations Not Wholly Due to Subjective Causes

The underlying reasons for embezzlements are so complex and manifold as hardly to be summarizable in brief form; but human weakness of one kind or another, coupled with opportunity (frequently with tempting opportunity), accounts for most cases. Occasionally a man will go wrong because he is ambitious to obtain wealth, or at least a competency. Far oftener, however, the reason for wrongdoing is altogether sordid: the defaulter has contracted evil habits, and he betrays his trust in order to gratify his base desires and to pay his dissolute debts. Wine, women, and dice loom large in the evidence in these cases. Extravagance outstripping one's income and attempts to even up by speculation lie at the root of many defalcations. Having treated at some length in the preceding chapter these subjective causes of breach of trust, we will consider now the external aspects of the matter—not so important as the other, but far from negligible.

24. Good Faith on the Employer's Side Essential

When I explained to an agent once that I felt unable to issue a certain fidelity bond because I found that the employer's business career had not been honorable, the agent at first protested that such a position was unjust and illogical. "Nobody asked you," he argued, "to guarantee the honesty of the *employer*. What has *his* character to do with your guaranteeing the honesty of his employees?"

It has a good deal to do with it, as a little reflection will show. In the first place, no surety company desires to deal, in this delicate business of writing fidelity bonds, with crooked people. Insurance in general, and fidelity insurance in particular, requires the best of good faith on the part of both insurer and insured. It seems a good general rule to follow, and one not calling for special justification, never to write fidelity bonds in behalf of a beneficiary who is known or believed to be untrustworthy or dishonest. It seems clear that a surety company is taking undue chances when it bonds even a presumably honest man in favor of a dishonest employer. The employee is likely to be affected by the example of the employer. If he remains in the service, it is not a good sign. If the employer is dishonest, he may easily force even a well-intentioned subordinate into wrongdoing. The whole situation is one that a prudent underwriter will avoid.

A curious and interesting illustration of the contagious effect upon subordinates of dishonesty is afforded by the increase of "nickeling" (the technical name for the street-car conductor's personal levy upon the fares he collects) that is said to be an invariable sequel of traction-company scandals. In one conspicuous instance of this kind, where the directors of a large public-service corporation were implicated in questionable transactions, the matter was widely discussed in the press, and it seemed to be the general opinion that the directors had misappropriated large sums of money. One curious result of the disclosures was a large increase in the pilferings of fares on the part of the conductors of the traction company. A good deal of such stealing was going on all the time, as the managers of the company well knew, but a comparison of receipts before and after the disclosures showed that the conductors were taking greater liberties than ever with the company's nickels. It is said that similar results have followed from similar causes in other cities. Truer words were never spoken than these by Emerson:

> Nor knowest thou what argument
> Thy life to thy neighbor's creed hath lent.

25. Audits and Good Accounting Methods Essential

Fidelity underwriters are guided in their work by various standards of life and conduct, but two basic principles have controlling force with them. In the first place, as we have seen, they decompose a man's character and career, and see whether the resultant elements indicate unflinching personal integrity. In the second place, and with hardly less insistence, they study with a microscopic eye the conditions under which the man will work, and see whether everything reasonable has been done to protect him from temptation. If they find that nothing whatever has been done or will be done, and that the man, so far as any accounting and supervisory safeguards are concerned, may steal when and how he will, they refuse to become his surety.

One who at common law brings against another an action for personal injuries must prove, in order to recover damages, not only that his injury was due to the carelessness of the person sued, but also that he himself was not guilty of such lack of prudence as to facilitate the injury. In a large proportion of defaults this just principle of the common law, known as "contributory negligence," has been violated by the employer, because he has failed to exercise proper supervision over his employees, and has not adopted reasonable safeguards to make wrongdoing difficult.

The freshman treasurer of a Greek-letter fraternity had the right idea. He was not overmethodical in keeping his accounts—not to speak of the fact that the society meetings were sometimes of so convivial a nature that even the most methodical of treasurers might well have been guilty of inaccuracies. As a result of these conditions there was a deficit at the end of the year in the treasurer's accounts of $247. He cheerfully made good the shortage; but when they asked him at the beginning of the sophomore year to serve again, he properly qualified his acceptance as follows: "I will act as treasurer this year only on condition that the society give me a bond guaranteeing me against loss."

Similarly a certain bank embezzler, now languishing in jail and deeply penitent, attributes his downfall to the laxity of his superior officers. He says that he fought hard to overcome temptation, and even prayed at his desk sometimes for strength to resist an unusually attractive opening. He reminds one in this respect of the famous Yale pitcher who was distinguished alike for his "in shoots" and for his piety, and of whom an envious Princeton poet wrote this touching couplet:

> He always prays before he plays,
> But he gets there just the same.

Generally speaking, surety companies will not bond a man whose work involves the handling of money and the keeping of books and accounts unless such books and accounts are periodically audited either (and preferably) by some outside expert accountant or, if not by such a person, at least by some superior officer or board within the organization.

26. A Recent Constructive Development

Some surety companies themselves now undertake to audit the accounts of the persons they bond. They do this either through some separate subsidiary or affiliated company or through an auditing department in their own organization. They charge for the fidelity bonds the regular Manual rate, and in addition collect a reasonable fee for the auditing service, in accordance with the complexity of the business audited, the number of persons bonded, and other varying conditions. This auditing charge is likely in any event to be much less than the assured would have to pay for similar audits bought in the open market, because the bonding companies perform the service, not for the purpose of making money out of it, but purely as an advantageous and protective incident of their fidelity suretyship. The audits are really a by-product of their bonding operations, furnished to the assured at or near cost; and the companies derive their profit from the transaction in a reduced fidelity loss ratio and in a strengthened hold upon the good-will of the assured because of their increased importance and value to them.

This surety-company auditing of fidelity risks marks a real and scientific advance in the conduct of the business, and the movement ought to grow. One possible and promising development of the idea would be for a number of companies, not now following the plan or doing so under the obvious disadvantage of a small volume of business, to get together and organize an auditing concern to care for all the audits of the participating companies, and also, perhaps, to do a general auditing business for the public at large. The agents of the companies would be encouraged to promote the interests of the auditing subsidiary, and it seems reasonable to suppose that in time a business could thus be built up that would not only be valuable in itself, but would also have beneficial reactions upon the regular underwriting activities of the parent organizations. The idea seems ripe and ready to hand for some organizing genius.

27. "Employers' Statements"

Underwriters inform themselves regarding an employer's existing and proposed accounting methods and audit system, if any, by means of a blank which has been especially prepared for the purpose of developing complete information in this respect, and which is known as an "employer's statement." The practices of the bonding companies regarding this aspect of underwriting fidelity risks have changed a good deal in recent years, and are not uniform today among the various companies, some underwriters requiring the completion of forms in cases where other companies would dispense with them. For a number of reasons surety underwriting in general has tended to become more uniform (and more skillful, it may be added) with the development of the business. Frequent conferences of underwriters upon difficult classes of risks have been educational to all concerned. Executives occasionally leave one company to go with another and naturally follow in the new position the methods found satisfactory in the old. The vastly increased reinsurance dealings of the companies with one another and consequent interchange of investigation papers have brought to the attention of all underwriters the best methods followed by any of them. Nevertheless, considerable diversity of practice prevails in the matter of these employers' statements and similar documents. The situation in that respect may be better understood perhaps through the following description of the development and gradual liberalization of fidelity insurance (sections 28-35).

28. Fidelity Insurance at First Extremely Narrow

Embarking upon a strange sea in untried craft, the early fidelity underwriters naturally so planned their virgin voyages that they could scurry back to the shores of cancellation and denial of liability at the first sign of a claim tempest. For a long time only such risks were ordinarily assumed as would now be regarded as the cream of the business; and the insurance provided even as to these gingerly accepted cases was subject to numerous and rigid provisions, stipulations, and conditions. As a condition precedent to the issuance of a bond covering an employee, the assured was required to describe minutely the duties of the employee and the conditions under which his work was to be performed, and to stipulate that these duties and conditions would not be changed while the bond remained in force. Since the surety company would not undertake the business unless the safeguards thrown about a bonded person's work were so stringent as to make a loss from dishonesty altogether unlikely, and since when such a loss did occur it was usually found that the employer had failed to keep effective some of the stipulated safeguards, and had thus forfeited his insurance, it is easy to understand why unpleasant claim situations continually arose.

Besides requiring the employer to make these precise and detailed preliminary statements as to the employee's duties and the supervision of his work, the bonding companies also exacted, in the early days of the business (and to some extent, indeed, up to a few years ago), at each annual renewal date, an "employer's renewal statement"; that is to say, the employer, as a condition precedent to the continuance of the insurance, was obliged to reaffirm the original statement, to stipulate that the employee's accounts had been checked up to the renewal date and found correct, that the duties and safeguarding conditions would remain the same, etc. This renewal statement was frequently, if not usually, warranted to be true. If a shortage afterward developed, an investigation was likely to show that the man was really in default at the renewal date, though the employer was unaware of the fact; but as the employer had warranted the truth of his statement that the man's accounts at that time were correct, it was at least possible for the bonding company to deny liability on the ground of a breach of warranty. One important surety company used to ask its patrons at renewal dates to sign a statement about the person bonded reading in part as follows: "Proper accounts are kept and adequate examinations of his transactions will be made." That last phrase is surely a gem, and must have vastly simplified the work of the company's attorneys (or at least might have done so) whenever a claim was made. All that they had to do was to confront the unhappy employer with his signed renewal statement, point to the word "adequate," and say, with an engaging smile, "Since you admit that your man embezzled some of your money, it is obvious that your 'examinations of his transactions' were not 'adequate.' We must regretfully advise you, accordingly, that there is no activity anywhere."

29. Applied Proverbs

A few years ago a surety company itself suffered a serious default on the part of a member of its staff. "Who is worse shod than the shoemaker's wife?" The defaulter was bonded by another surety company, and liability was denied because of the assured's failure to fulfil the stipulations embodied in the preliminary and renewal statements. This interesting dog-eat-dog episode suggests one of Chaucer's sage observations: "He must have a long spoon that eats with the Devil." If anyone objects to my dragging in Mr. Chaucer, on the ground that his authority is too ancient to have weight in the matter, I would cite the analogy of the case of Sagebrush Sam of Catamount Crossroads, Arizona. At a critical point in that case the stranger laid down four aces and scooped in the pot. "This game ain't on the level," protested Sagebrush Sam, at the same time producing a gun with which to emphasize his remarks, "that ain't the hand I dealt ye."

30. Representations and Warranties

A vast amount of litigation over fidelity bonds has been concerned with the legal effect of the preliminary declarations of the assured regarding the conditions of the risk, heretofore referred to as the "employer's statement," and the similar, reaffirming declarations made at the annual premium-anniversary dates and known as the "employer's renewal statement." Sometimes these documents have been held to be, in legal parlance, "representations," and in such cases their falsity has not invalidated the bond, unless they have related to facts material to the risk. Sometimes, however, they have been held to be "warranties," and in such cases their falsity has *ipso facto* nullified the insurance, since any statement warranted by the assured to be true is regarded in law as necessarily material, and the validity of the insurance is conditioned upon its truth.

It is easy to see that warranties are more likely than

representations to prove troublesome to the assured, and block the path to recovery in the event of claims. While it seems reasonable enough on general principles, when an insurer has assumed a given risk in reliance upon the statements made by the assured and warranted by the latter to be true, for the insurer to hold the assured to his agreement, yet in practice this doctrine of warranty was frequently found to facilitate inequitable results. The average man will not read his bond, and even if he does and thus finds himself "warranting" the truth of certain statements, he rarely realizes how important the phraseology is or understands its legal connotation. Many states, therefore, have passed laws that virtually annihilate the distinction between representations and warranties; and in such states bond forms that have been narrowly drawn in this respect will be automatically broadened by the local statutes.

31. Benevolent Attitude of Courts

Even without the aid of statutory law and in reliance solely upon general principles of justice, the courts have ever been prone to temper the invalidating wind to the shorn bond-holding lamb in a closely litigated case. The primary indemnifying purpose of the bond will always loom large in the mind of the court, and will be effectuated, even at the cost of rather ingenious reasoning if necessary, when only such an end would square with the demands of ultimate justice.

In the old days of private suretyship one who gave a bond was regarded as a "favorite of the law," and the person in whose favor the bond ran was held rigidly to its terms, and frequently lost all its benefits by some negligent deviation therefrom. This rule of *strictissimi juris* (as it is called in the law books) has been greatly relaxed under present-day conditions of compensated suretyship; and the courts show a natural and justifiable tendency to favor the assured in close cases involving this principle. But the law still requires, and ever will require, no doubt, the best of good faith on the part of the assured. There must be no misrepresentation of material facts, no failure to answer fully and frankly all reasonable questions concerning the risk, no intent to deceive. If under such conditions the insurer suffers loss because he has not used proper diligence in ascertaining the liability involved, he cannot escape the consequences of his own negligence. "The law stands between the parties perfectly impartial, ready to rebuke fraud, concealment, or misrepresentation on the part of either; but carelessness and want of proper vigilance are left to their own fruits."

32. Liberalized Bonds Due to Various Causes

In the long run no business can survive and prosper unless it serves a useful public purpose and serves it well. Fidelity premiums in the United States in 1921 aggregated about $23,500,000 (as compared with surety premiums of over $36,000,000). This imposing volume of fidelity business could not have been built up unless the insurers had radically changed their practices as described above, and had sold to their patrons a product of far greater value than the old-fashioned narrow fidelity instrument. Almost from the beginning the more broad-minded executives saw that they could not permanently do business on the existing illiberal basis, and they began gradually to modify their requirements. While continuing to insist that the assured make and warrant preliminary and renewal statements, they did so less with the idea of standing strictly upon their legal

4

rights in the case of just claims than with the idea of insuring close supervision of the employee's work by the employer, or perhaps of providing themselves with a technical defense against unjust claims. In the case, for example, of the company referred to above as exacting from employers a preposterous renewal statement— a company that has always been noted for the liberality of its treatment of the assured—I am confident that the company never availed itself, in handling a fair claim, of the legal advantage accruing to it because the employer had innocently and without substantial fault failed to make "adequate examinations."

These preliminary statements, and to a less extent renewal statements, are still required by the bonding companies in many cases; but such statements are no longer as a rule warranted or otherwise made a part of the contract, and their falsity would not now, in the absence of fraud, invalidate the bond. It is natural and reasonable for a surety company, before bonding a man in an important position, to ascertain from the employer what accounting methods are followed; and this information may be conveniently obtained by means of the printed form still called an "employer's statement." This is done, however, in connection with and as an aid to the underwriting, and not as an essential, and possibly invalidating, feature of the contract between the parties.

33. Broadening Outside Influences

It is thus apparent that the change from the early narrow forms of fidelity bonds to the present comprehensive instruments has come about largely from causes operating within the surety companies; but the development was due, also, in the case of two important causes, to influences outside the companies. More and more have the various states, through their insurance departments, fastened watchful eyes upon the operations of the surety companies; and in certain cases changes in bond forms in the direction of broader protection and freedom from confining conditions have been the direct result of the regulatory supervision of these departments. Sometimes, probably, the state officials have exceeded their real authority in forcing the companies to issue simpler and broader policies; and frequently, no doubt, they have attained their ends more by the pressure of practical considerations than as a matter of admitted and undoubted right. The net effect, however, in any case has been to secure for the public a greater degree of fidelity protection, and to confront the insurers with the problem of procuring from some source sufficient revenue to meet the resultant higher loss ratios.

Another important outside influence promoting the liberalization of fidelity bonds may be found in the nature of the laws enacted by many state legislatures. Quite commonly, for example, public officials have been required by statute to furnish bonds conditioned "for the faithful performance" of the duties of their office; and in such cases the surety companies simply wasted good ink and paper if they tried to modify the bald requirement of the statute by interjecting limitations upon their liability. In some states similar laws have been passed in regard to officers of banks and certain other quasi-public officials, with the same automatic and inescapable broadening effect upon the bonds given in behalf of such officials (cf. section 50).

34. Competition the Chief Broadening Force

By far the most important reason for the liberalization of fidelity policies has been the aggressive and persistent competition of the bonding companies. Not content with building up their volume through the creation of new business—not a hard thing to do in view of the virgin field and the recognized need of the protection afforded by the policies—the companies have always preferred to make a short cut to their goal by preying upon each other's preserves. Formerly their favorite tool for prying loose a choice line of bonds was rate-cutting; but when, about fourteen years ago, the organization of the Rating Bureau put an end (just in the nick of time for some companies) to that form of slow suicide, they concentrated their competing energies upon the point of liberality of bond forms. Such a policy once begun necessarily spread quickly. Every time a broader policy was issued by any company the continued existence of the older and narrower forms became impracticable. Even if executives could reconcile with their ideas of fair and proper methods of doing business the withholding from old clients of concessions made to new ones under the stress of competition, the alert and zealous agents and brokers could be depended upon to see to it that their clients obtained the best and broadest policies anywhere obtainable.

35. Standard Form of Fidelity Bond

The wholesome injunction embodied in the Greek proverb, "Do nothing too much," was so far ignored by the companies in this matter of broad bond forms that they finally came to err as much in the direction of unnecessary and unwarranted liberality as they had in the early days in the opposite respect; and it ultimately came to be pretty well agreed among executives that a halt should be called. Some years ago, accordingly, the matter was brought up before the Surety Association of America, and a certain wag, who tries to be funny in season and out of season (and who sometimes unwittingly succeeds), introduced the following resolution:

> Whereas, the companies are now issuing fidelity bonds of great diversity of protective scope, ranging from instruments composed of a rivulet of insurance lost in a meadow of limiting conditions to instruments consisting of an ocean of obligation and an attestation clause; and
>
> Whereas, there would be manifest advantage in the adoption by the companies generally of a standard, uniform fidelity bond form affording all necessary and reasonable protection to the obligee, but conceding, to the extent of a comma or two, the right of the obligor to live—if for no other purpose than to draw the obligee's check:
>
> Resolved, That a committee of five experienced fidelity underwriters, distinguished for their broadmindedness, but known to be sane, be appointed by the chair to draft a standard fidelity bond form, and to submit the same to the Association for fastidious consideration and possible adoption.

That resolution was adopted by the Surety Association; and the committee so appointed, after holding a number of meetings and giving the subject much thought, reported to the Association a proposed form of bond. The form was adopted, and is known as the "Surety Association Standard Form of Fidelity Bond." A few years ago this form would have been regarded as extremely liberal, and none of its provisions can reasonably be criticized as in any degree unfair to the assured. Some companies are, however, still using in many cases forms of bonds that give the assured more privileges and rights than they really need and surely more than they pay for at current premium rates. Other companies are using the standard form freely, and have no difficulty in procuring its acceptance by the assured. (See section 68 for an analysis of this form.)

36. "One-Man Banks"

Most underwriters would avoid altogether if they could, even at the relatively high rate obtainable, fidelity bonds covering small country banks. Usually only one or two men are bonded—sometimes only the cashier or the president; and it is clear from the whole situation that the important underwriting safeguard so much emphasized in this chapter, supervision of the bonded employee's work, is likely to be largely absent in these cases. They are known in surety parlance as "one-man banks," and underwriters steer clear of them, as indicated, when they can do so without imperiling other and desirable business or without disobliging a valued agent.

Usually the one man who dominates the bank is the president, and that circumstance does not improve the risk from the underwriter's point of view. It may seem odd to some people, but the simple fact is that, generally speaking, underwriters regard all presidents of small banks with suspicion, and would rather not bond them. This attitude should not be deemed unduly severe on bank presidents—it applies equally, and indeed with more force, to the presidents of any small organization where the bonded chief is free to a large extent to do what he will with the trust funds under his control. Almost always, of course, the presidents of small banks are excellent fidelity risks; but underwriters cannot assume risks on an "almost always" basis; to do so would mean ultimate disaster. Their one safe course is to go ahead only when every known condition is favorable; even then they suffer losses from unknown conditions.

37. Savings Banks

While the rate for bonds covering the officials and staffs of savings banks is no higher than that prevailing in the case of other kinds of banks, many underwriters believe the risk to be distinctly more hazardous in the former class. This is so because of the greater opportunity for wrongdoing open to dishonest tellers and other employees in a savings bank dealing with ignorant depositors. A savings bank in a large city has scores of thousands of depositors (one in Philadelphia has 265,000) scattered far and wide. Many of the accounts are dormant, and the pass-books sometimes remain out for years without being compared with the ledgers. A dishonest teller, receiving $100 on such an account, can credit the correct amount in the pass-book, but enter only $50 (or nothing whatever as for that) in the ledger; and if he has chosen his depositor with judgment, the crime may not be discovered for years.

An interesting mechanical method of guarding this danger point is available and seems worthy of trial by a savings bank. The receiving teller must enter all deposits in pass-books with a machine that prints in duplicate; and when the entry is made in the pass-book a duplicate entry is simultaneously and inevitably made on a ribbon of paper enclosed in a locked box. At the close of the day this enclosed tape is taken from the box; and every entry thereon, originally a credit to a depositor, becomes now a debit to the teller and an automatic check of his work. The device registers totals, also, and the exact amount of the day's receipts for which the teller must account is shown at once.

38. Rotation and Vacations Desirable

An underwriter counts it a good sign when a bank or other bonded institution occasionally shifts its clerks without warning from one post to another. In a large proportion of the defalcations forced upon the unhappy

attention of the bonding companies, the defaulter is
allowed to keep his books and handle his cash exclusively
for long periods.   In many British banks no clerk knows
when he leaves his desk today to what department he
will be assigned tomorrow.   That is one important
reason why bank defalcations in Great Britain are so
rare.

When an underwriter finds that an employee holding
a responsible position is permitted by the management
to remain at his post indefinitely without a vacation, he
should suggest as politely as may be the expediency of a
change of air for the faithful servant; such a proposal
will often be received in good part and adopted.

39. The "Handles-No-Cash" Fallacy

Surety companies are often asked to abate their
regular charge for a fidelity bond, or to waive some
usual requirement as to audits and supervision, because
the person bonded "handles no cash."   Both antecedent
reasoning and experience in painful abundance show the
weakness of this argument.

For some reasons, indeed, a company takes less chance
when it bonds money-handling positions.   Usually
people who handle cash all the time are subject to daily
audits and to rigid supervision otherwise, while people
who do not handle money are able to find undetectable
ways of getting ultimate cash.   All the surety companies
have repeatedly paid claims on bookkeepers, for example, who have had no access to the cash-drawer, but
who have forged checks or have made out checks to
fictitious payees and have collected the proceeds themselves, or have in some other ingenious way gotten possession of their employer's cash.   They have held non-
money-handling positions; but they have contrived in

some way to handle their employer's money just the same.

40. Overlooking the Obvious

It seems strange that it should be so, but experience shows that corporation officials and other employers will often fail to put two and two together when they see their salaried people living far beyond their incomes. Fidelity-claim adjusters continually find that the defaulter was known for some time to have been living in a style of luxury quite inconsistent with his moderate salary, and that everybody, including his own superiors or employer, took it for granted that he had additional and legitimate outside sources of income. Fidelity underwriters, if they know their business, do not thus complacently accept a situation on its face anomalous and requiring explanation.

A flagrant but otherwise typical case of the kind in question may be cited from my own experience. This was the more remarkable from the fact that the defaulter did not live in a large city, where an extravagant establishment and lavish outlays might easily escape the notice of superior officers, but in a little Massachusetts town, where every man's life is an open book to all the countryside.

We had been bonding the man, a bank officer, for years, and our information about him was uniformly good. One day, however, in pursuance of our policy of investigating periodically the home life and domestic conditions of important "risks" of this kind, we sent an investigator to look up the man thoroughly on the ground. The fact soon transpired that the man was living in a manner by no means justified by his moderate salary in the bank. Everybody apparently knew that he was spending money freely, but nobody could tell the investigator where the money came from. They all seemed to think that it was all right, some people suggesting speculation and others a legacy as the explanation.

The investigator also thought at first that it was all right, but he did not fall into the error of *assuming* so and letting it go at that. On the contrary, he thought it proper to assume just the other thing, and to make the man show him that such a view was wrong. When he put it up to the bank official, the latter's explanation was so unconvincing and his general attitude so little reassuring that the bond was cancelled. A short time afterward it was discovered that the official had stolen a large amount of money from the bank.

41. The Principal's Salary

Other things being equal, a surety company's risk is greater when the salary of the person bonded is not sufficient to enable him to live comfortably and in a style reasonably accordant with the requirements of his business life and his general position in society. This point comes up particularly with underwriters who handle bonds covering officials and clerks in banks; and sometimes they prefer not to accept a given line of bonds, because they do not see how the persons bonded are going to be able to get along upon the meager salaries paid to them. The point is naturally a delicate one to discuss with the employer, but the alternative in some cases is to decline the business.

All this, of course, applies to exceptional cases and not to the general run of bonded positions. The salaries paid to the officers and clerical staffs of banking institutions are commonly thought to be unreasonably small; and when a cashier or similar official entrusted with the custody of other people's money goes wrong, the newspapers are prone to ascribe the trouble to the "niggardly" salary paid to the unfortunate defaulter. While such implied criticisms of bank management have sometimes seemed warranted by the facts disclosed, it appears, from an investigation made a few years ago by the Comptroller of the Currency, that the average salary of the 66,000 officers and employees of national banks was then $110 a month. The figure is somewhat higher than might have been expected, in view of the fact that a very large proportion of the employees are mere clerks, and that the compilation includes a vast number of banks located in the smaller cities and towns, where salaries are likely to be low. It is probable, too, that a similar investigation made to-day would show an average considerably higher than the one previously obtained.

From the same source it is found that the presidents of national banks having a capital of $50,000 or less received, at the time of the investigation, an average salary of $1,008 per annum and that the presidents of national banks having a capital of $5,000,000 or more received on the average $44,400 per annum. Many people would regard the former figure as too small; and more the latter as too large. It is to be remembered, however, that the presidents of small banks are frequently engaged in other occupations, and give the bank comparatively little time.

CHAPTER IV

SPECIAL CLASSES OF FIDELITY BONDS

42. Attorneys Specializing in Collections

Large business concerns and other creditors are continually forwarding claims for collection to attorneys in all parts of the country. It is said that Lincoln, when asked whether a lawyer could be an honest man, made no reply, but remained buried in thought for some time, and then began to talk about something else. The story is presumably apocryphal, like so many other Lincoln anecdotes, but large forwarders of claims know from abundant and painful experience that not all attorneys exemplify in their dealings with distant clients the qualities of efficiency and integrity that are undoubtedly characteristic of the legal profession in general. As a result of this admitted condition of things, many so-called "bonded lists" of attorneys have come into being; that is, some central organization will publish a list of attorneys located in all cities, county seats, and other important commercial centers, who will undertake to collect, at fixed moderate rates, claims sent to them by subscribers to the service. One of the common inducements held out to prospective subscribers is a guarantee that all listed attorneys will faithfully account for the proceeds of claims sent over the list. The bond is limited in amount and is valid only when certain details of recording and notifying are observed by the forwarder, but, in general, adequate and highly useful protection is available to forwarders under the system described. The central organization makes a single comprehensive contract with some surety company whereby the latter undertakes to become surety as described for all the attorneys listed. While "trouble notices" concerned with these bonds are frequent, and resultant vexatious correspondence is a common incident of the business, and while actual losses must occasionally be paid, yet the bonds as a whole are looked upon by the companies with favor.

Sometimes individual attorneys, eager to build up a large commercial law practice, apply to surety companies for similar bonds running in behalf of only the individual applicant and in favor of only his particular clients. Bonds of this variety, guaranteeing that the given attorney will faithfully account for the proceeds of claims entrusted to him for collection, are regarded likewise as desirable business, provided an investigation develops none but normal or exceptionally favorable information regarding the personal, professional, and financial aspects of the risk. The form of bond, however, may occasion a little difficulty because of the necessity or desirability of limiting the aggregate amount at risk. The following form is used by one company:

> WHEREAS............(the collecting attorney) of........ hereinafter called the *Principal*, is engaged in the mercantile collecting business, and will receive claims for collection from persons, firms, and corporations, hereinafter called the *Obligees;* and
>
> WHEREAS it is the purpose of the Principal in conducting the said business to indemnify the Obligees from and against any and all loss by reason of the defalcation of the Principal:
>
> NOW, THEREFORE, THE GIBRALTAR SURETY COMPANY OF NEW YORK, hereinafter called the *Company*, does hereby agree that it will reimburse the Obligees for the direct loss, not exceeding in the aggregate...........dollars (........), of any money through the dishonest appropriation thereof by the Principal during the term of this bond in connection with

any claims filed by the Obligees with the Principal during the said term.

The foregoing agreement is subject to the following conditions:

1. The term of this bond begins on the.........day of ....192.., at noon, standard time, at the Principal's address hereinbefore stated, and ends on the.......day of ......192.., at noon, standard time, at the said address.

2. The claims of the Obligees hereunder shall be settled in the order in which they are received by the Company, the first claim received by the Company being the first claim for settlement, and so on. Every payment made by the Company hereunder shall be accounted in diminution of the insurance hereunder, and in no event shall the Company's liability for any and all claims exceed the sum of.......dollars (......).

3. No claim shall be made hereunder unless the dishonest appropriation of the Principal is discovered within the term of this bond or within six months from the termination thereof; and no action shall be brought against the Company under or by reason of this bond unless it shall be brought within six months from the date of the discovery of the loss for which the action is brought.

4. The Company may at any time terminate its liability under this bond by a written notice stating when such cancellation shall be effective served on the Principal, or sent by registered mail to the Principal, at the address hereinbefore stated. The date on which the cancellation is to be effective shall not be less than thirty days after the date on which the cancellation notice is mailed or served.

43. Fraternal Orders

There are in the United States not far from two hundred "fraternal societies"—voluntary groups of persons who have formed themselves into organizations for some meritorious purpose other than commercial. In many cases life insurance is the chief, or at least an important, purpose of the organization. Sometimes these "orders" cover the entire country and include a vast number of

bonded officers.   There will be a few large bonds ($100,-
000 or more) covering the high officials holding office in
the "Supreme" or "Grand" organization, and a multitude
of small bonds (up and down from $500) covering the
collectors of monthly dues and similar officers in the
local or subordinate bodies.   Position forms of bonds
(cf. Chapter V) are commonly issued in the case of large
fraternal orders—that is, the bond covers the office
irrespective of the temporary incumbent, so that the
insurance is not affected by changes in the official personnel.

Sometimes subordinate bodies of fraternal orders procure bonds locally covering their own officers; and sometimes, especially in the case of large societies, the supreme body makes a contract for bonds covering not
only its own roster, but also all the officials of subordinate bodies wherever located.   In this latter case a vo-
luminous schedule, in a constant state of flux, is attached
to the main bond, and shows what positions are covered,
and in what amounts, everywhere.

Fraternal-order business as a class is regarded by most
underwriters as exceptionally desirable.   The high officials of the big organizations devote their entire time to
the work and are liberally compensated; but the great
bulk of the bonded persons, the officers of the subordinate bodies, commonly serve without pay or for nominal
salaries, and are chosen because of their well-known
probity and trustworthiness.   That is one reason why
the position form of bond is practicable.

44. Three Degrees of Fraternal Insurance

Fraternal-order bonds of three kinds are issued, in
accordance with the amount of protection provided, as
follows:

Form A bonds provide insurance against losses due to dishonest appropriation only. They are ordinary fraud or dishonesty bonds.

Form B bonds include all the insurance afforded by Form A bonds, and in addition guarantee that the officials bonded will faithfully perform their duties and comply with the constitution and by-laws of the order.

Form C bonds provide all the insurance afforded by Form B bonds, and in addition important and comprehensive protection of other kinds, including the insurance of money deposited in banks. They guarantee the safekeeping of all funds and an absolute accounting therefor in accordance with the constitution and by-laws of the order.

For a number of reasons it seems desirable to issue Form C bonds whenever the order is willing to pay a corresponding premium. The persons who negotiate for the bonds are not, ordinarily, except in the case of the large orders, keen business men who appreciate the difference in the coverage of the three classes of bonds, and realize that the lower-priced instruments necessarily carry less protection. From the nature of the case full protection is highly desirable, and is expected by the public; and an unpleasant claim situation arises if a loss occurs that is not covered because of the narrow form of bond in force. The Form C instrument costs so little that agents would be well advised to place it in every practicable case. Under it a lodge is protected against virtually all contingencies. A loss, for example, due to the failure of a bank in which an official has deposited lodge money, or a loss due to a robbery of lodge money from an official on his way home from a meeting, would be covered by a Form C bond, but not by either of the other bonds.

45. Fraternal Rates Incomprehensible

In view of the vast number of fidelity and surety classifications that must be separately rated, and of the baffling complexity of the subject generally, the ease and certainty with which surety executives and fieldmen are able all the time to ascertain the correct rate in any given case demonstrate beyond question the excellence of the Rating Bureau's work. This general statement, however, does not apply to fraternal-order rates, in the confident opinion of the author, who regards them as confused, illogical, impracticable, and generally indefensible. There is no difficulty in the case of isolated lodges applying to local agents for their particular bonds; but when the supreme body makes a contract for the bonds of the entire order, the rate depends upon the aggregate volume of suretyship so placed, and changes every time a fresh risk is added to the schedule. The rule is obviously unworkable in practice, and cannot be followed consistently by any company. Most of the big fraternal-order schedules have been monopolized by a few companies, and the absurd premium regulations have tended to strengthen their hold upon the business. All the large orders should be specifically rated, the sliding-scale rule abolished, and the other orders made subject to a simple and uniform rate.

As the matter stands now I defy anybody, when a large fraternal-order schedule is in question, to ascertain the rate even with prolonged and expert study of the Manual. I have the highest regard, in general, for the Towner Rating Bureau; and as for the Rate Manual, in my mature and Britannically authoritative opinion that is the greatest product of the human brain since Moses (if it was he) wrote the Pentateuch (if that was it). They do say, and with justice, that the Towner Manual makes

5

Kant's "Kritik of Pure Reason" look like a baseball score-card. However and nevertheless and notwithstanding all the aforesaid, I do wish that the learned, genial, and outstandingly capable manager of the Rating Bureau would take a day off sometime and set his crystalline intellect to work upon the fraternal-order pages of the Manual and clear up some of the mystifications embodied therein. It is about as clear now as an income-tax blank decoded into Hottentot.

When I find it necessary to obtain a fraternal-order rate, I summon thirty of my most learned and expert statisticians, provide them with the latest treatises on differential calculus, with slide-rules, logarithmic tables, and the Giants' batting averages, and tell them to strip off their coats and go to it. When they hand in their results at the end of the day I add together the thirty different answers, divide the total by thirty, and there's my rate.

Sometimes I apply a simpler method to the problem as follows: Having decided on general principles what the rate ought to be—22½ cents, say—I paw around among the Manual pages until I find a combination of paragraphs, parenthetical exceptions, and brilliant-point footnotes that together demonstrate the rate to be exactly 22½ cents. I adopt this method when my time is short, as I can always find such a combination in an hour or two.

The other day when a stupid agent wrote to me that he had been unable to make out the rate from the Manual, I replied as follows:

> I am surprised that you thought it necessary to consult me about this simple matter.
> It is clear from section 7 on page 16 of the Manual that the rate is 24 cents. This section, though, is so modified by para-

graph b of section 2 on page 36 that the rate becomes 17 cents instead of 24. However, these two sections are inoperative under the conditions laid down in the last sentence but one on page 47-h, so that the rate there mentioned, 32 cents, is correct.

You understand, of course, that all this is subject to Supplemental Tissue no. 1323, sent to you April 1, 1911, whereby the 32-cent rate otherwise effective becomes 37 cents if the tide is high when the rate is quoted, 26 cents if the tide is low, and intermediate rates in accordance with tidal conditions at the moment of quoting.

While I give you a rate on this occasion, as requested, do not bother me next time, but look it up for yourself in the Manual.

46. Charitable Organizations

Under various classifications in the Rate Manual it is permissible to quote exceptionally low rates for fidelity bonds given in behalf of officers and ordinary staff employees of societies and organizations devoted to philanthropic purposes. The theory upon which these low rates were originally authorized was, no doubt, that the incumbents of such positions would naturally be persons interested in charitable work and thus presumably persons of exceptionally high character.

That theory is clearly sound as applied to directors, trustees, and similar officials in general charge of the affairs of eleemosynary institutions; and it is sound also, though perhaps in less degree, as applied to the active executive officers of such organizations; but the theory may well be questioned when it comes to the rank and file of staff employees. By some strange perversity of suretyship chances these latter risks not infrequently have turned out bad. One reason for that, perhaps, is that benevolent organizations are not likely to be conducted with high efficiency, and especially are their managers not likely to be looking for embezzlement trouble or taking suitable precautions to guard against it.

Not long ago, for example, one company paid a considerable loss in behalf of a trusted bookkeeper of a large hospital. This man was unusually resourceful in his fraudulent methods: he raised checks; he bought drugs ostensibly for the hospital and upon the hospital's credit, but really that he might sell them privately to physicians and pocket the proceeds; he stole valuables belonging to patients and placed in his charge for safe-keeping; and even, when an operatic performance was given for the benefit of the hospital, appropriated the $750 representing the proceeds of the concert, evidently on the theory that the opera had been given for *his* benefit.

When the science of fidelity underwriting has made further progress, through the accumulation of statistics and the research of students of the subject, it may be conjectured that the present uniform rate for the bonds in question will be split up, and a higher rate named for ordinary staff employees. Such a course would seem to be justified both by *a priori* reasoning and by the experience of the companies.

Some time ago I received in one mail from the same manager a large batch of fidelity applications covering cashiers and ticket-sellers of a big race-track association and another smaller batch submitted by the staff of a local Y. M. C. A. I questioned the judgment of the manager in accepting the former piece of business. A few months later he properly rebuked me by reporting a Y. M. C. A. claim and accompanying it with the statement that the loss ratio under the race-track bonds, upon which liability had already terminated, had been nil.

47. Assigned Accounts

Many manufacturers, jobbers, and other business men borrow money upon the security of their receivables—

they pledge to the lenders the accounts owed to them. They sell merchandise in the ordinary course of trade upon credit and assign the accounts thus created to some banker, who lends to them upon such security 90 per cent, say, of the face of the amount of the accounts. Since the borrower prefers not to have it known to his customers that he needs accommodation of this kind, the banker agrees not to notify the customer of the assignment of the account, and the customer pays his indebtedness at maturity directly to the borrower. The latter is then bound, both by his explicit agreement with the banker and by all the dictates of common honesty, to turn over at once to the banker the amount received from the customer. A situation thus arises that seems made to order for fidelity bonds, and such bonds were written in large volume a few years ago and are still frequently called for.

Most underwriters would not at first regard such business as abnormally hazardous. Losses cannot arise unless the principal is guilty of the grossest bad faith, and is willing to run the risk of a state's-prison term and of permanent business ruin; and the theory of underwriters for a long time was that such a contingency was extremely remote in the case of long-established business houses of high financial rating and excellent reputation in the trade. The experience of one large company with the line was for some time satisfactory, but it became increasingly bad, notwithstanding the adoption of elaborate auditing systems and of every other precaution that seemed practicable to make the business safe. This experience covered six years of time, a wide variety of industries, most parts of the country, and a volume of business producing premiums of about $30,000 a year. This company's final view of the business is shown by the following extract from a letter that it now writes to agents who submit assigned-accounts risks:

> Although we drew our underwriting lines closer and closer, and advanced rates to a point that evoked protests to the Bureau from other and less experienced companies, we were finally forced to conclude that some factors overlooked or insufficiently weighed by us counterbalanced all the antecedently favorable reasoning, and made the business unwritable under any conditions. Unless the moral standards of the commercial world advance materially or our underwriting skill improves greatly, this must continue to be our attitude. While we are optimistic as to the first arm of the alternative, the outlook in the second respect seems so dubious that we throw up our hands.

The method of underwriting assigned-accounts bonds recommended by the author is the following: Investigate the proposed principal with microscopic thoroughness, by means of mercantile-agency reports, banking references, and every other known device; obtain a fresh, completely itemized financial statement, sworn to before a notary with all solemnity, and verified as to every item at all susceptible of such treatment; procure indemnity agreements from everybody in sight; arrange to have auditors inspect the principal's books at weekly intervals: and when all this has been done, with no adverse development or faintest hint of danger—turn down the business!

48. Warehouse Custodians

A business concern sometimes borrows money from its bank upon the security of merchandise which it agrees not to dispose of without first or simultaneously paying off the loan, and which it often agrees to keep in some designated place, termed a warehouse, pending such disposition and loan repayment. Under such conditions application is frequently made for a bond covering the business concern itself as principal, or perhaps one of the officers or employees of the concern as principal, and conditioned for the faithful carrying out of the agreement described. Bonds of this general character seem to most agents, and indeed to most underwriters early in their career, little more than ordinary fidelity bonds, and thus not hazardous in the case of principals for whom fidelity bonds would readily be written as a matter of course. Painful and costly experience, however, has caused underwriters to view warehouse bonds of this kind with a critical eye. The trouble is that when a warehouse-bond principal finds himself in a financial corner, it is not hard for him to extricate himself, for the time being anyway, either by issuing duplicate warehouse receipts and thus raising fresh funds upon the same merchandise or by selling the merchandise and appropriating the proceeds, notwithstanding the fact that the property has been pledged to a bank or some other lender.

While warehouse bonds of this nature are not regarded by most underwriters as altogether unissuable, they rarely feel able to provide such suretyship except in behalf of principals of high personal and financial standing; and even then only when they are permitted to check at frequent intervals the merchandise supposed to be in the warehouse. These risks bear a painful resemblance, from an underwriting point of view, to the assigned-accounts bonds just discussed.

49. Certificates of Character

Several times companies have tried, with scant success, to build up a business in the issuance of "certificates of character"—statements evidencing the fact that the person in whose name the certificate is made out has been investigated by the surety company and is eligible for a fidelity bond to be issued by such company. The theory is that a person holding such a certificate and seeking employment will have a distinct advantage in competing for a given position over a person without such credentials. The theory seems sound, but in practice the plan has' fallen flat. One company, for example, advertised its certificates rather exclusively in the "Help Wanted" columns of papers specializing in that field, at the peak of the unemployment troubles of 1921, when, if ever, conditions seemed ripe for such a service, without getting back enough revenue to defray the cost of advertising.

The applicant for a certificate completes a form similar to an ordinary application for a fidelity bond, and signs a statement at the end as follows:

> I hereby declare that the foregoing statements are true, and I apply to the Gibraltar Surety Company for an investigation of my character and career, that it may thereafter, if it shall be willing to do so, issue a Certificate of Character concerning me. I hereby agree to pay to the said company a fee of $5 as compensation for such investigation. I understand that the fee is payable in advance, and that I shall receive no rebate in case the company, because of the unfavorable nature of the information received about me, shall decline to issue a Certificate.

The certificate of character, after identifying fully the certificated person (name, birthplace, age, residential address, height, color, and autographed signature), reads as follows:

> The Gibraltar Surety Company does hereby certify that it has made a thoroughgoing investigation, up to the date shown below, of the character and career of the person named above; that this investigation disclosed no unfavorable features; and that the company is willing at this date to issue a bond in behalf of the said person covering him or her in any appropriate capacity and amount.

It seemed to the author worth while to record all this, because every little while some company has this same brilliant idea about certificates, and the foregoing information may be of interest and value to any such company.

"There is a best way of doing everything," says Emerson, "even if it be but to boil an egg"; perhaps the companies that have failed to make their certificates of character go did not boil their eggs expertly.

50. Statutory Quasi-Public Fidelity Bonds

Fiduciary and public-official bonds are largely fidelity instruments, and in their case underwriters take it for granted that the bonds will be written upon prescribed forms, and will be straight-out faithful-performance-of-duty obligations. As for all other classes of fidelity bonds, where the obligees are private and where the state as a guardian of the public is not directly interested, the companies are able to issue bonds of their own designing, which are intended to cover only losses due to dishonesty, and which otherwise embody conditions deemed essential to the prudent conduct of the surety company's business and in no wise unjust to the obligee. The competition of the companies has made even these every-day mercantile bonds extraordinarily liberal, but none of them (with rare exceptions not concerned with the present point) indemnify the assured for losses other than those due to dishonesty of some kind.

The general situation outlined has changed in a few states, and seems likely to change in additional territory, and perhaps to change still more in all the places affected, with the growth of paternalistic and socialistic thought and legislation. Already a considerable number of states have enacted legislation requiring banks organized under the laws of such states to bond their officers, or certain of them, in ways involving more than mere dishonesty protection. The statutes are not uniformly phrased, but almost always they call for bonds broader than those ordinarily issued by any company to mercantile concerns; and sometimes they are so worded as to cover losses arising out of pure negligence—losses, for example, due to the mishandling of securities by a bonded official, or his careless overpayment of checks, or even perhaps his poor judgment in making loans. Similar bonds are required in certain states from the officials of insurance companies, the managers of public warehouses, and the like. At present the statutory bank bonds referred to are more numerous than any other bonds of this class.

While a somewhat higher premium is obtained for these bonds than for the corresponding company-form bonds customarily issued, it may be doubted that the differential adequately covers the increased hazard. Partly because bank managers desire to save the difference in premium, and partly because surety companies prefer it so and encourage the practice, many state banks take out small bonds upon the statutory form, in order to satisfy the requirements of the law, and simultaneously procure what they regard as their real protection by purchasing, at the lower rate, company-form bonds of much larger amount. This device has been used pretty freely for some years in the states concerned, and apparently the surety companies have no fear that the statute will be read into their forms in the case of a loss not covered thereunder but falling within the broader terms of the legal requirement. Let us hope that this confidence is justified; but stranger things than that have happened to the surety companies in their adventures with the courts.

CHAPTER V

POSITION FIDELITY BONDS

51. Position Insurance Explained

The position form of bond provides insurance identical with that afforded by ordinary fidelity bonds, but differs from the latter in the important respect that while the usual bond covers defaults on the part of a *particular person* designated by name, the position bond covers the defaults of *any person* holding a *particular position* designated by name. If, for example, the cashier of the Brown Manufacturing Company, John Jones, is bonded in the sum of $5,000 in the ordinary manner, and Jones is discharged or resigns or for some other reason ceases to act as cashier, and if his successor, not bonded through inadvertence or delay, steals $5,000 from the B. M. Company, the latter is out that amount; but if, under the conditions described, not Jones personally, but the position of cashier, had been bonded in the sum of $5,000, the B. M. Company would have been protected regardless of the identity of the person who happened to succeed Jones.

52. Description of a Position Bond

The insuring clause is much like that of an ordinary fidelity bond, and embodies the undertaking of the surety to indemnify the obligee for losses due to the dishonesty of persons (any persons) holding certain designated positions. A schedule attached to the bond shows clearly the scope of the protection as to personnel by setting out:

(a) The titles of the positions covered (treasurer, secretary, cashier, bookkeeper, branch-office manager, etc.).

(b) The place where the incumbents of the given position are located.

(c) The number of incumbents of each position (sometimes only one, but sometimes, in the case of large organizations, a considerable number).

(d) The amount of insurance provided in the case of each incumbent of the given position. The named amount is the maximum liability of the surety for the default of any one incumbent of the given position; and if an employee has held more than one of the positions listed and has been guilty of dishonesty in each position, the surety's liability is limited to the largest amount recoverable on account of any one of the positions covered.

(e) The aggregate insurance provided for each position (depending upon the number of incumbents) and the aggregate for all positions.

The forms of position bonds used by the various companies are not identical, but they all substantially fit the foregoing description.

53. Position Bonds Are Not Blanket Bonds

It should be noted that the protection afforded by position bonds, broad as it is, falls short nevertheless of blanket-bond insurance. The employer in case of loss must do more than show merely that he has sustained a loss—he must show that the loss was due to the dishonesty of some employee holding a position listed in the schedule (not any position whatever—unless, indeed, all positions are listed).

54. Data Required from the Employer

Before the bond can be written the assured must give the surety information that will enable the latter to complete the schedule in accordance with the plan outlined in section 52 above. While the employer must, for his own benefit and safety, give close attention to all the items of this schedule, it is especially important that he consider carefully how many incumbents he should list for each position. Indeed, the whole theory of position insurance, from the standpoint of the surety's premium income, pivots on this point. Since the premium depends upon the number of employees listed in the case of each position, the surety must protect itself against failure on the part of the employer to list and pay for the full number of incumbents of a given position. If, for example, a large corporation, employing regularly ten cashiers and desiring to have the position of cashier covered in the sum of $5,000, say, as to all ten incumbents, should list only five persons as holding that position and should pay a premium as to that position upon $25,000 only, and if one of the cashiers should steal $5,000, and the fact should transpire in the investigation of the loss that twice as many cashiers were employed as the schedule indicated—such a situation would obviously be unpleasant for all concerned. If the employer has deliberately understated the number of incumbents for the sake of saving half the premium, a denial of liability by the surety would doubtless be justified; but the employer may not have meant to deceive the surety, and the false statement may have been due to mere inadvertence on his part, to the carelessness of a clerk, or to some other innocent cause. The surety nevertheless has received only half the premium due, whatever the cause may have been. In order to provide for a contingency of this nature, with justice to all concerned, some companies include in the bond a clause that limits the surety's liability, under the circumstances described, to a proportionate amount; that is to say, the surety would pay in the case cited only $2,500, instead of $5,000, and would pay $4,000 if eight cashiers had been listed, $3,000 if six had been listed, and so on. This provision seems entirely reasonable, and perhaps the companies that do not now make it a part of their bonds will ultimately do so.

55. Changes in the Schedule

An employer's business may expand after the bond is issued, or he may decide to protect certain positions not originally listed, or he may desire for various other reasons to change the schedule. Printed forms are furnished to the employer that enable him conveniently and easily to effect such changes when new positions are added, existing positions eliminated, or the amount of insurance assigned to given positions increased or decreased.

56. Fresh Premiums Due When Claims Are Made

When an employee bonded under an ordinary fidelity instrument is found to be in default, the premium is regarded as fully earned as soon as the default is discovered, and when a successor is appointed fresh fidelity insurance covering him is paid for additionally as a matter of course. In the case of position bonds the surety's liability remains constant so long as the position continues to be filled, regardless of defaults by prior incumbents. In order to protect the surety's premium income under these conditions, a clause in the bond provides that when a claim is made the amount of insurance allotted to the position held by the employee in default shall not be diminished by any corresponding loss payment, but shall be kept intact in the original sum, in return for a pro-rata additional premium. If, for example, one of five incumbents of the position of cashier bonded for $5,000 at a 50-cent rate is known or thought to be in default, and a claim is made accordingly three months after the bond is issued or renewed, the employer pays an additional premium of $18.75 and continues to have protection for the remaining nine months of the year as to the four cashiers originally covered and the new one taking the place of the defaulter. This inclusion in the schedule of the new cashier is instantaneous and automatic, without the need of notice from the employer, and the latter's only obligation concerned with the incident is to pay upon due demand a pro-rata premium from the day when the claim is made up to the end of the current premium year. This premium is due regardless of the amount, if any, that may afterward be paid upon the claim, and is based upon the fact that the premium has been fully earned upon the employee concerned with the claim, and that a fresh element of risk to the surety, subject to proper compensation, comes into being as soon as the new cashier begins to function.

57. Premium Rates

Position bonds have been written thus far upon the same premium basis as that prevailing in the case of ordinary fidelity bonds. It may be doubted, however, that the Rating Bureau will deem it advisable indefinitely to recommend ordinary fidelity rates, since antecedent reasoning would rather indicate the need of increased rates.

58. Kinds of Risks Suited to Position Bonds

The practice of the companies as to this point is divergent, some underwriters going much farther than seems to others prudent in providing position protection to concerns of certain types. The attitude of conservative underwriters in this respect ("conservative" now, but possibly normal before long) may be seen from the following statement issued to its agents by a certain company:

> We are prepared to provide position fidelity insurance only
> for high-grade concerns and only for certain classes of employees of such concerns: that is to say, the employer must be a
> concern of high standing and reputed good management,
> whose auditing and supervising arrangements we suppose to be
> thoroughgoing and adequate, and whose staffs are reasonably
> permanent; and the schedule of positions must include only
> executives and clerical employees located in home and branch
> offices. Outside salesmen, delivery people, collectors, agents,
> and the like will not be covered under position bonds; though
> the employer may, of course, secure fidelity insurance as to
> these latter classes of employees by taking out, concurrently
> with his position bond, an ordinary fidelity schedule bond
> covering employees holding places not acceptable under the
> position form.

59. Applications and Investigations

Obviously, of course, under position forms of bonds, on the face of things, neither the employer nor the surety receives the distinct benefits incident to the investigation of the persons bonded; that is to say, the employer does not know that his staff is composed of persons who are at least supposed to be thoroughly trustworthy, nor does the surety know that its chance of loss is minimized because all the persons bonded have risen superior to temptation in the past. Such a state of affairs would seem, to many people at least, unsatisfactory on both sides; but employers are not always wide-visioned in this matter, and underwriters as well seem to think investigations under many conditions dispensable. At all events, whatever the reason may be, the practices of the companies that write position bonds as to investigating the persons covered lack uniformity. The company referred to in the preceding section covers the point as follows:

> While we shall be bound under the position bond as to any person holding the given position, whoever he may be, yet it is not our purpose to provide this insurance without due regard to the character of the people whom we expect to be our risks. At the outset, therefore, when the employer makes known to us the positions to be bonded and the number of incumbents thereof, we shall require the names of all such incumbents and applications from them, in order that we may make the usual investigations. Sound underwriting principles necessitate this course, and wise employers will welcome rather than oppose it. It must be understood, too, by the employer, that applications will be expected from all new incumbents of the listed positions, and that they will all be investigated in the usual manner. The insurance, of course, will not be conditioned upon our receipt of such applications, and the new employees will be inescapably and automatically covered as soon as they begin to serve, regardless of the application incident of the risk; but we shall take steps from time to time to ascertain what persons in fact we are bonding and to enforce the foregoing program, if the employer has been lax in carrying out his part.

60. Underwriter's Attitude toward Position Bonds

Every once in a while some surety company breaks away from the beaten path and brings out a new form of bond or develops an existing form in some novel fashion. In that direction lies progress, and the business is all the better in the long run because so many keen and fertile minds are all the time striving to devise ways and means of extending it and increasing its utility. In many cases these brilliant ideas fall flat, and after a short time nothing is heard of them; while in other cases the new departure marks a genuine advance in the development

6

of the business, and becomes a prominent feature. In which of these classes should position bonds be placed? Not in the first, surely, because they have been used now for two years or so, and are still much in evidence; but perhaps not in the second either—at least not yet. It is thought that comparatively few underwriters are *pushing* position bonds, or are issuing them at all except when forced to do so to save business already on their books. The attitude of many underwriters is perhaps reflected more or less clearly in the subjoined extract from a circular issued to its agents by the company quoted above:

We regard the position bond as an unnecessary and unwise departure from tried fidelity practice and sound underwriting principles. We think it unnecessary, because any well-ordered concern can procure through ordinary schedule bonds the same and even greater and more closely adaptive protection than that afforded by the position bond, without the serious drawbacks of the latter; and we think it unwise, because it measurably changes a scientific achievement of underwriting, expressly carried out for the benefit of the employer, into a blind speculation of which he may be the victim—or one of the two victims. A company that guarantees an employee's honesty, after an exhaustive and satisfactory investigation of the employee's character and career, is not only moving on safe ground itself, but it is also rendering a service to the employer that is by no means limited to the mere monetary insurance embodied in the bond; while a company that agrees to cover without investigation anybody and everybody that may be conveniently available for a given position is not only taking an unwarranted chance itself, but is also subjecting the employer to unnecessary risks, and is withholding from him assistance of a valuable nature. In practice, moreover, position bonds may easily lead to awkward situations and misunderstandings, unless extreme care is taken by both the assured and the surety to see that all the employees as to whom protection is expected are properly classified, enumerated, and otherwise covered. Under a system of bonding by name no embarrassment of this kind is possible. While we shall try to overcome, to a large extent, in the manner indicated above, the dangers of position bonds to both the employer and the surety, we realize that in practice difficulties will arise. We earnestly urge our agents, therefore, not to recommend position bonds to their clients, but to try to place with them instead ordinary fidelity schedule bonds of the tried-and-tested type.

CHAPTER VI

SPECIAL FIDELITY-BOND TOPICS

61. Individual Bonds and Schedule Bonds

Ordinarily a fidelity bond covers only one person. If, however, there are many or even several persons to be bonded in favor of the same obligee, a schedule bond may be issued; though even then individual bonds will be issued, if the assured prefer it so. Schedule bonds are so called because no individual is named in the text of the bond as a principal, but a schedule is attached, showing the names of all the persons bonded, the positions held by them, and the amount of liability assumed in each case. Additions to or deductions from the list of persons bonded when the bond is first issued, or the amount of liability assumed in any given case, may be made upon notice to the company by the assured. Pro-rata premiums are charged for such additions to the schedule, and, subject to such minimums as may be in order in the given case, are credited for deductions therefrom.

Schedule bonds are commonly used in the case of banks, corporations, and large business houses. They are a great convenience to the assured when the staff is large and changes therein are frequent. When a schedule bond is issued the employer may cause a person to be bonded immediately by simply sending a "change notice" to the company. The notice is binding upon the company from the time the person enters the service of the employer, provided that the company receives the notice, as shown by its acknowledgment, and provided further that the employer notifies the company promptly of the additional risk. The company may thereafter, of course, cancel the risk, if its investigation of the person bonded discloses adverse features; but the bond is nevertheless in force until the cancellation notice takes effect.

Each person bonded under a schedule bond fills out an application blank as in the case of individual bonds.

62. Explanation of Schedule-Bond Rates

Page 3 of the Rate Manual shows as to unclassified business what premiums are to be charged for schedule bonds, the rate changing with the aggregate amount of liability. The following points are sometimes not understood by agents:

(a) The rate is determined by the *aggregate* amount of the bonds carried by the insured, whether or not they are carried in one company. If, for example, an insured has a schedule bond with a certain company involving an aggregate liability of $150,000, and desires to favor the agent of some other company with half the business, say, leaving half with the original company, the rate for the new $75,000 schedule would be, not 40 cents, but 30 cents—not the rate appropriate for a schedule bond of $75,000 only, but the rate made upon a $150,000 schedule. The fact that the business is split up among two or more companies has no bearing on the rate.

(b) When a line of bonds is not classified, thus taking the general rates shown on pages 1–2 of the Manual, and is sufficient in volume and number to warrant a schedule rate, and when in addition some of the risks included (executive officers, for example) could be covered by means of individual bonds at rates lower than the schedule rate appropriate to the given volume, such risks may be included in the schedule for the purpose of determining the general schedule rate, but may nevertheless be charged for in accordance with the lower individual rate. If, for example, six persons are bonded in the aggregate amount of $32,000, and two of them are executive officers bonded in the aggregate amount of $14,000, the rate for the entire schedule will be $139—$3.50 per thousand for the executives and $5 per thousand for the rest of the schedule.

(c) The $1 minimum earned premium is intended to be the surety's minimum compensation for each name on the schedule. The charge is necessitated by the accounting and underwriting work incident to frequent changes. It is not an annual minimum for bonded employees who continue year after year in the assured's service; but when a new name goes on the schedule the surety earns at once a minimum of $1 for the term of that employee's service, no matter how short the term may be.

(d) When a risk is classified a schedule rate is sometimes mentioned (in addition to the individual rate), and sometimes not. If none is mentioned, there is no schedule rate for that particular class of fidelity bonds—the rate is the same, however large the volume. The schedule rates on page 3 of the Manual have nothing to do with such a case, applying only to unclassified business.

(e) If a line of bonds is not classified, and is thus theoretically entitled to the schedule rate shown on page 3, some companies object nevertheless to conceding, and it seems illogical to concede, those rates when the line consists exclusively or largely of risks normally taking a much higher rate. If, for example, an assured conducting a business not classified attempts to bond a large number of drivers or branch-office managers, say, and hardly anyone else, at the low rate appropriate to a considerable volume of normally diversified risks, including executive officers and other inside people, the business would be regarded by some underwriters anyway, and perhaps by most, as unacceptable on any such basis.

63. Leaning Backward

I heard not long ago of a manager who was asked to name a rate on a fidelity schedule aggregating about $90,000, and who promptly quoted 40 cents without explaining to the assured that he could get a rate of 30 cents by slightly expanding the schedule so as to make the aggregate liability $100,000. The manager did not make this suggestion to the assured, I was told, because he felt that doing so would be inconsistent with his determination to maintain Manual rates under all circumstances. He seemed to me to be leaning backward and to be carrying a virtue so far as to make it a vice. What would he do if he were engaged in a really respectable business, and were selling oranges, for example, at 5 cents apiece or 50 cents a dozen, and if an old lady—a poor widow, say, with nine small children dependent upon her for maintenance and college educations— should come in and order eleven? What would the conscience-racked manager do, I ask, if placed in that appalling predicament? The situation is painful, whichever way you look at it. If, on the one hand, he resolutely puts aside temptation and maintains the Manual rate of 5 cents, the poor widow loses a nickel, and may have to give up her limousine. If, on the other hand, he relaxes his moral vigilance, and explains to the widow the advantage of ordering oranges in wholesale lots, his subsequent remorse over such a fall from rectitude is distressful to contemplate.

64. Bonding without the Knowledge of the Principals

Occasionally surety companies are asked to issue policies of fidelity insurance covering employees who have made no applications for such policies, who presumably will not know of their existence, and who have undergone no investigations by the bonding company. This insurance is sometimes sought by employers who desire to have fidelity protection, but who are reluctant to let their employees know of any such frame of mind. While it is thought that some companies are willing in certain cases to supply this want, at a rate somewhat higher than that prevailing under the usual conditions, fidelity underwriters in general do not look with favor upon the plan, and are not willing to adopt it.

The whole proposal seems to them inconsistent with the general theory upon which the employer buys and the surety sells this form of protection. Just as people do not want their boilers to explode or their elevators to fall, even though they carry boiler and elevator insurance, so they do not want their trusted employees to become defaulters, even though bonds might afford partial or complete indemnity from loss; and just as preliminary inspections render boiler and elevator insurance effective and cheap and scientific, so antecedent investigations give to fidelity insurance the same desirable and necessary qualities. Moreover, when the person does not know that he is bonded, one considerable advantage in the normal practice is lost—namely, the fact that knowledge of the existence of the bond on the part of the person bonded reacts upon him in a manner favorable both to him and to his surety.

Insurance at best is highly speculative, and any development of this kind tending to make it a pure gamble is a step in the wrong direction. It is thought that very few bonds issued under these conditions are in force.

65. Cumulative Liability Sometimes Incurred

In the case of continuing fidelity risks, bonding companies were able up to a few years ago, in virtually all cases, and are still able in a vast majority of cases, to obtain a full fresh premium at the beginning of each year as compensation for carrying the risk for that year, with no cumulative liability, however long the risk might continue thus to be renewed. It is now true, however, that under certain conditions the surety companies as a whole, while receiving altogether no larger premiums than before, are nevertheless subject to an aggregate liability equal to the former liability multiplied by the number of times the risk is renewed. That is so, for example, in cases where an obligee changes surety companies every year, and procures always a form of bond with no cut-off clause. Under such conditions a bank, say, might give its $500,000 schedule bond to a fresh company every year for ten years, and at the end of that period, though it would have paid throughout the term only the premium supposed to be sufficient to warrant a company's providing insurance in the sum of $500,000, it would have the right, unless some statute of limitations prevented, to call upon each of ten companies for that amount, or for an aggregate amount of $5,000,000. Moreover, in some cases, where an official is required by law to give a new bond each year or at stated longer intervals, a single surety company, if it desires to retain the bond of a given official, must shoulder this same indefinitely cumulative liability for successive annual premiums of only the normal amount.

The unpleasant condition of things described, while theoretically a matter of some concern, has not yet in practice developed, and seems likely not soon to develop, into anything really serious. It is thought that few private obligees will go to the trouble, the considerable trouble, of changing sureties year after year; and while additional laws may be enacted from time to time similarly calling for new bonds every year, rather than term bonds, in the case of certain public or quasi-public officials, there seems to be no particular trend of legislation in that direction. The trouble referred to, so far as it is practically remediable at all, would seem to be a matter to be cared for by the Rating Bureau. Probably nothing need be attempted in that respect by the Bureau, because of the present negligible importance of the matter, in the case of bonds issued in favor of private obligees; while as for bonds required recurrently by law in such a way as to fasten cumulative liability upon the surety, a higher annual rate may be imposed in accordance with the plan already followed by the Bureau in a few cases, notably in that of Massachusetts bank officials.

66. Foreign Fidelity Bonds

Underwriters deem exceptionally hazardous bonds conditioned for the honesty and right conduct of persons employed by domestic concerns, but located in foreign countries, for the following reasons:

(a) Usually such foreign employees are necessarily entrusted with high authority and wide discretionary powers—with vastly more authority than would be given to employees of similar rank located in the United States and thus within easy reach of the home-office of the employer. Branch-office managers and traveling salesmen, for example, located in this country, are all the time under considerable supervision on the part of the home-office of the employer, making frequent reports thereto, and occasionally visiting the home-office or otherwise meeting their superior executives; but no such supervision is practicable for foreign employees.

(b) While the underlying extrinsic conditions of foreign risks are thus in two important respects highly unfavorable, from the bonding company's point of view, as compared with similar domestic risks, the conditions on the subjective side are likewise as a rule decidedly unsatisfactory in the case of foreign risks as follows:

(1) Frequently the persons whose honesty is to be guaranteed are foreigners about whose characters and careers it is extremely difficult, if not impossible, for the surety company to obtain full and satisfactory information.

(2) If the bonded persons are not foreigners, but are American citizens transferred to a foreign post of duty, the investigations of their past offers no unusual difficulty, but the subjective aspect of the risk is still relatively unfavorable in the fact that a man is more likely to give way to temptation when he is located in a far-off foreign city, deprived of home ties, and with perhaps unusual opportunity and leisure for wrongdoing.

(c) Finally, in the matter of the settlement of losses foreign bonds are deemed materially more dangerous to surety companies than are similar domestic instruments. The precise facts of the loss are harder to ascertain; salvage even in small amounts is rarely recoverable; and the conviction of the defaulter, however certain his guilt, is usually impracticable.

Nevertheless, while foreign bonds are unattractive, underwriters do not refuse absolutely to issue them under all conditions. On the contrary, they are prepared to cover a comparatively small number of foreign risks in connection with a large number of domestic risks carried in the same schedule. A much higher rate is charged for foreign than for corresponding domestic risks.

67. Salvage on Fidelity Claim

When a surety company makes good to the holder of its bond the amount that the person bonded has stolen, the company considers that it has a valid claim upon the defaulter for the amount so paid. It keeps close track of him, and pursues him relentlessly, if he gets back upon his financial feet, and forces him to satisfy this claim. Sometimes surety companies are criticized for taking this course. It seems to be thought that, having received a premium for guaranteeing the man's honesty and thus, as it were, taken a sporting chance, the bonding companies ought to play the game consistently and call everything off as soon as claims are adjusted.

It seems easy to see that it would never do for surety companies to act upon any such plan as this. There is no doubt that frequently bonded persons, when perilously near the brink of wrongdoing, are kept from falling over by their certain knowledge that the surety company will pursue them to the bitter end if they yield to temptation. It is certain, too, that on the basis of present loss ratios fidelity rates would need to be vastly increased, if the sureties were debarred from making recoveries. In the case of some companies anyway, and perhaps in that of most companies, salvage on fidelity claims in normal years equals from a third to half the losses. These gross recoveries, however, are subject to considerable reduction on expense account.

There are cases, of course, when it would be little less than cruel, even if strictly legal, for the surety company to enforce its claim against the defaulting principal; but fidelity adjusters know how to temper the wind to the shorn lamb, and in practice they are continually doing it. It is not so widely believed now as it used to be that corporations have no souls; and the belief would be still further shattered by the disclosure of the secrets embodied in the fidelity-claim papers of many bonding companies.

An important question concerned with salvage arises

when the default exceeds the amount of the bond and partial recovery is effected. If, for example, a person bonded in the sum of $10,000 steals $16,000, and the surety company, after paying the full amount of the bond, recovers $6,000, is it at liberty to retain the $6,000, as so much salvage towards the $10,000 paid; or must it turn over the amount to the obligee, so that the latter will then have complete indemnification; or should the obligee and the surety share the $6,000 in some proportion, and if so, in what proportion? Would the answer be different if the obligee rather than the surety company made the $6,000 recovery?

In practice, situations of the kind referred to have been handled in various ways by different companies, and indeed in various ways by the same company, as the circumstances of particular cases varied. Upon the principle that the obligee under the conditions described took out less insurance than the exposure required, and thus paid the bonding company a correspondingly reduced premium, many claim-adjusters hold that the surety company should not be made to suffer because the obligee has underinsured his property, and that the demands of equity will be satisfied if the salvage is divided in accordance with some such rule as this: "The surety and the obligee shall share any recovery (excluding insurance and reinsurance) made by either on account of any loss in the proportion that the amount of loss borne by each bears to the total amount of the loss." Under this rule the surety company, in the case cited, would keep five-eighths of the $6,000, or $3,750, and would turn over to the obligee three-eighths, or $2,250; and the same disposition of the salvage would have been made if the obligee had effected the recovery instead of the surety company.

Formerly in most cases, perhaps, and still to a large extent, it is thought, recoveries made under these conditions are disposed of in accordance with the rule quoted. The competition for fidelity business, however, has been so keen in recent years that some companies have inserted in their most liberal forms of bonds (used only in the case of business deemed particularly desirable) a provision that makes *all* salvage inure to the benefit of the obligee, by whomever recovered, up to the point where the obligee is completely indemnified. If, however, in such cases the recovery is effected by the surety company, the expenses incurred by the latter in procuring the salvage may be deducted from the amount payable to the obligee.

68. The "Standard Form" of Fidelity Bond

I have explained elsewhere (section 35) the circumstances under which this form of bond came to be prepared and adopted by the Surety Association as a standard form. The committee to which the drafting of the bond was entrusted gave much thought and painstaking work to the task, and their product seems deserving of wider use than it may have received. A brief analysis of the bond may be of interest and value as follows:

(a) There is no reference in the bond to an "employer's statement" (cf. section 27), and if anything of the sort is obtained by the surety company (as may easily and properly be the case), the insurance is not conditioned upon compliance with the statement. Having satisfied itself that normal and efficient accounting systems are followed, the surety company proceeds on that assumption, and does not complicate and perhaps impair the insurance provided by conditioning it upon rigid compliance with preliminary representations.

(b) Similarly no legally binding statements are required at yearly intervals as a condition precedent to the continuance and validity of the insurance. If the employer is asked to give the bonding company some simple form of assurance that, so far as he is aware, there is no reason based upon the character and record of the employee why the insurance should not be continued, this statement does not form a part of the bond or of any agreement between the insurer and the employer. It is obtained and used solely as an underwriting aid, and for the benefit of all concerned.

(c) The insuring clause of the bond is comprehensive and liberal. Some variance of view as to the proper scope of the insuring clause developed in the committee when this part of the bond was under discussion. One opinion was that it would be well to prepare two forms of bonds, to be sold at different rates, alike in every part except in the insuring clause, one form to be a "larceny and embezzlement" instrument, and the other to provide insurance against dishonesty broadly defined. This plan was rejected because it seemed open to several serious objections—the dual rating would be a fruitful source of confusion and misunderstanding among agents and patrons; in practice patrons would select the cheaper form, not understanding, and not being made to understand by zealous one-eyed agents, that they were getting less than they supposed and reasonably required; and claims not covered by the narrow bond would continually arise, with resultant friction, litigation, and general disrepute of the business of corporate suretyship. It finally seemed better not to recommend a "larceny and embezzlement" instrument even as an alternative form. Few buyers of bonds, it was thought, would accept this form if fully aware of its limitations, or ought to be allowed to accept it by a seller anxious to provide what the buyer really needed and presumably expected to receive. Where the situation as first developed was such (the argument ran) as to suggest to the underwriter the expediency of assuming only a narrow obligation, the better course was thought to be either to insist upon safeguarding methods of audit and supervision, or to charge a premium higher than normal to meet the abnormal hazard.

The committee accordingly adopted, and the standard form of bond now has, an insuring clause substantially like that used by many companies in their latest and most liberal forms. It is true that the clause does not contain the word "misapplication" found in some broad forms. A principal may misapply funds without any sort of dishonesty, and yet with resultant loss to an obligee; and valid claims based upon that word have arisen under circumstances which were not contemplated in advance by either party to the contract, and which would not have been regarded by either party, if considered in advance, as claim-culture material.

The precise phraseology of the insuring clause is not important in the ordinary crude case of plain theft; but fidelity bonds are constantly issued in behalf of principals holding high executive positions, where the dishonesty involved, while effective equally with that of the usual kind and perhaps even more blameworthy, is yet of a type so subtle as to escape the meshes of a limited form of bond. The operations of the gentry in question are carried on so cunningly that they seldom fail to clear the edge of the criminal law, albeit by a hair's breadth, but they would one and all fall within the protection of a broad fidelity bond.

(d) The insurance is not conditioned upon the employee's remaining in any one position, certain lines in the bond permitting interchange of positions and duties without limit.

(e) The bond is made continuous by certain other lines —it contains no stated term, but runs indefinitely until and unless cancelled by either the assured or the surety. This feature is of great value to the assured in two respects: (1) There is no danger that the insurance will lapse at the end of the premium year because someone whose duty it is to continue the bond fails to care for the matter; (2) a more important advantage in the continuity feature of the bond lies in the fact that losses need not be discovered, in order to be reimbursable under the bond, within a definite term, but may be discovered at any time so long as the employee remains in the service and the bond remains in force.

(f) The bond provides for a simple and just procedure on the part of the assured in the event of claims. Five days are allowed in which the assured may notify the surety company of the discovery of loss ("immediate" notification is often required), and three months are allowed in which to make a complete investigation and file a proof of loss. Many bonds have complicated and highly technical provisions in this respect.

(g) The bond gives the assured six months in which to discover losses and make claims after the termination of the bond. Shortages are frequently not discovered until the person bonded has left the service and his books are examined. This provision of the bond gives the assured ample time in which to discover any such losses. This cut-off clause has no meaning, of course, so long as the bond remains in force, the remarks made under paragraph (e) above applying in that case; the cut-off clause becomes effective only if the bond is cancelled or

7

terminated in any way. It is true that bonds have occasionally been issued (they are thought to be comparatively rare) containing no limitation whatever as to the period in which, after the termination of the bond, the assured must discover losses and notify the surety. Such liberality, in a mercantile fidelity bond where the form is controlled by the surety, seems unnecessary.

(h) In case the assured has failed to buy sufficient protection and a loss exceeds the amount of the bond, the assured and the surety share with each other, upon the pro-rata basis explained in the preceding section, all recoveries. Some forms of bonds provide that *all* salvage shall be turned over to the assured until the latter is completely reimbursed, only subsequent salvage inuring to the benefit of the surety. In this respect, as well as in that referred to in the preceding paragraph, bonds are occasionally issued on terms more liberal to the assured than those embodied in this standard form. Neither concession seems called for by any mandate of fair dealing or justice—both appear to be gratuitously due to excessive competition.

(i) While the foregoing points of positive merit are to be noted, it is also true that none of the few conditions inserted in the bond are in the least objectionable from the point of view of the assured: they are all provisions such as any fair-minded business man or attorney would deem to be appropriate in such an instrument.

69. An Interesting and Fruitful Field

Fidelity bonds deserve more attention than they receive from the average fieldman. Almost all classes of fidelity bonds are deemed excellent business by surety companies generally, and are written by them freely— a point of considerable importance to the agent. While many kinds of surety bonds serve their useful purpose and come to an end after the agent has profited from them to the extent of a single premium only, a good line of fidelity bonds, like Tennyson's "Brook," runs on forever, to the permanent advantage of the agent and with slight corresponding trouble for him after the initial stages of the transaction.   Fidelity business, as everybody knows, is harder to "switch" than almost any other line of insurance.   Moreover, fidelity bonds keep the agent in close touch with the assured, and thus frequently lead to other business of various kinds.   On all accounts the fieldman would do well to cultivate intensively this branch of suretyship.   Here more than in most lines lies an opportunity to *create* business, since many employers who do not now protect themselves and simultaneously improve the morale of their staffs by means of fidelity insurance would do so on a proper presentation of facts.

In like manner, too, it is feared, fidelity bonds receive from the average home-office executive less than their fair share of his crowded activities.   Because applications for fidelity insurance may sometimes be handled with a certain lack of judgment or even with more or less carelessness without serious resultant trouble, while even a little laxity shown at a critical stage of a piece of surety underwriting may mean a heavy loss, executives as a rule have been tempted to neglect the former division of their business in favor of the latter.   Perhaps a more accurate way of putting it would be to say that their surety problems have been so numerous and knotty that every last atom of their judgment and mental power (not always so much at that) has been needed there.   The fact remains that the fidelity end of the bonding business will always yield rich results to the diligent and expert producer, organizer, and underwriter.

CHAPTER VII

BANKERS' BLANKET BONDS

70. Origin of the Bond

For a long time banks constituted about the most important class of patrons that the surety companies had in their fidelity-bond departments. Competition for the business was bitter from the start, and rates quickly reached a point where, when the cost of investigations was taken into account, little or no profit remained for the companies. Yet the banks were ever striving, through associations and by individual effort, for lower rates and broader forms of bonds. There was, indeed, justification for such an attitude on the part of the banks—at least for their insistence upon broader protection; because in numberless instances they suffered losses that were found not to be covered by their outstanding bonds and insurance policies, nor even to be coverable under the existing *systems* of fidelity suretyship and burglary insurance.

This was true, for example, when, after having purchased from a surety company a full line of fidelity bonds covering every important member of the staff in amounts consistent with the practice of the best banks, some defalcation occurred that exceeded in amount the largest bond in force or the bond of the particular defaulter; or when some defalcation surely occurred, but could not be charged with certainty to any particular bonded person, so that the surety company would be in a position to deny liability, perhaps with entire fairness, perhaps from an excess of technicality in its claim department, but with results to the bank equally unhappy in both cases. It

was true, too, when a defalcation in all probability
occurred, but only the disappearance under suspicious
circumstances of money or securities could be proved, so
that a similar but even more awkward situation arose with
the bonding company; or when, after burglary insurance
and hold-up policies of the broadest type procurable had
been purchased, a loss occurred, and the claim-adjusters
found that some important condition of the policy,
deemed essential by the underwriter and accepted by the
insured with full knowledge of the limitation, had been
overlooked by the bank, with consequent impairment or
perhaps nullification of the insurance.

Under the system described a bank was forced to
revise its fidelity schedules continually, and to use equal
or even greater vigilance in keeping track of its burglary
and hold-up insurance; and even then losses of an insur-
able nature were frequently found not to be susceptible
of proof under any of the numerous bonds and policies
that the bank had taken out in its determination to provide for every loss contingency. Since all this and more
was true in the old days, the banks naturally and justi-
fiably searched high and low for the comprehensive,
automatic, and unfailing protection that they deemed
essential to their safety. They finally found what they
wanted in London. For more than two hundred years
a body of underwriters there, known collectively as
"Lloyd's," have been furnishing insurance of a high
order of excellence. At first they operated exclusively,
as they still do chiefly, in marine lines; but the seven-
hundred-or-so underwriting members are free to enter
into any engagements that commend themselves to their
adventurous spirits, and in practice they do not hesitate
to make at times what seem to outsiders to be highly
speculative and riskful commitments. They will insure,

for example, a prima donna's voice or a dancer's foot or a grandstand's profit on a coronation day that may turn out to be stormy.

71. London Underwriters Satisfy an American Demand

In that fertile nursery of insurance vegetation American bankers were able, as stated, to buy the protection that they desired. What they obtained for their money was an agreement executed by a group of these Lloyd's underwriters—thirty or forty, perhaps, each assuming a definite stated part of the risk—whereby the underwriters engaged to indemnify the given bank, up to $100,000, say, for any loss of money or securities sustained by it on account of the dishonesty of its employees, theft on the part of outsiders, burglary, hold-up, etc. The instrument so issued, entitled a "banker's blanket bond," was incomparably the broadest contract of indemnification ever offered to bankers up to that date, and they lost little time in possessing themselves of it. They realized the unfavorable aspect of the transaction in one respect—the fact that they were dealing with a lot of men concerning whose character and financial responsibility they knew little or nothing; that the insurance provided was not authorized, supervised, or taxed in this country; and that, in the event of contested claims, enforcement of the contract would be difficult and perhaps ·in practice quite impossible, because the underwriters would be amenable only to the jurisdiction of the courts of a foreign land. The bankers here would have much preferred to deal with regularly organized American companies, but they wanted the wholesale insurance so much that, in default of a domestic source of supply, they bought the foreign product in large volume. Indeed, the movement finally reached such proportions that

American bonding companies found themselves losing a large part of the cream of the bank fidelity business of the country—that is, the bonds of the big metropolitan banks.

72. The Last Word in Bank Insurance

Hardly any of the American companies, at least in the beginning, viewed the new insurance with favor, or had the slightest disposition to provide it; and for some time, as good business continued to go off their books, they watched the process with the stoicism of an Indian at the stake.   At last, however, the strain proved too much for poor human nature—for a white man's nature anyway— and they resolved to meet the London competition.   In August, 1915, five companies joined forces, agreeing with each other to underwrite in equal parts all bonds issued by any of the venturesome five.   Almost at once another similar group of co-operative underwriters was formed; and quickly thereafter all the important surety companies in the country began to write blanket bonds in the usual independent manner, and without special antecedent reinsurance arrangements.

There are two ways in which the insurance of a given hazard develops in practice.   Frequently the earlier attempts of the insurers to cover the field are more or less crude and inefficient.   In their effort to feel their way into unknown and perhaps dangerous ground, and to "play safe" in any event, the underwriters put out at first policies that are full of conditions and otherwise unwarrantably narrow.   They gradually acquire confidence, however, and drop one condition after another, broad-minded competition expediting the process, until the given exposure is adequately covered in an instrument reasonably satisfactory to both sides.   Sometimes, however, the evolution of the final product is just the reverse of this, and that seems likely to be true in the case of blanket bonds.

"When nature wants a thing done," says Emerson, "she overloads the tendency." The thing that the companies wanted done was to stop the London advance into their territory and to regain the ground already lost, and they overloaded the tendency by bettering the London instruction and making the bond extraordinarily liberal. In fact, they overdid it, and most of the changes since then have been in the direction of foreshortening the first expansive outlook upon the universe of hazards, defining more narrowly the insurance provided, and applying additional premium charges to points of exceptional exposure. The blanket bond first issued by the American companies seemed susceptible of such an interpretation that hardly any losses sustainable by a bank, aside from those due to uncollectible loans and public forgery, fell outside the enormous arc delimiting the protective scope of the bond; and the same thing is largely true of certain forms of blanket bonds still issued.

73. Bond Forms Standardized in All Respects

While the Surety Association of America has scrupulously refrained, for the most part, from attempting to prescribe for the use of its members stereotyped and unchangeable forms of bonds (though one or two recommendatory forms have been promulgated), wisely holding that any such course would obstruct the natural and healthful development of the business, yet it has made an exception to that practice in the case of blanket bonds, and has rigidly standardized all forms of blanket bonds, including the main text and all permissible endorsements. At present two kinds of blanket bonds are issuable for banks, Form 1 and Form 2, differing chiefly in the fact that Form 1 includes the word "misplacement" in its insuring clause, while Form 2 does not. The standard forms of blanket bonds have been changed frequently in the past, and no doubt the existing forms will undergo further modification.

74. The American Underwriters Overleapt Themselves

As stated above, the American bonding companies, in their determination to rescue their bank fidelity business from the London despoilers, did more than merely follow in the footsteps of the gentlemen at Lloyd's. They *meant* substantially to do only that, but they acquired so much momentum in running down their rivals over the beaten track that they found themselves, before they could stop, some way beyond the point at which they intended to stop. They planned to give banks extraordinarily liberal insurance, but they had no idea at the start that the bond would or could be used as an instrument by means of which a shortage of any nature or due to almost any cause could be cleared and liquidated by a mere debit entry in the surety company's account with the insured bank. The companies meant, generally speaking, to cover only losses resulting primarily from dishonesty on the part of officers and employees of the bank, or from crime on the part of outsiders in cases of burglary, hold-up, and the like. There was no intention to cover, and it may confidently be asserted that the banks did not expect the insurer to cover, losses due to errors of judgment in granting credit, to carelessness in delivering securities, and to miscarriages incident to similar administrative functions. Likewise it was surely not supposed on either side at the start that the bonding companies could be held liable for mere account-book differences which might or might not

represent real losses, and which in any event would be
unaccompanied by proof that such differences were due
to dishonest or criminal acts.   No doubt it would be
extremely convenient to a bank to have its judgment and
its general efficiency absolutely guaranteed in this way;
but it was never the purpose of the bonding companies to
provide any such protection in their blanket bond, even
if it be conceded (as it cannot be) that any such universal
and multiform hazards could be legitimate subjects of
insurance.

75. The "Misplacement" Coverage

This was not so bad a world to live in until a certain
lady (as usual a lady), named Pandora, opened a certain
box and permitted countless human ills to escape therefrom and spread out over the earth.   Similarly the surety
world was a calm and peaceful affair until, a few years
ago, some ill-starred underwriter permitted to escape
from his disordered brain into the insuring section of the
bankers' blanket bond the word "misplacement."   Ever
since that fatal day the surety companies have been
afflicted with claims essentially invalid, but nevertheless
filable with some semblance of legitimacy upon the
ground of loss through "misplacement."   As the thrice-
wounded Hibernian said that he expected to recover
from two of his wounds, but the third one would undoubtedly prove fatal, so many an adjuster, confronted with a
blanket-bond claim based upon three alleged breaches of
the bond, has survived the assault with ease so far as two
of the accounts were concerned, only to succumb utterly,
upon the third, "misplacement" contention.   Long ago
our exhausted blanket-bond adjusters began to say with
Hamlet, "There's 'something too much of this' misplacement business."

While most bankers have realized that losses of the kind indicated are not within the scope of a blanket bond, and could not reasonably be so regarded even under an omnibus "misplacement" clause, yet the presence of that word in the bond has facilitated unpleasant controversies with the assured, and has sometimes forced the companies to pay claims that they felt to be unjust. Since it was not the banks, but the companies, that wrote the bond, the banks are not to be criticized perhaps for giving to the word "misplacement" the most expansive interpretation warranted by any dictionary, as helped out by a gifted imagination. When I was asked to define, "with particularity," the word "misplacement," I answered that, in the light of claim experience, the following definition, originally applied to metaphysics, would exactly fill the bill: "A blind man looking in midnight darkness for a black hat which isn't there." Two recent cases in one company's experience show how the word is interpreted by some bankers. In the first case an imposter opened an account with the assured by means of forged documents, and thereby obtained a genuine credit with the bank for $1,000. Two days later the bank cashed his check for $500, drawn against this $1,000 credit. When the bank discovered the fraud that had caused it to open the account, it demanded reimbursement from the company on the ground that the $500 was "misplaced" when it was handed out to the imposter. In the other case the assured cashed for a stranger a check drawn on a small bank in a distant part of the country. The check was good at the time, but before it could be collected the bank upon which it was drawn failed. As the stranger could not be found, the bank was out the amount of the check, and demanded reimbursement from the company under its blanket bond on the ground that it had "misplaced" its money in passing it over to the stranger. Whatever the bank may have done with its money, it certainly misplaced its confidence in the surety company, if it really expected the company to pay the claim.

76. Two Contributory Causes of Trouble

Some readers may deem far-fetched, if not altogether absurd, the suggestion made above that evidence of inability to locate securities immediately, or mere book-keeping indications of loss, may be made the basis of claims provable under Form 1 blanket bonds, even if there is otherwise no reason to suppose that a real loss has been sustained, and surely no reason to suppose that a loss has been sustained because of anyone's dishonesty or crime; but claims have frequently been made, and perhaps in some cases have been paid, under precisely such conditions. They have been possible primarily by reason of the existence of the word "misplacement" in the insuring section, and secondarily by reason of two contributory, two aiding and abetting, features of the insurer's obligation—namely, the fact that negligence on the part of the bank, however gross, may not be advanced by the insurer as a defense under the circumstances referred to, and the further fact that the bank is not re-quired to identify the specific securities alleged to have been lost. Many banks, for example, handle constantly large quantities of Liberty Bonds, and some banks have in their possession at all times millions of dollars' worth of such bonds. On and near coupon dates and during conversion periods the transactions in Liberty Bonds have been so heavy, and the necessary haste and con-fusion in dealing with them have been so great, that numberless mistakes have been made, in the records particularly, and to some extent in the handling of the securities themselves.

77. Some Startling Claim Possibilities

Several cases have been reported in which the number and aggregate value of the Liberty Bonds found to.be on hand differed by large amounts from the number and value of such bonds shown by the books of the bank to be on hand. In one notable instance involving a large blanket bond, the bank's Liberty-Bond account was out of balance at one time to the extent of several hundred thousand dollars. It was not thought at the time that the bank had really sustained any such catastrophic loss, and in fact it had not, as months of laborious research by expert accountants ultimately showed. For a long time, however, it looked as if such a loss had occurred—that is to say, it looked so only because one very long line of figures, when added together, fell several hundred thousand dollars short of another very long line of figures, and not because there was otherwise even the slightest indication of a loss. Yet the bank was camping on the front steps of a bonding company from the moment that the bookkeeping discrepancy came to its notice, with its little proof of claim all ready to be sent in as soon as the door should be opened. Boiled down to its essence, including what was plainly visible between the lines, this "proof" amounted to about the following:

> We submit, gentlemen, in Exhibit A a statement of all the Liberty Bonds received by us in the last twelve months, according to our books; in Exhibit B a corresponding statement of all the Liberty Bonds delivered by us in the same period, as indicated by such receipts as we have been able to turn up in our files; and in Exhibit C a statement of all the Liberty Bonds now on hand, as indicated by a careful count by eighteen members of our staff. You will observe, gentlemen, that the

41,248 items constituting Exhibit A, when added together, equal $542,767,423, while the 37,792 items constituting Exhibit B aggregate $517,413,223. The difference between these two amounts is thus $25,354,200. The aggregate of Exhibit C, as you will further observe, is only $24,599,999; and this difference of $754,201, constituting a loss under our blanket bond, you will kindly remit to us in settlement of such loss. It is true that we are quite unable to give you the denominations and numbers of the bonds thus indicated in a general way by our books to be missing, or even to specify the particular issue or issues of bonds involved. It is true, also, that all our people are absolutely honest in our confident opinion, and that no robbery or theft from the outside has ever come to our notice or been suspected. It is true, too, that nobody is now demanding from us more bonds than we are prepared to supply, and that nobody has ever demanded any bonds from us when our books did not show that they were due to the claimant and on hand. The fact remains, however, as you can see for yourselves, that these three sets of figures do not hang together at all. We must ask you, therefore, as stated, to send us by an early mail, in accordance with this proof of claim, your check for $754,201.

What, then, is the answer? A problem clearly stated is, they say, half solved; and if all the foregoing were even muddier than it is, the malodorous concoction would still be clear enough to show the answer. Obviously the word "misplacement" should be lifted bodily, with a pair of sterilized tongs, from all blanket bonds, and catapulted through planetary space to the outermost confines of the solar system.

78. Extremely Broad Protection Nevertheless Intended

While most experienced underwriters hold the views outlined in the preceding section regarding the necessity of eliminating the word "misplacement" from blanket bonds, yet it must not be supposed that anybody desires thereby to withhold from the banks the protection to which they are legitimately entitled under the general

blanket-bond system of insurance as originally understood by the London and American underwriters and by
the bankers themselves—all of the latter at least who
gave the matter sustained consideration.   Indeed, about
the only argument in favor of the retention in the bond of
the word "misplacement" that has any weight with the
author and with others, no doubt, is the fact that its
presence will occasionally enforce the payment of a valid
claim that might otherwise be turned down by an adjuster possessed of a single-track mind so full of legal
niceties as to leave no room for a little horse sense.   It
must not be supposed, for example, from the references to
negligence above, that the surety should be permitted to
set up negligence on the part of a bank as a defense upon
a claim otherwise proved—not in the least.   If that
could be done, the bond would be of slight value to the
bank; and in fact the surety companies are constantly
paying, if not with alacrity and pleasure exactly, at least
with philosophic composure, losses due in part to the
negligence of some officer or employee of the bank.   If,
for example (an extreme example), the cashier of a small
country bank should go home some night and forget to
lock up his safe, and burglars should happen along and
avail themselves of his kindly forethought for them, no
surety company would think of denying liability because
of the cashier's accommodating disposition.   Similarly,
it was not intended to suggest, in the citation of the
Liberty Bond case above, that a bank should be unable
to prove a claim under a blanket bond, merely because
it could not give all the "names, dates, and specifications," when it was otherwise clear that a loss had really
been sustained, and when it seemed reasonably clear
that the loss was due to some hazard covered by the
bond.   If, for example (in this case not an unusual

example), a completely identified $10,000 Liberty Bond is known to have been received by the cashier, to have been turned over by him to an appropriate member of the staff, and to have been left by the latter in a more or less exposed position accessible to a number of staff employees and possibly at times to an outsider, and if that certificate vanishes into thin air, the bank has a perfectly provable claim under a blanket bond.

What the companies object to in the present situation is the tendency of bankers to use their blanket bond as a convenient means of balancing their books when an awkward deficit arises in some unexpected quarter, whether or not the deficit can be shown to be even probably the result of a mischance covered by the bond.

79. Computation of Premiums

The cost of blanket bonds depends upon the form of bond (whether Form 1 or Form 2), and whether or not it carries endorsements; the amount of the bond; the number of officers and other employees covered; the number of branch offices of the bank, if any; and the amount of concurrent insurance carried, if any. In determining the premium, all officers and employees on the pay-roll whose duties relate to banking or require their presence at any time within the banking office, however subordinate their positions in some cases may be, must be included in the count. The premium is collected annually. No additional charge is made for employees temporarily taken on or permanently added to the staff after the premium is determined; and no deduction is allowed for employees temporarily absent or permanently leaving the service. On chains of banks, or banks under a common ownership, the rates are computed separately for each bank having a distinct corporate organization, except that affiliated banking institutions occupying adjacent premises in the same building may be regarded for rate-computing purposes as one bank.

80. Primary and Excess Coverage

A blanket bond is said to be a "primary" bond when no concurrent bonds are carried by the bank, and an "excess" bond when the bank carries concurrently a primary blanket bond or ordinary fidelity bonds. Whether or not an excess blanket bond is also a primary one under certain conditions is a question that seems not to have been definitely settled. If, for example, a bank carries a primary Lloyd's policy for $100,000, and an American-company excess policy for the same amount, and a $100,000 loss occurs of such a nature that it would not be covered under the Lloyd's form, but would be under the "excess" bond, is the American company liable? How would the matter stand if the London underwriters denied liability, and the bank could not collect from them, while both the bank and the American "excess" underwriters believed them to be liable? The point is extremely important, and seems not to be clearly disposed of in the existing standard form of bond, or to be uniformly understood by underwriters. Perhaps the ultimate view will be that an "excess" bond can never be a primary instrument, and that somebody other than the excess insurer must always stand a primary loss up to the point where the excess coverage applies before any·demand can be made upon the excess underwriter. So far as the latter is concerned, it makes no difference who this somebody is; and if it happens to be the bank itself, owing to its poor judgment or hard luck in selecting primary insurers, the unfortunate fact is of no direct concern to the excess underwriter.

8

81. Possible Obligees of Blanket Bonds

The rules of the Surety Association of America limit the issuance of blanket bonds to the following classes of obligees: national and state banks, savings banks, trust companies, title-insurance companies, safe-deposit companies, companies organized by banks to deal in securities, private bankers, and stockbrokers.

One reason why many executives vigorously opposed, and for a long time successfully blocked, the movement in favor of writing blanket bonds was because they feared that such bonds could not be limited to banks, but would soon spread to large mercantile houses, and would ultimately be issued generally, with the net result of converting the entire field of fidelity underwriting into a virtual gambling operation. These fears seem to have been groundless. Although many big commercial and industrial concerns have tried to obtain blanket bonds, the companies have steadfastly adhered to their determination not to extend the system. Possibly some modification of the present practice will come about some day, but there seems to be no indication now of any such development. It would not be lawful, indeed, for the companies to go outside of the present permissible obligees named above, in a number of important states, in the absence of additional legislation enlarging the range of beneficiaries authorized by existing law.

82. Commissions, Brokerage, and Reinsurance Allowances

Since it was known that blanket bonds represented a new and untried field of suretyship, and since it was feared that the premiums obtainable would prove to be inadequate, the companies that originally wrote the bonds agreed to limit brokerage, commissions to their own agents, and reinsurance allowances. Afterward the

Surety Association ignored the agency element of acquisition costs, but passed a resolution regarding brokerage and commission allowances that finally (March 31, 1921) took the following form:

> RESOLVED, That as to Bankers' Blanket Bonds and Bankers' Excess Blanket Bonds, the originating company shall be entitled to receive or retain from co-insurers and/or reinsurers a commission of fifteen per cent and no more; and be it further resolved that no company or any of its agents shall pay to any broker, or to the agent of any other company, on any such bond, a brokerage in excess of ten per cent.

It is thus open to the companies to pay any commission they please to their own agents upon blanket bonds, although if they pay more than 15 per cent they will be directly out of pocket as to any parts of such risks that they reinsure. In practice some companies pay their agents the latters' regular commission upon any blanket bonds reinsured in no part, but pay them only 15 per cent upon any parts of blanket bonds that are reinsured. Other companies pay their agents only 15 per cent upon the entire bond, regardless of reinsurance. These discordant practices have brought about unsatisfactory situations in the field at times, and it seems probable that the existing rule will some time be changed as regards this point.

83. Investigation of Persons Covered

Under the old system of individual bonds or schedule bonds covering named individuals in stated amounts, it was the practice of the surety companies (the orthodox practice at least) to investigate thoroughly every person in the service of the bank who was bonded. Some bankers valued this service highly; many of them, indeed, continued to carry American bonds largely for the sake

of this investigation service after they had procured
blanket bonds in London and before the latter were
obtainable here. Many bankers, however (strangely
and shortsightedly enough), prefer not to have their
people "bothered" with applications and the other
incidents of a thoroughgoing surety-company investigation, and they even in some cases make it a condition of
the awarding of the business that investigations shall
not be made. In the confident opinion of many underwriters no such attitude on the part of bankers should be
tolerated—it is better in any such case, in their judgment,
to let the other fellow have the business. The views
and practices of underwriters, however, are not uniform
in this matter; and it is thought that some companies
make few investigations of people covered by their
blanket bonds. One company has disposed of the point
by issuing to its blanket-bond underwriting staff the
following instructions:

> Since it has always been our practice to investigate rigidly
> individual applicants for bank bonds, and since under a blan-
> ket bond we are more than ever exposed to danger (formerly
> we could lose, generally speaking, only because of our princi-
> pals' dishonesty, whereas now even their laxity or carelessness
> may involve us in serious loss), it seems to be essential to make
> investigations. In cases where we reinsure, or where our
> position is that of co-surety with some other company, we
> will assume that this investigation is made by the con-
> trolling company. In cases where we are the originating
> company, we will conduct this matter along the following
> lines:
> (A) In the case of newly organized banks, where the bank
> officials cannot attempt to sidetrack investigations on the
> ground that their people have already been investigated in
> connection with existing bonds, we will obtain application
> blanks from everybody covered by the blanket bond, and will
> make investigations as usual. The issuance of the bonds need

not be held up pending the completion of such investigations, but it must be understood by the bank, in advance, that investigations will be made.

(B) Where we issue a bond in behalf of a bank whose staff is already covered upon ordinary bonds issued by some company other than our own we will ascertain, by means of stock letter no. 666, what employees have been satisfactorily investigated by such other company; and upon receipt of this information we will seek, by means of stock letter no. 629, permission from the bank to investigate as usual all other members of its staff.

(C) Where in these latter cases the bank objects to our obtaining applications and making investigations therefrom, we will select from the list of officers and other employees, for special treatment, all members of the staff holding important positions—the executive officers, paying and receiving tellers, chief accountants, etc. These people we will investigate as follows:

(a) We will obtain from commercial agencies, local attorneys, or similar sources, individual reports. If these reports are favorable, no further action will be taken. If the reports are unfavorable in any case, we will develop the facts through detective agencies or otherwise, and cancel the risk in case the situation seems to warrant such a course.

(b) If, at the anniversary date of the bond, our experience with the risk has shown the advisability of full investigations based on applications, we will take up vigorously with the bank the question of obtaining such applications, and if the bank is still unwilling to require its people to complete them, we will cancel the bond.

(c) In the case of all blanket-bonded banks we will investigate in the usual way officers and other employees of the bank newly taken into the service after our bond is issued. In most cases it will probably be better to arrange this detail of the matter through the agent or broker who obtains the business, but in some cases stock letter no. 630 may serve the purpose. The ideal method is for the agent or broker to suggest to the bank that it keep on hand a supply of application forms and require each new employee to complete one when he enters its service. The procedure is so reasonable, and so much in the

interest of the bank, that few bank executives will object to
it. Where they do, we must either refuse to take the business
on any other basis, or make our investigation through commercial-agency reports, detective agencies, etc.

84. Securities Owned by Outsiders

Banks frequently undertake to care for Liberty Bonds
and other securities for their customers or even for the
general public, making no charge for such service. This
practice was particularly common during the Great War,
when hundreds of thousands of small investors bought
Liberty Bonds and had no safe place in which to keep
them. Many banks protected by blanket bonds, finding
themselves in this way in possession of large quantities
of outside securities entrusted to them for safekeeping,
asked the surety companies whether or not the blanket
bonds covered such securities. The answer was not
altogether easy. A blanket bond indemnifies the bank
for the loss of property "in which the Insured has a
pecuniary interest or for which it is legally liable." If,
therefore, the banks, under the conditions described, are
liable to the depositors for the securities left with the
banks, then the blanket bond unquestionably covers
such securities; but if the banks are not liable, then they
sustain no loss when the securities cannot be returned to
the depositors, and are thus in no position to call upon
the surety company for indemnification. To indemnify
means to make good a loss, and when there is no loss
indemnification is obviously out of the question.

When this was explained to the banks, with or without
the additional statement that the surety companies saw
no reason why they should gratuitously extend the protection of their bonds to the public, from which they had
received no premium and with which they had no con-

tractual relations, the resultant situation was not particularly satisfactory to the bank; nor was it helped materially if the surety company went on to say that in
practice its bond would probably extend to these outside
securities, because the courts would in all likelihood hold
the bank liable on the ground that it had agreed to take
charge of the securities primarily for its own ultimate
benefit, regarding the procedure as a piece of excellent
advertising and deeming itself adequately compensated
by the good-will and prestige thus acquired.

As the banks desired *certainty* of insurance above all
else, and more and more demanded that the surety
companies assume complete liability for outside securities,
regardless of the banks' own responsibility, endorsements were finally authorized, for an additional premium,
covering the point unequivocally. For some time only
Liberty Bonds were thus provided for; but a later endorsement extended the protection to all other kinds of
securities.

85. Permissible Modifications of Standard Forms

Since it would be idle to standardize blanket-bond
forms and then permit those forms to be amended or
endorsed by any company in its own underwriting discretion, a Surety Association rule provides that the
standard forms may be changed or endorsed only in
accordance with corresponding prior action by the Association. Endorsements, accordingly, designed to meet a
great variety of conditions have been authorized from
time to time. The Surety Association changes its mind
about these matters with feminine facility, and it would
be futile to include here a set of endorsements as they
stand now, because some of them would surely be changed
or eliminated while the book was in press.

86. Brokers' Blanket Bonds

Special forms of blanket bonds of several varieties have been prepared for use when stock-market brokers are the obligees. Only a few companies are willing to provide this insurance, antecedent reasoning having indicated its exceptionally riskful nature, and actual experience having abundantly confirmed, amplified, and accentuated such *a priori* conclusions. It is hoped, however, by the sunny-tempered underwriters still in the game, that the augmented rates, chastened forms of bonds, and soberer conditions now prevailing in Wall Street will ultimately take the color out of the red-ink figures; they hope, so to speak, to take the red out of the redolent record.

CHAPTER VIII

PUBLIC-OFFICIAL BONDS—GENERAL CONSIDERATIONS

87. Multiform Hazards Embodied in These Bonds

Almost everywhere nowadays persons holding public office are required by law to give a bond conditioned for their faithful performance of duties. To a very large extent formerly this suretyship was furnished, as it is to some extent even now, by private individuals, but more and more it is becoming the practice to provide corporate bonds in these cases. This is so partly because governmental bodies have found it impossible in numerous cases to collect from private sureties, and have therefore facilitated or required the filing of corporate bonds, and partly because painful loss experiences have made people reluctant to assume this liability. Increasingly in recent years and with eminent wisdom legislatures and similar bodies have enacted laws prohibiting personal suretyship and authorizing officials to procure corporate bonds at public cost.

Almost always the only bond that will satisfy the requirement of the law is one that baldly guarantees the faithful performance by the official of the duties of his office. Quite commonly these precise words, "faithful performance," are used by the lawmakers; and even when that is not the case, no bond-approving official who knows his business will accept an instrument that does not substantially guarantee absolute performance of the duties of the office. In other words, public-official bonds are necessarily wide-open instruments.

Now, what does that mean? It means that all the

money of the city, county, state, or nation, as the case may be, that the official receives, or would receive if he discharged his duty properly, must be paid over to the governing body. No excuse whatever, other than an act of God or the public enemy, will save the official or his surety. If he puts the money in the best bank in town, and the bank fails; if he is overpowered by thugs on his way to deposit the money; if he receives it during evening office hours and loses it the same night to burglars who break into his strongest and best style of safe; if he does anything, indeed, whatever may have been his good faith and diligence, except pay over the money, he is liable, and his sureties are, too.

Whether you comprehend it or not, whether it seems to you proper or not, such is the law, established by innumerable decisions. It is so even in the case of private sureties, those "favorites of the law"; and as for corporate sureties, they haven't a ghost of a chance before any judge or jury in any such case. It is absolutely and undeniably true that when surety companies bond a public official their obligation includes a negligence bond, a fidelity bond, a theft policy, a burglary policy, a fire policy, and numerous other varieties of insurance and suretyship.

88. Subjective Underwriting Considerations

Most students of suretyship, at first anyway, regard public-official bonds as little more than fidelity instruments. We saw in the preceding section that they were vastly more than that; but it is true that public-official bonds are primarily, and in most cases preponderantly, pure fidelity risks. The character and capacity and general responsibility of the office-holders are thus of the highest importance from an underwriting point of view.

Aside from the external aspect of these bonds (audits, countersignatures, depository conditions, office staff, etc.), to be considered later, there are three of these subjective features of public-official risks deserving of attention—namely, the character of the principal, his business experience and capacity, and his financial responsibility.

It goes without saying, of course, that a surety company will never knowingly bond a man as an important public official unless it at least supposes him to be a person of integrity. It is true, no doubt, as some cynical readers may be already telling themselves, that office-holders, in some localities especially, are not always men whose characters and careers would survive the searching investigation of a competent fidelity examiner; but the fact remains that public officials are more and more resorting to the surety companies for their bonds, and are getting them from such companies, although they could not do that unless the underwriters found them to be persons of good character. In view of our numerous political scandals and of all that we read (especially in the opposition papers at election periods) about the infamies of our office-holders, the fact that a very large proportion of them are able to offer corporate suretyship seems to me significant and, from the standpoint of civic welfare, highly reassuring.

Mere honesty, however, though a prime essential in an applicant for an official bond, is not enough, since an official may be as honest as the day is long, and may nevertheless misuse the public money because of his inexperience in business affairs, his inability to apply intelligent methods to strange and somewhat complex situations, and his general incapacity. Not infrequently, in our land of golden opportunities, laborers, mechanics, and other estimable gentlemen are elected to important public offices to which they may bring spotless characters, but for the duties of which, in many important respects, nothing in all their prior career has in the least equipped them. Whoever writes their bonds under such conditions is taking more than a normal chance.

The third consideration, financial status, is considerably less important than the other two, but nevertheless needs attention, since even an official who is both honest and able may under conditions readily conceivable default on his bond for causes beyond his own control. Even, therefore, when all the other incidents of the risk are favorable, prudent underwriters will not bond in a large amount a money-handling public official who has little or no personal means. Sometimes, however, a defect in an applicant's credentials as respects this last point (lack of means) may be cured by indemnity of unquestionable value.

89. External Incidents of the Risk

In the chapters relating to fidelity underwriting the importance of the external features of a given risk was pointed out—the opportunities for wrongdoing, the checks and safeguards designed to minimize such opportunities, and the like. Similar objective considerations, correlative to the subjective considerations discussed in the preceding section, apply to public-official bonds—perhaps, indeed, with greater force.

In the first place, a large number of bonded officials handle little or no money. It does not follow, of course, that these officials are necessarily preferred risks; quite the contrary is sometimes the case (cf. sheriffs and other police officials). Yet it is true that officials whose duties involve no collection or custody or distribution of money are, *ceteris paribus*, safer people to bond than money-handling office-holders.

In the next place, there are numerous gradations of risk among officials who receive and disburse money, in accordance with the nature of their contact with the money—whether it comes to them in checks or in currency, whether it stays with them or is promptly disbursed or turned over to some other official, whether it is paid out upon vouchers signed only by the official or signed by him and countersigned by another official, etc.

Again, there are differences of distinct underwriting significance in offices as regards auditing checks and other conditions affecting the concealment of shortages. Sometimes the circumstances are such that no considerable deficit in an official's cash is likely to remain undiscovered long; while under other conditions, characteristic of certain offices, shortages at one date may readily be covered up with current receipts that need not be accounted for until a year or more perhaps has elapsed, with the net result, in the case of long-term offices especially, of postponing for years and perhaps indefinitely the uncovering of defaults.

Expert and experienced public-official underwriters know pretty well from the nature of the office which of the foregoing considerations apply to a given risk; and the application blank, supplemented by good work on the agent's part, should likewise develop the facts in this respect. It is clear that these features of the risk will have much to do, in many cases, with an underwriter's decision as to the acceptability of a given offering.

90. The Incidental Depository Risk

Since a public official is absolutely liable for the safe-keeping of the money received by him in his official

capacity, it follows, generally speaking, that the failure
of a bank in which he has deposited public funds will not
absolve him from responsibility, with whatever care he
may have selected the bank, and however high its reputation may have been. The delightful possibilities in
this respect are shown by the following telegram sent to
a surety company by the attorney-general of a certain
state:

> The state treasurer, for whom your company is surety in
> the sum of $500,000, wrongfully deposited $547,000 in a sus-
> pended bank, and is, therefore, short that amount. You are
> advised that the state looks to you forthwith to make good to
> the treasurer the amount of your guaranty bond. The busi-
> ness admits of no delay. Will expect an answer by wire to-
> morrow.

This delicious exhibit of strong-arm work on the part
of the attorney-general naturally tickled the surety
company nearly to death. There seems to have been, by
the way, a slight error in transmission in the last sentence, which presumably read, "I expect to receive the
amount of the bond, $500,000, by wire tomorrow."

The welfare of the state is paramount, of course, and
the rule fastening liability for deposits on public officials,
or some equivalent regulation, is essential to the public
interest; but in practice that rule was found (and was
bound) to work grievous hardship upon deserving officials. In many states, therefore, a plan is now followed
that equally protects the body politic, and yet relieves
the official and his surety of an unwarranted hazard.
This plan provides that if officials deposit their public
funds in certain designated banks or trust companies,
following at every step the precise procedure prescribed
by law, and exceeding in no case the amount allotted to a
given bank, no liability is sustained by the principal and

the surety for losses due to the failure of such depositories. Where laws of this nature prevail the underwriter
must see to it that they are followed to the last detail
by the officials bonded.

91. Favorable Depository Laws in Certain States

The following states have enacted depository laws in
which public officials may relieve themselves of liability
for losses due to the failure of banks:

Alabama, Arkansas, California, Florida, Illinois, Indiana, Kansas, Louisiana, Michigan, Minnesota, Mississippi, Missouri, Montana, Nebraska, New Jersey,
New York, Ohio, Oregon, Pennsylvania, South Dakota,
Tennessee, Virginia, Washington, West Virginia, Wisconsin, Wyoming. In the case of the following states
special depository rates, as shown in the Manual, apply
to certain funds: Minnesota, Tennessee, Virginia, West
Virginia, and Wisconsin.

Officials located in states other than those mentioned
in the preceding paragraph (and states that may hereafter enact similar legislation) are subject to the old rule
fastening absolute liability upon them for deposited
funds; and in such states underwriters ordinarily think
it necessary to protect their companies by requiring the
official to take out depository bonds. This requirement
is sometimes waived, however, when the banks used by
the official are particularly strong.

Depository bonds written, not by corporate, but by
personal, sureties will not ordinarily be acceptable to
underwriters. Sometimes, however, and especially
when the depository risk continues for only a short time,
bonds executed by personal sureties of known responsibility will be taken, if the other and better plan seems
impracticable. Some companies are willing to write

themselves such incidental depository bonds, while other companies prefer to have this part of the risk carried elsewhere.

92. The Incidental Office-Staff Risk

Almost always in the case of large bonds, and frequently in the case of smaller risks, the bonded officials cannot perform their duties with efficiency and with the dispatch essential to the public convenience unless they have assistance. This condition of things is recognized and provided for in governmental budgets, which frequently assign to an official, at appropriate salaries, one or more deputies, clerks, and the like. The official himself, however—and it could not well be otherwise— is held absolutely responsible for the performance of *all* the duties of his office, even though some of those duties, and frequently a considerable share of them, are necessarily delegated to others. Obviously under such conditions the safety of the official, no less than that of his surety, calls for the bonding of all assistants whose work is so important that their dishonesty or incapacity might involve the principal in default. Here, therefore, as in the analogous matter of depository liability, underwriters desire full information regarding staff members as follows:

(a) The name of each member and position held by him or her.
(b) The amount of the bond in each case, if any bond has been issued or is contemplated.
(c) The name of the company that issued the bond.
(d) The date of termination of the bond in each case (they should, of course, be coterminous with the official's own bond).

Actual copies of the bonds will serve the purpose better, and will supersede items (b), (c), and (d) above.

Bonds covering staff members written by personal

sureties will not ordinarily be acceptable to underwriters. Some companies are willing to issue themselves, when they bond the chief official, these bonds covering subordinate staff members, while other companies deem it rather illogical to carry that part of the risk themselves even upon a normal premium basis. In practice the circumstances are sometimes such that personal sureties of demonstrable responsibility are acceptable to underwriters in the case of these minor officials.

93. Hold-Over Bonds

Public officials who are elected or appointed to succeed themselves in the same office are called in surety parlance "hold-overs." They are deemed undesirable risks, except under circumstances not always existent and upon conditions not always fulfillable. Hold-overs are regarded as subnormal risks because of the danger that shortages really arising in the earlier term will be covered up and carried into the new term, and will *thereafter* become known and be charged against the subsequent bond. Such cases have been by no means infrequent in the history of public-official suretyship, and they may easily occur in the case of any hold-over. The official who has been clever enough to create a shortage without detection and to conceal the shortage up to the end of his term will find it no great draft upon his powers of falsification and manipulation to carry the shortage into the new term; and while, in theory at least and in strict justice to the second company, this shortage should be cared for by the first surety, in practice it rarely works out that way. In the first place, it is usually impossible to fix the exact date of the defalcation, which, indeed, may have no exact date, having run along in various amounts for an indefinite period; and in the second place,

9

even if the fact of a shortage in the prior term is reasonably well established, the courts are likely to hold that the second surety is liable anyway for all amounts that the principal should have had on hand at the beginning of the succeeding term, including the amount of the shortage.

While applications for hold-over bonds are not fought for by surety companies with their customary competitive abandon, yet under some conditions such bonds are acceptable. In all such cases the following underwriting safeguards are regarded by underwriters as essential:

(a) A copy of the official's latest account should be obtained. This ought to be of recent date, and should show the approval of the official or board whose duty it is to oversee the official's accounts.

(b) A statement should be obtained from the bank or banks in which the official keeps his public funds showing that the bank balances are consistent with the official's books.

(c) A satisfactory explanation of the need for the new suretyship should be obtained. Perhaps, for example, no bond was required before. Perhaps personal suretyship was furnished in the prior term, and the official prefers not to burden his friends longer but to substitute corporate suretyship. In any such case, of course, it is highly important to ascertain who the personal sureties were, and to find out what *they* have to say about it. Usually these changes of surety companies come about from the competition of local agents; and under such conditions the succeeding company should state the situation frankly to the prior company, and find out whether or not the official stands well with it. Oftentimes the succeeding company can, with grace and self-service, throw a sop to Cerberus by reinsuring part of the risk with the earlier surety.

When officials do not handle money, there is less difficulty over a change of companies at the beginning of a new term of office.

94. Mid-Term Bonds Occasionally Called For

Public officials, generally speaking, must give a bond when they take office conditioned for the faithful performance of the duties of such office.   If they fail to do that within a prescribed time, they will definitely forfeit the office in some states, while in other states they will conditionally forfeit it, but will be automatically reinstated by the subsequent approval of a proper bond.   In all states the bond so given (and whenever given) covers the full official term.   This is necessarily so, because the imperative condition would not be satisfied, if the bond were filed for a period falling short of the full term. When the term is two years or more, the premium for the bond is frequently paid initially only for the first year; but that fact has no effect upon the term of the bond, nor would it matter, indeed, if the bond itself purported in such a case to run for one year only.   In the eye of the law the bond will always be deemed to have been given in accordance with the statute requiring the official to furnish a bond conditioned for his faithful performance of duty; and any surety company that permits the official to file its bond will be so bound, and so bound throughout the full term, regardless of premium payments or non-payments and equally regardless of any provision in the instrument itself inconsistent with this fundamental and inevitable intent and meaning of the bond.

The official cannot qualify for his office without filing a bond, and if the bond is once filed it stands and, generally speaking, may not be withdrawn or cancelled. Not infrequently when surety companies have written official bonds in haste and afterward repented at leisure, they would gladly have given back many times the premium paid for the privilege of cancelling; but no such way out has been open to them. When Josh Billings in a certain emergency was admonished to take the bull by the horns, he said that he preferred to take him by the tail, since he could hold on just as well and could let go a good deal easier. Unfortunately there is no way in which an underwriter can take an official bond by the tail—when he once signs and delivers the bond he must hold on grimly until the end of the term (still generally speaking), however much he may have been deceived regarding the character of his principal, or for whatever other reason he may desire to withdraw or to cancel the bond.

95. Mid-Term Bonds Usually Undesirable

Because an official bond when once filed is uncancellable (except under exceptional conditions and with infinite trouble), surety companies will not ordinarily bond an official in the course of his term, nor permit him to file their bond in presumed replacement of an existing bond. To do the latter would be grossly unfair to the original surety, and would be contrary to all the rules of the game as played by the bonding companies. The effect upon the first bond of the filing of the second bond would vary with the circumstances of the given case and with the jurisdiction, but under no conditions probably would the first surety be released. Under some circumstances and in some jurisdictions it might be regarded as a cosurety with the second company, and to that extent might benefit from the performance of the intruder; but it would presumably obtain no premium (since the official would not pay two premiums) for thus carrying half the risk. Similarly the legal position of the second company involves doubtful and difficult questions of law the answer to which would vary with the circumstances and with the jurisdiction. Always, no doubt, the new company would be liable in some degree and for a certain period. It would surely be liable from the time its bond was filed, and many courts perhaps would antedate its liability to the beginning of the official term, on the ground that the bond necessarily covered the official for his full term, notwithstanding the date of its filing, and notwithstanding the incidental and irrelevant fact that another company, now to be deemed a cosurety, had also filed a similar bond.

While, therefore, it is both inconsistent with inter-company comity, and altogether unwise generally, to become surety for a public official in the course of his term of office when another company is already on the risk, there are nevertheless two conditions under which mid-term bonds may be issued: (a) Unfortunately surety companies sometimes become insolvent, and when that happens public officials are required to furnish new bonds; (b) sometimes an official who has provided personal suretyship is forced by the disqualification of some of them, or desires for reasons of his own, to furnish new sureties and decides to replace his personal with corporate suretyship.

Mid-term bonds even under the foregoing conditions are not choice business; but some company must write them, in the public interest, and they are not necessarily so bad. If the other aspects of the risk are good, and if the official does not handle money, or, if he does, if an audit shows everything to be apparently all right when the new bond becomes effective, most underwriters will deem the bond issuable.

96. Reindemnifying Bonds Frequently Required

In a few benighted regions public officials are still required by law to. furnish personal suretyship; and in a good many places (a little further removed from the Stone Age) personal sureties are frequently offered and accepted. Sometimes in these cases the official, while complying with the law or the custom of his habitat, is nevertheless so far in advance of his age and generation that he desires to indemnify his bondsmen against loss that they might otherwise sustain in connection with their guaranty of his faithful performance of duties. He applies to a surety company, accordingly, for a bond running in favor of his personal guarantors and giving them a right to demand reimbursement from the surety company in case they have to pay any claim upon their own undertaking to make good the defaults of the official. An instrument of this kind is known as an reindemnifying bond. It is often called for in surety practice.

Since the companies do not hesitate to bond public officials directly, it would seem, on general principles, logical and reasonable to do the same thing indirectly by issuing these reindemnifying bonds; and so it would be in all normal cases, and where no circumstances exist such as might give pause to an underwriter handling a direct application. It is important, therefore, and indeed quite necessary, whenever reindemnifying bonds are requested, to ascertain just what the circumstances are that underlie the application. Possibly the official's record and character were such that he was unable to obtain a corporate bond and so fell back upon personal sureties as a last resort, agreeing to indemnify them as soon as the matter could be arranged. Perhaps the personal sureties volunteered their services in the beginning, but learned disquieting facts afterward and are seeking a release correspondingly.   It is not a good sign, anyway, if a man's own friends and neighbors require indemnity in such a case—if they *do* require it.   Obviously complete information is essential regarding the reason for indemnification.

Usually there is a good reason—one that reflects credit rather than discredit upon the official; but it is necessary, nevertheless, to find out what the reason is.   One of the commonest reasons, and one of the most satisfactory, is that the directors of some bank, eager to obtain the deposit of the public funds, have agreed as a *quid pro quo* to sign the official's bond.   Other excellent reasons are often found to explain the desire for indemnification and thus to warrant the issuance of the bond.

97. Partial Indemnification Sometimes Proper

The form of reindemnifying bond issued by the surety company deserves a word.   Since the personal sureties must always assume the broad liability characteristic of official bonds, and since the surety company undertakes to indemnify them for losses incurred under *their* bond, it follows that, in fairness to the personal sureties and in the absence of exceptional circumstances, the corporate bond should be as broad as the other.   Sometimes, however, the circumstances are such as to justify the surety company in asking the personal sureties to accept a narrower bond than the one that they themselves have signed in behalf of the public official.   In the case of the bank directors, for example, referred to above, the surety company will ordinarily exclude from its bond any liability for loss due to the insolvency of the bank.   Sometimes other limitations upon the normal liability of the surety may fairly be embodied in the re-indemnifying bond—non-liability, for example, for losses

occasioned by the defaults of deputies or clerks; and
sometimes the surety reserves in its instrument the right
of cancellation—something, of course, that it could not
do in the case of a regular public-official bond. Since
personal sureties, when they sign these public official
bonds, are invading the legitimate field of the surety
companies, the latter may be pardoned perhaps for not
going out of their way to make things easier for their
unnatural competitors. There should, of course, be no
sort of deception about the matter, and whenever the
corporate bond is so drawn that claims provable under
the personal bond and thus a possible source of loss to
the personal sureties would not fall within the terms of
the reindemnifying instrument and would thus not be
reimbursable thereunder, such a condition of things
should be made clear to the personal sureties. They
would naturally, and in default of such an explanation,
expect complete indemnification.

98. Premium Rates Not Uniform

Since the amount of the official bond is sometimes made
by law much larger than the real exposure seems to the
personal sureties to require, the latter, in order to save a
part of the premium charge, frequently agree to accept a
reindemnifying bond in an amount smaller (perhaps
very much smaller) than that of the instrument executed
by them: they may, for example, think themselves
sufficiently protected by a reindemnifying bond of $25,-
000, say, when they have themselves signed a $100,000
bond. The premium charge is not reduced *proportionately*, of course, in these cases—that would be altogether
unfair to the surety company because of the concentrated
and overweighted liability; the rate has been carefully
worked out by the Bureau and graded in accordance

with the ratio between the amount of the official bond and that of the reindemnifying bond (cf. page 123 of the Public Official Manual).

99. A Bond of Uncertain Temperament

Reindemnifying bonds are rather common, and are regarded by most underwriters as desirable business, provided a thoroughgoing and satisfactorily-resulting investigation of their origin is made. Occasionally, however, claims arise that are both costly and difficult to adjust with the obligees; and this happens just often enough, in the course of an experience favorable on the whole, to give reindemnifying bonds an unpleasant resemblance to the little girl in the nursery rhyme, who, when she was good, was very very good, and when she was bad, was horrid.

100. Cumulative Liability

A public official furnishes a qualifying bond when he enters upon the duties of his office, and usually that is the only bond filed by him. Sometimes, however, he must give one or more subsequent and additional bonds, because of fresh legislation requiring him to handle more money than was originally contemplated or for other reasons; and in some places the authorities demand from officials a new bond at the beginning of each year of their term. These latter bonds are sometimes called "superseding" or "substitute" bonds. Both terms are complete misnomers, because the subsequent bonds do not in any case, and whatever their cause, release the original bond; and the net result of the additional suretyship is simply that two or more bonds instead of one safeguard the obligee from maladministration of the office.

That is so because in all these cases of multiple bonds

the liability of the surety is cumulative. If, for example, an official elected to an office for a four-year term is required to give a $25,000 bond, say, at the beginning of each year, the surety company will be carrying during the last year of the term a liability of $100,000, although the premium paid for that year will be computed on the basis of a $25,000 liability only. A situation of this kind is regarded by surety companies as unfair to them; and when, as sometimes happens, bonds running in favor of private obligees are reissued in behalf of the same principal and in favor of the same obligee, or changed in amount, an endorsement is attached to the new instrument intended to forestall cumulative liability. Nothing of the sort is possible in the case of public-official bonds; no approving officer would accept the bond so endorsed, nor would the endorsement ultimately stand in all probability, even if it got by the approving officer, in case the bond afterward figured in a lawsuit against the surety.

Sometimes underwriters would rather not have business of this class at all than have it on the cumulative basis indicated; while in other cases, although the amount nominally at risk pyramids upward in a somewhat startling manner, in fact the real liability is not greatly affected by the plurality of bonds issued in behalf of the official. This is so, for example, when he is required to clean up and turn over to some other official his collections and receipts so promptly that the defaultable fund in his hands never rises much above the uniform amount of the successive bonds.

101. Public-Official Application Blank

Many fieldmen seem not to appreciate the importance of the forms that applicants for public-official bonds are expected to complete for the guidance and information of underwriters. The same agents who take it as a matter of course that applicants for ordinary fidelity bonds shall give the surety company full and accurate information about themselves sometimes ask the home-office to waive applications altogether or to accept inadequate documents from public officials. In fact, full information is more important, generally speaking, in the case of official bonds than in that of ordinary fidelity bonds. Frequently special information, not expressly called for by the printed form, but of distinct underwriting relevancy, will come to the knowledge of fieldmen; and the home-office, while deeming itself entitled to such information (whichever way it bears upon the acceptability of the business), nevertheless feels grateful to the fieldmen for imparting it.

In the case of important bonds few underwriters are willing to waive the completion of a full application blank. A briefer form, however, has been adopted by most companies as a concession to the easy-going field tendency referred to and in weak submission to a regrettable competitive departure from sound underwriting practice. They use the shorter form particularly for federal officials, but make it do likewise in other cases where the duties and incidental features of the office are fairly well understood anyway, and where the character of the applicant is the chief underwriting factor to be developed.

102. Form of Public-Official Bond

Delightfully simple and satisfactory, from the standpoint of the obligee, is the ordinary public-official bond—a clear-cut, unqualified avowal by the principal and the surety of liability to the obligee in a named amount, a recital of the fact that the principal will hold a given office for a stated period beginning at a certain date, and a final conditioning of the entire obligation upon the principal's failure faithfully to perform the duties of his office. If he serves without default, everything is off— otherwise the obligation stands. There is no condition in the bond the fulfillment of which would defeat recovery thereunder, nor any other sort of qualification of the surety's undertaking, nor any right of cancellation reserved to the surety. All this, of course, is as it should be, since the absolute validity of the bond under any and all conditions is essential to the public welfare.

A form of bond drafted along the foregoing lines is usually prescribed by the obligee—in the case of the more important bonds anyway—and it would be idle for the surety to attempt to change the form, even if any disposition to do so were present; all that the surety company can do in such cases, if it desires the business, is to sign on the dotted line. It is true that once in a while a concurrence of unusual conditions makes possible the issuance and perhaps the valid acceptance of a public-official bond containing a cancellation clause, a provision excluding liability for depository loss, and other limitations of the normal official-bond exposure. The statute, for example, creating some office may say nothing about any bond requirement, and the controlling political unit concerned (state, city, etc.) may never have enacted any general law calling for faithful-performance-of-duty bonds in *all* cases, and the immediate political unit in whose favor the bond runs may not have counsel charged with the duty of procuring an adequate bond, and the official with whom the bond is left may not be sufficiently well advised to insist upon the filing of a proper bond. Even when all these coinciding conditions enable an official to qualify with a narrow bond, if a loss occurs recoverable under a normal bond but apparently shut out by some restrictive provision of the special bond actually issued, it may be doubted that the bond would stand as drafted—it may well be that the court would find some ingenious way in which to construe the bond as an ordinary faithful-performance-of-duty, public-official obligation. The cases where narrow bonds may be filed are so rare and unimportant as to be negligible for most practical purposes, and they are so treated in this volume. Perhaps, indeed, it would be better in the long run if official underwriters, having in mind the good name of their companies and the general welfare of the state, would refrain from taking advantage of the situations described, and would issue in all cases, regardless of any statutory requirement, the usual broad form of public-official bond.

103. Certain Information Particularly Important

While it is highly important in the case of all bonds issued by fieldmen that exact copies of the form used be sent to the home-office or to the proper branch office, in the case of public-official bonds the requirement is imperative. The surety company's files should always contain either (and preferably) a complete carbon copy of the original bond or such an identification of some standard or official form used as will enable the company to reproduce at will a perfect copy of the bond actually issued.

The application papers concerned with official bonds are frequently deficient as to one of the most important aspects of the risk—they do not show precisely what the term of the bond is to be. Usually the term of the bond is the same as the term of the office to which the official is elected or appointed; but in a surprising number of cases the papers do not show what that term is. Sometimes the statutory requirement is that the bond shall remain in force until a successor qualifies, so that the term of the bond may exceed the regular term of office. Obviously the surety company must have exact information upon this important point.

104. Cancellation Evidence

When a bond is once entered in a surety company's records as a live risk, it must so remain, and the company must carry a corresponding reserve until adequate evidence is procured that all liability under the bond has, in fact, expired; and this evidence that the risk is dead must be such as to satisfy not only the underwriter, but also the Insurance Department examiners who will sooner or later come across the item in the records and demand to know why the reserve was taken down, if convincing evidence of termination is lacking. It is not enough in one of these cases to show merely that the term of the official, according to the surety company's files, has expired; because he may remain in office pending the failure of some successor to qualify, or (as occasionally happens) the underwriter may have been misinformed regarding the term. Obviously the company must procure from some source and must have in its file with the other papers, before it can safely mark off the risk, affirmative and compelling evidence of the termination of active liability. The term "active liability" is used, because for years to come, and until the statute of limitations rescues the surety company, there will remain a latent liability—the possibility that some loss provable under the bond will turn up to plague the underwriter. Surety companies are not required, however, to carry a reserve against claim conceivabilities of that nature— perish the thought!

It is not practicable, of course, in many cases to obtain complete proof of termination of liability under a public-official bond.   Underwriters, however, have recourse to various forms and devices that serve the general purpose fairly well.   What they need, preferably in the shape of official, authenticated documents, is:

    (a) A copy of the principal's final account showing a complete audit of his office up to the end of his term.

    (b) Evidence that the principal's successor in office has duly qualified.

    (c) Evidence that he has turned over to his successor all moneys and other property.

    (d) Evidence that the new bond has been approved and filed, and that a satisfactory audit, with verification of bank balances, was made as of the end of the previous term, when, as sometimes happens, the principal succeeds himself in the same office, but gives his new bond to another agent (by way of passing around the plum, perhaps).

105. "Renewals" of Public-Official Bonds

While public-official bonds, as emphasized above (cf. section 94), are necessarily issued when the official takes office for his full term, four or five years in duration perhaps, and are never "renewed" in any real sense, and while the constant references in surety practice to "renewals" of official bonds are illogical and misleading, yet there is a certain justification for the word as a matter of accounting and underwriting convenience.   The premium for official bonds, for example, when the term exceeds one year, is commonly paid, not in advance for the full term, but in annual instalments; and the "renewals" that we all talk about at such premium-anniversary dates are in fact only the bills, receipts, and similar accounting adjuncts concerned with such subsequent premium payments.   Once a year, too, if not oftener, in the case of

long-term official bonds, prudent underwriters will deem
it worth while to look over the principal's latest official
account, to ascertain what unusual developments, if
any, there have been within the twelvemonth, and, generally, to consider the whole case afresh. It is true that
the underwriter, however prudent or expert he may be,
cannot cancel the bond, even if the said developments
have been seriously adverse; but he can point out and
correct dangerous tendencies, and he can sometimes
improve a bad situation or perhaps cure it altogether, by
taking appropriate remedial action with the principal or
with the latter's superior official.

Not infrequently public officials themselves hold confused and incorrect notions about the continuing validity
of their bonds, and they sometimes demand from the
surety company a "renewal" of their bond. In all such
cases the underwriter must patiently explain the situation to them, and must be careful, whatever else he does,
not to give them any form of instrument that fastens
cumulative liability upon the surety. In practice, almost
always, after such an explanation, it is found that a
simple receipt for the annual premium such as would be
furnished anyway will satisfy the official.

106. Official Bonds Gradually Improving

Public-official bonds seem to me to be getting safer
for the surety companies with the lapse of time, partly
because of improving conditions outside the companies
and partly because of better and more uniform underwriting practices. Notwithstanding many occasional
disheartening setbacks, the character and efficiency of our
governmental bodies seem to be showing slow improvement all the time, and incidentally to be making official
bonds less hazardous for the surety companies. More

and more,. for example, are states and other political units adopting the practice of auditing regularly and thorqughly the accounts of their public officials. As for the companies' contributions to the lessening loss ratio that I hope to be characteristic of present-day official business, it seems to me that the experience of the companies has shown the underwriters the necessity, as modern co-operative methods have shown them the practicability, of enforcing the adoption of the safeguards described in this chapter. Depository protection, for example, is more and more regarded as a matter of course by underwriters, and officials unwilling to comply with their sureties' requirements in this respect find it more difficult than it used to be to obtain bonds from another company.

Plenty of room for improvement in this respect remains, however, and losses are all the time occurring because competition, real or presumed, has caused some underwriter to waive a safeguard that he knew to be reasonable and essential to his safety. When the claim comes in and the reason for it is apparent, the underwriter resolves not to be so weak the next time; but when the next time arrives, if the bond is particularly attractive and the agent eloquently insistent, the bars are likely to be let down again:

> The Devil was sick: the Devil a monk would be.
> The Devil was well: the devil a monk was he.

CHAPTER IX

PUBLIC–OFFICIAL BONDS—CERTAIN IMPORTANT SPECIES OF THE GENUS

107. Treasurers' Bonds (State, County, City, Town, School, etc.)

I take up treasurers' bonds specifically because they constitute the largest and on the whole most important class of public-official risks with which surety companies have to do; but I think of no weighty underwriting consideration affecting them that has not already been discussed in the preceding chapter. No one, for example, would think of bonding a money-handling public official of this type who was known or suspected to be constitutionally incapable of distinguishing his own from other people's property, or who was notoriously lax and incompetent and generally irresponsible in the conduct of business affairs. The section, too, concerned with the external features of a public-official risk (89) has special force and relevancy when applied to treasurers' bonds, and the underwriter should run down this point until the whole situation is laid bare. Sometimes treasurers receive the public funds largely in the form of cash, and hold them indefinitely, without special supervision, and disburse the funds under their sole signatures. Sometimes, on the other hand, the money comes to them chiefly in the form of checks payable to them only in their official capacity or directly to the particular political unit, and it is not disbursable by the treasurers upon their own initiative, but only in connection with other signatures or warrants. Between these two extremes there are found in practice all the intermediate gradations of supervision afforded by audits, countersignatures, concurrent authorizations, and similar safeguarding systems.   Obviously this aspect of the situation is of vast practical importance in the underwriting of treasurers' bonds.

The incidental depository risk (section 90) is more important in the case of treasurers' bonds than in any other division of the public-official department, and no experienced, careful underwriter will finally approve a bond of this type until he is satisfied that the depository hazard has been cared for adequately.   If there be in the given jurisdiction some provision of law under which the official can take refuge, as shown in section 91, no pains must be spared to make sure that every last requirement of the law is fulfilled, because the least irregularity may have fatal consequences in the hour of need; and if in the given case no statutory life-saving station is available, corporate depository bonds or some supposedly equivalent security must be procured for the protection of the principal and the surety.

The office-staff risk incident to public-official bonds in general is present, of course, in the case of treasurers' bonds, and must be considered by underwriters, particularly in connection with important offices where deputies and other assistants are likely to be employed. Frequently, however, this feature of the risk in the case of treasurers is found not to require special attention.

The unpleasant possibilities involved in large bonds for treasurers may be understood from the fact that in November, 1921, the Attorney-General of the state of Illinois instituted suits against five former state treasurers and their sureties, alleging shortages (interest on public funds not accounted for) of approximately two and one-half million dollars, and demanding restitution of that amount.

108. The Sad Case of the Ambidextrous Official

One hazard incident to treasurers' bonds recognized by all experienced official underwriters may be described as "the dual-capacity risk"—the danger that the person holding the official treasurership may simultaneously hold some other money-handling position by means of which a shortage in the official position may be temporarily or perhaps indefinitely cared for. Officers of banks, for example, are frequently town treasurers or custodians of other public funds. This is a natural and entirely legitimate situation, of course, but it nevertheless contains the seeds of danger from the point of view of an official underwriter. The history of defaults upon bonds of this class abounds in examples of this hazard, where a person acting in the dual capacity has made good the shortage in one position for the time being, and not infrequently for years, through a species of kiting of funds.

An interesting case in my own experience illustrates this danger. In a little country town in Massachusetts one man officiated as town treasurer and at the same time served the local bank in the capacity of cashier. The town frequently borrowed money from the bank, giving its notes for the loans; and the double-headed official would, with his right hand as treasurer of the town, make out the notes and pass them over to his left hand, and at the same time, with his left hand as cashier of the bank, turn over the money to the town—when he did it, the trouble being that his left hand was not so well trained as his right and sometimes failed to function. The latter fact, however, transpired only after this ambidextrous manipulation had been going on for years, and after the official had succeeded in stealing about $600,000 from the bank and the town together in some unknown proportion.

The bank sued the town for amounts alleged to be due on notes given by the town to the bank, while the town stoutly maintained that it had paid the notes through its treasurer to the bank through the latter's cashier. The man had undoubted authority to act for the town in paying over the money and equally good authority to act for the bank in receiving it. And there you are: I do not know myself where you are, but perhaps some bright little boy or girl in the class can tell us.

109. Tax-Collectors' Bonds

Next to the bonds called for by the many varieties of treasurers, these are the most numerous and the most important of official bonds; and they overtop all other classes perhaps in the matter of underwriting complexities and inherent hazard.   Some tax-collectors' bonds, indeed, are so dangerous as to have gained the dubious distinction of a prominent position in the prohibited list of certain companies. The bonds vary markedly in loss content in accordance with the laws and customs of the controlling jurisdiction.

The business of a tax-collector is, of course, to collect the taxes—every last penny due from the unfortunate owners of real·estate and personal property. For any number of reasons it is not possible for even the most energetic and grasping official to collect absolutely every item of the tax levy, especially every item based upon the alleged ownership of personal property; and the wide variance in hazard characteristic of these bonds is due to the different degrees of rigidity with which collectors are held to the assessment rolls by the laws and practices of different jurisdictions.   In some places "exonerations," as they are called (release of liability as to specific items in the levy), may be procured by the collector with comparative ease—his mere affidavit perhaps that the item is uncollectible will be accepted. In these innocent regions the authorities evidently agree with the cynical judge who insisted that the truth would come out "even in an affidavit." In some places, too, tax-collectors are treated with even greater liberality in this respect, inasmuch as they are held directly liable only for actual collections and are permitted, as a matter of course, at the end of the tax year, to turn over all uncollected items to an official who kindly relieves them of all responsibility from that date. On the other hand, in many states just the reverse of all this is true, and collectors are absolved from liability for unpaid items only upon incontrovertible evidence that they have exhausted all ordinary means of collection and every legal resource without avail. Sometimes they cannot convince a reviewing official or board that they have done that, and the unpaid items then remain charged to their account and must be included in their return and liquidated in cash exactly as if they had been collected. Because this severe interpretation of the collectors' duty sometimes involves worthy officials in unmerited loss, lawmakers nowadays seem disposed to lay down definite and practicable rules for the guidance of collectors and to give them a clearance regardless of results if they can show compliance with such rules. Until, however, this more reasonable attitude of the authorities becomes general, underwriters will hardly be able to work up much enthusiasm over tax-collectors' bonds as a class.

110. Fidelity Underwriting Considerations Particularly Relevant

Though collectors' bonds include much more than a mere fidelity hazard, and though a surety may sustain heavy loss under such a bond even when its principal has been guilty of no dishonesty whatever, yet the fact remains that the risk is primarily and preponderantly a fidelity one, and that all the underwriting principles applicable to fidelity bonds have equal validity in the case of collectors' bonds. One of the first safeguards, however, that an underwriter thinks of when handling ordinary fidelity risks is frequently absent altogether or largely from collectors' bonds and is at all events beyond the control of the underwriter—namely, adequate supervision of the principal's work by some competent and interested superior. All this in the case of official bonds is a matter of law and practice and almost a matter of chance, the conditions varying enormously in different states and jurisdictions, and even in the same state to a considerable extent, in accordance with the efficiency and discipline and general moral and business capacity of particular supervisory officials. In many places the greatest laxity in this respect prevails, and collectors do their work under no supervision worthy of the name and have every chance in the world to be dishonest if they feel so disposed. Successive levies of taxes on various accounts (highways, schools, county, state, etc.) are given to them for collection at frequent intervals, and no attempt is made to enforce quick and separate settlements of each such levy. It is easy in case of need so to manipulate the various funds as to cover up defaults for a considerable time. If, for example, highway construction progresses so fast that the contractors must be paid large amounts, and if the highway levy, presumably available for the purpose, has been collected and converted, there may be an opportunity to care for the contractors with money taken from one of the other funds.

Collectors, however, have less chance to use their public funds unlawfully than might be expected, because of the fact that most states, counties, cities, and other political units in our ambitious and progressive land are not noted for their businesslike budgetary methods, are likely to spend their money before they get it, to anticipate collections by bank borrowings, and otherwise to adopt the devices characteristic of those who are chronically hard up. Official treasurers, therefore, are all the time pressing collectors for funds; and to a certain extent this favorable factor offsets the unfavorable consideration emphasized above—the lack of close and intelligent supervision.

One of the commonest methods of concealing a shortage adopted by tax-collectors is to report as unpaid taxes that have really been paid. This subterfuge would, of course, be immediately detected and defeated if confirmatory notices were sent to such alleged delinquents; but in many jurisdictions there is no provision for any such rudimentary checking operations. Reasonable officials will not object if the surety company supplies this obvious defect in the system.

The incidental depository and office-staff risks described in sections 90–92 apply to tax-collectors. The former risk, however, is ordinarily not serious, because collectors commonly turn over their funds to treasurers or similar officials at frequent intervals. Collectors are, however, in the absence of special provisions of the kind referred to in section 91, absolutely liable for the solvency of banks in which they may keep their collections during the month or so during which they retain them; and this point should be considered by the underwriter in connection with the other features of the risk. Sometimes the conditions are such that prudent underwriters deem depository bonds reasonably requirable; while in other cases, because of the small amounts involved, brief period of exposure, and high standing of the bank, the depository risk is regarded as ignorable.

111. Sheriffs, Constables, and Other Police Officers

These bonds have a bad name in surety circles, and with good reason. Some companies, indeed, will not write them at all. The losses have not been due so much to dishonesty. Ordinarily, indeed, a sheriff does not receive much money, and is not permitted to keep long the little that he gets, because the litigant entitled to it loses no time in demanding it. The losses have been due rather to wrongful and excessive appropriation of fees and to damage suits arising from errors in the serving of process.

Formerly to a large extent sheriffs were not compensated by fixed salaries but upon a fee system, as they still are, especially in rural regions, in great part. Not infrequently the statutes regulating the fees left room for doubt as to precisely what fees were authorized, and the sheriffs naturally resolved such doubts in their own favor. Sometimes, after one of these broad-visioned, fee-paid sheriffs had been generous with himself for years, some district attorney, ambitious for political preferment and perhaps of a different party persuasion, would sue the sheriff and the surety for a huge amount because of the unlawful appropriation of fees. Heavy losses have been sustained by the bonding companies in this way, and narrow escapes from such losses have been numerous. A notable situation of this kind arose in Maryland a few years ago, where enormous losses upon bonds issued in behalf of sheriffs long dead would have been incurred if a benevolent legislature had not passed a law relieving the sureties. In many cases the fee system resulted in compensation so scandalously high that the law was changed, and the sheriff was made a salaried official. In this respect, therefore, sheriffs' bonds are less dangerous than they used to be.

The average official underwriter looks askance at sheriffs' bonds chiefly because of the second danger referred to above—the chance of damage suits due to the unlawful use of official authority by a willful or careless or ignorant sheriff, when he is preserving the peace, or giving practical effect to court judgments as regards persons in his custody, or executing process. He may sell or attach or replevin the wrong property, may arrest or imprison someone without due cause, and may otherwise abuse or exceed his authority.

112. Developments Helpful to the Surety

In this respect, too, as in the other, sheriffs' bonds are somewhat safer than they used to be. At common law a sheriff was bound at his peril to perform his duty in accordance with the law and the facts of the given case; and he was liable to the plaintiff for a false return if he failed to levy on any property subject to the writ, while he was liable, at the same time, in an action of trespass, if he levied on property not subject thereto. This severe common-law view of the matter has been greatly modified by statutes in favor of the sheriff, who now almost everywhere may require indemnity before proceeding with the execution of a writ in all cases where he reasonably assumes that he will subject himself to some liability by proceeding. Bonds of this kind given for the protection of sheriffs and their sureties constitute an important part of the judicial business of the surety companies.

In the matter of sheriffs' bonds, as in so many other respects, surety companies benefit from the slow but constant improvement in general commercial and industrial conditions.   The whole business of the modern sheriff's office is conducted in a more conservative and orderly and scientific manner than was formerly the case. An experienced and well-informed sheriff is rarely confronted nowadays with a situation which is strange to him or which he cannot handle safely and efficiently; and in many jurisdictions he is at liberty, at the cost of the governing body, to call upon able counsel for help and guidance in any unusual or difficult case.

Section 92, "The Incidental Office-Staff Risk," has special applicability to sheriffs' bonds, since in many places the sheriff cannot possibly perform all the duties of his office himself, but must delegate them largely to deputies and other subordinates.   Every deputy, therefore, and every other important member of his staff should be bonded, for the protection of both the sheriff and the surety.

The office of tax-collector is sometimes joined with that of sheriff, and under such conditions the resultant bond is correspondingly more serious.   In such cases the considerations cited in sections 109–110 should be deemed equally applicable here.

113. County Clerks and Clerks of Courts

I group these officials in this way partly because in many states the two offices are combined, and partly because the duties and underwriting factors are not greatly different in the two cases.   These officials are generally elected for short terms (two years, say), but in a few states they are appointed by the judges and hold office during the pleasure of the appointing power.   As court clerks they keep a record of the proceedings and orders, docket cases for trial, issue process and writs, enter judgments rendered by the court, certify to the correctness of transcripts, and preserve the property and money in the custody of the court—all, except the last, rather harmless functions, from the standpoint of the surety. As county clerks, however, they frequently have duties other than ministerial—for example, the issuance of many kinds of licenses and collection of corresponding fees—in connection with which they sometimes handle considerable sums of money and assume responsibilities of a comprehensive nature; and the surety's risk is not only that they will fail faithfully to account for the fees received, but also that they will, through carelessness or ignorance of the law or general inefficiency, fail to collect all the fees that are lawfully payable. Rather serious claims of this latter nature have occasionally arisen under these bonds.

114. Federal Officials

Most of the underwriting considerations discussed in this and the preceding chapter apply to the bonds required from vast numbers of persons in the service of the United States. In the Post Office Department alone, for example, about 243,000 bonds were outstanding in March, 1922, of which 9 per cent were personal and 91 per cent corporate. Formerly all federal official bonds were personal. Corporate suretyship was not legal until Congress made it so, about thirty years ago, largely because the Secretary of the Treasury reported that the government had at that time judgments against individual sureties amounting to more than $35,000,000 that were uncollectible and would prove a total loss.

While a few classes of federal bonds require rigid

underwriting, both antecedent reasoning and experience indicate that federal bonds in general are less dangerous than are those covering officials of states and smaller political units. This is so for a number of reasons: The depository risk is incomparably less serious in the case of federal officers (because the money is quickly transferred to the United States Treasury); the office-staff risk is likewise relatively unimportant (most subordinate staff members being required by law to furnish bonds); the methods of collecting, taking care of, and accounting for federal funds have been highly systematized and perfected, and are far superior, as a rule, to those of the average state, county, or smaller governmental body; the "Secret Service" permanently maintained by the federal government, of enormous advantage to surety companies, has no counterpart in the case of the other class of bonds; Congress has repeatedly relieved in the past, and may confidently be expected to relieve in the future, federal officials from liability for the loss of public money not due directly to their own theft or blameworthy default.

CHAPTER X

JUDICIAL BONDS

115. Provisional-Remedy Bonds

The law's delay is proverbial. Contested actions drag along for months and frequently for years, and by the time the successful (?) litigant obtains judgment there may be nothing left with which to satisfy the judgment. While such an end in many cases cannot be foreseen, in other cases the circumstances are such as to indicate clearly, even when the action is begun, that an ordinary trial of the cause would surely lead only to an empty result. All this is so sadly and undeniably true that the law under certain conditions sanctions what would be, except for the existence of these conditions, highly irregular proceedings; that is to say, when these exceptional conditions are present, as shown to the satisfaction of the court, plaintiffs may have recourse to certain anticipatory remedies, in virtue of which they are allowed, so to speak, to satisfy judgments before the latter are obtained and upon the assumption that they will ultimately be obtained.

Because this rather arbitrary procedure sometimes works injustice to defendants, and because the privilege of adopting it might easily be abused, the law further provides that any plaintiff desiring to procure a court order that will enable him to make use of one of the remedies must first furnish a bond guaranteeing that, if the defendant recover judgment, or if it is finally determined that the plaintiff is not entitled to the order, the plaintiff will pay all costs and damages that the defendant may sustain by reason of the issuance of the order. This general statement is subject to exceptions, since security may be waived in some jurisdictions in the discretion of the court; but in practice bonds are commonly required.

The three most important provisional remedies are arrest, injunction, and attachment; and the remedy of replevin is much like the others so far as the bond features are concerned. These four classes of bonds, together with the corresponding counter-bonds concerned with each remedy, constitute an exceedingly important part of the judicial business of the surety companies.

116. Order of Arrest

In the old days defendants were arrested as a matter of course, even in civil cases, as the first step in the action, and in some states now an order of arrest against a defendant pending an action may be procured and executed in certain cases (breach of promise to marry, for example, slander, malicious prosecution, false imprisonment, and conversion). No such order will be issued, however, unless (in addition to other essentials) the plaintiff furnishes a bond conditioned to indemnify the defendant for all damages resulting to him from the arrest, in case the order is ultimately found not to have been warranted.

While the court will not issue orders of arrest unless the statute authorizing them under certain conditions is plainly applicable, and all the affidavits and other moving papers make out a clear case, and while in practice defendants are not often able to prove damages, yet, when they are so able, the full penalty of the bond may easily be awarded. Unless, therefore, the principal is abundantly responsible and the bond is one of moderate amount, full collateral security is proper in cases like these.

117. Bail Bonds

In civil cases always, and in criminal cases usually, a person arrested may obtain release from custody by giving a bond conditioned for his appearance at the order of the court under penalty of forfeiture of the sum named in the bond. Personal sureties are frequently provided in these cases, partly because under most conditions little or no expense is thus incurred by the person requiring the bail, and partly because in many cases it is found impracticable to obtain corporate suretyship; but a considerable volume of bail-bond business is nevertheless transacted by the surety companies. This latter statement is particularly true of New York City, and other highly civilized and more highly criminalized communities.

The theory underlying the practice of admitting defendants to bail is that they are merely transferred from the custody of the court to that of their sureties, who may surrender them at any time, and who have authority, for the purpose of making such surrender, to arrest them; and that procedure is often quite practicable in the case of personal sureties. While it is true that companies specializing in bail bonds and possessed of a personnel expertly familiar with this important aspect of criminal practice do in some cases exercise more or less supervision over the movements of their principals and recommit them to the custody of the court upon occasion, yet in general the surety companies do not execute bail bonds upon any such theory as that described. The principal goes whithersoever he listeth as soon as the bond is issued, so far as the surety company is concerned, and the latter forgets him completely unless and until it is unpleasantly reminded of him by a forfeiture of the bond. Except in the case of the bail business discussed in the next section, surety companies write bail bonds upon the theory that they are guaranteeing the payment of a sum of money that will surely become due upon a definite date in the near future; and unless they are entirely confident (as they rarely are) that the principal is abundantly good for the amount, they will not execute the bond unless they are first secured with cash or unquestionable indemnity. In two classes of cases, it is true, neither cash nor outside indemnity seems necessary—where the real defendant is a large corporation or business concern whose employee has been arrested in connection with his work for the employer (a street-car motorman, for example); and where the defendant has been arrested for some comparatively trivial offense like going to a ball game in his twin-six at a speed of fifty miles an hour. The indemnity of the corporation, always procurable in the former case, sufficiently safeguards the surety; while in the second case the standing of the principal, and his virtually-certain compliance with the mandate of the court, render special security unnecessary. Generally speaking, however, bail bonds are written only upon the security of cash or quasi-equivalent indemnity.

118. Bail Bonds in New York City

To a large extent in New York City, and perhaps to some extent elsewhere, bail bonds have long been issued in accordance with theories of underwriting not succinctly definable (in parliamentary language anyway). They are surely not written, generally speaking, upon the basis of cash collateral, because in a large proportion of the cases no collateral is received; and they are not written upon the strength of indemnity of the usual character, because the indemnitors, though deemed responsible in

the case of bail bonds, would hardly be accepted in the
same capacity in connection with appeal bonds. The
surety's risk upon bail bonds is, of course, that the defendant will not appear at the appointed time and place,
and *anything* that tends to make him appear helps the
surety. If, therefore, a principal refrains from forfeiting
his bail because of his relations with his indemnitor, the
result to the surety may be the same, for all practical
purposes, as if collateral security had been deposited.
At all events, and whatever the explanation may be,
principals do appear in a surprisingly large proportion of
cases, and the business of writing bail bonds upon the
underwriting basis referred to has proved to be profitable
for most, if not all, of the companies engaged in it.

It has proved, also, to be productive of criticism in
certain quarters, and has been made the basis of official
investigations. These criticisms are thought to be
largely unwarranted; and surely anyone who knows
about the shocking conditions that usually prevail in
criminal courts where personal bail is the rule must
realize that corporate suretyship marks a great advance
and is far preferable to the older practices. Yet it may
be doubted that the system of writing bail bonds now
under consideration is free from objectionable features.
Some executives at least are of the opinion that abuses
are certain to develop, notwithstanding close and continuous supervision of the business, so long as the practice is followed of writing bonds, not at the offices of the
surety companies, but at the courts, through licensed
agents having powers of attorney that enable them to
issue bonds in their own discretion. These executives
believe that the only way in which the companies can
surely safeguard themselves from deserved criticism is
to abolish the present system of transacting the business

through scattered, commission-compensated, power-holding agents, and do it only through salaried, home-office underwriters stationed at and working out of branch offices located near the courts. So and only so, in the judgment of these executives, is it possible absolutely to control charges, indemnity and security arrangements, and the other incidents of the business subject to abuse. Probably it would not be practicable to conduct the business in this way, except through co-operative action on the part of all the companies writing bail bonds. It surely would be easy to do so with such co-operation; and there would seem to exist in New York City and similar great centers of criminal practice an attractive opportunity for the surety companies to subordinate their individual activities to the public good and contribute a joint service to the courts, to district attorneys, and to members of the bar, in this important detail of judicial administration.

119. Plaintiff's Bond to Procure an Injunction

When a plaintiff is able to show, to the satisfaction of the court, that the defendant is about to dispose of his property with intent to defraud the plaintiff, or contemplates doing or suffering to be done some act involving a violation of the plaintiff's rights and likely to make nugatory such judgment as the plaintiff may obtain, the court will apply the remedy of temporary injunction and thus impose upon the defendant such restraint as may be necessary to keep matters *in statu quo* during the determination of the issue and forestall the threatened injury to the plaintiff. No such injunction order, however, will ordinarily be granted, unless the plaintiff files a bond guaranteeing that he will pay to the party enjoined any damages resulting to the latter from the injunction, if the order is afterward dissolved.   This protection to the defendant is altogether just, since the practical effect of the injunction is to give the plaintiff at the very beginning of the action the fruits of an anticipatory judgment, though he may not ultimately prevail in the suit; and if he should not prevail, the defendant would have no remedy against the plaintiff for damages incident to the injunction, unless he could prove that the action was malicious.   With a bond, of course, no such proof is necessary.

While most bonds written in behalf of plaintiffs in connection with provisional-remedy proceedings are not particularly hazardous, these injunction bonds are often required under circumstances dangerous to the surety; and the facts of each case must be carefully analyzed with a view to determining how far the defendant may be damaged by the issuance of the injunction in case such damage becomes a charge against the bond.   Sometimes, for example, a defendant is enjoined from collecting a note that is quite collectible at the time; and if, in such a case, the injunction is vacated and the note cannot then be collected, the plaintiff or the surety must pay the note.

Sometimes a defendant is prevented by injunction from carrying on a profitable business.   It may be alleged, for example, that he is infringing the plaintiff's patent, or pirating the plaintiff's trade-mark, or affixing to his own product labels simulating those of the plaintiff, with intent to mislead the public; and if, in any case of this kind, where the remedy of injunction has been successfully invoked by the plaintiff, and the defendant restrained from proceeding with his normal and prosperous business—if, under such conditions, the defendant finally prevails in the action and the judgment of the court is that the plaintiff is not entitled to the injunction, then obviously there may be a heavy bill of damages for the plaintiff or his sureties to settle.

Sometimes, too, when a public-service corporation promulgates new and increased rates for gas or electric-current, and the city served by the corporation passes an ordinance intended to enforce the old rates, a court is persuaded that it would be contrary to equity and good conscience to require the corporation to furnish its products at the lower rates, and enjoins the city from interfering with the new tariff. Under such conditions the corporation is commonly required to give security that it will refund to its patrons the difference between the old and the new rates, if the latter are not finally upheld. Sometimes this litigation drags along for several years, and if the public-service corporation loses and is required to pay back this difference, the amount may be enormous.

In these and in numerous like instances injunction bonds may involve heavy hazard to the surety. Collateral security in all such cases is appropriate. When the circumstances of a given case do not indicate abnormal hazard, injunction bonds in small amounts are frequently written without collateral for principals of undoubted responsibility.

120. Defendant's Bond to Dissolve an Injunction

The first paragraph of the preceding section shows under what conditions an action may be instituted to secure a judgment of injunction. The person against whom the injunction is obtained may be convinced that he has a perfect right to do the things that he is forbidden to do (to cut timber, perhaps, on land that he supposes himself to own); or the defendant may be very much averse to doing the things that the court deems essential to justice and commands the party to do (e.g., a railroad may be ordered to interchange freight and traffic facilities with a connecting line). Under such conditions the defendant will often make a motion to vacate the injunction order, and the court will often grant the motion with the proviso that the defendant give a bond conditioned for the payment to the plaintiff of all damages resulting to the latter from such vacation.

While *plaintiffs'* injunction bonds are regarded by most underwriters as sufficiently dangerous for all ordinary purposes, the corresponding bond given by the *defendant* in the same proceeding is deemed more hazardous still. The court will not order the injunction unless at least a *prima facie* case has been made out by the plaintiff; and for other reasons the presumptions all favor the validity of the plaintiff's contention. As a rule, therefore, these defendants' bonds are written only upon full collateral security.

121. Plaintiff's Attachment Bond

The provisional remedy of attachment is more common and more important to the bonding companies than any of the others. The conditions under which the remedy may be availed of by plaintiffs differ markedly in the several states, but almost if not quite everywhere warrants of attachment are obtainable upon numerous grounds—the non-residence of the defendant, his departure from the state with intent to defraud creditors, his removal or concealment of property with like intent, etc.; and almost if not quite everywhere plaintiffs are able, upon demonstrating by means of affidavits the existence of the facts essential in the given jurisdiction to the issuance of such warrants, to obtain them and procure corresponding action by the sheriff—namely, the attachment of so much of the defendant's property as will satisfy the plaintiff's demand. The rights of the absent defendant, however, are not forgotten by the law, and plaintiffs are not permitted thus summarily to levy upon the defendants' property precisely as if they had already obtained judgment against such defendants, unless they first file a bond conditioned for the payment of all damages sustained by the defendants because of the attachment, in case the warrant is vacated or the defendants recover judgment.

These bonds are commonly called for by established business concerns of high standing and by individual creditors of repute, under circumstances indicating the entire regularity of the proceeding and the improbability of any undeserved damage to the defendant. The bonds are written freely, therefore, for responsible principals of the kind referred to, and in most cases without security. If, however, the conditions are not of the usual character described, or if the principal is irresponsible financially, or if the damages may be serious, collateral security should be obtained.

Fortunately it is not difficult, in the case of most attachment bonds, to estimate somewhat closely in advance the damages that a defendant may sustain by reason of the particular levy, if it is ultimately found to have been unwarranted. While the statutes under which plaintiffs are required to furnish security before attachments will be ordered are commonly phrased rather broadly in describing the damages covered by the bond, and frequently, indeed, make the bond chargeable with "all damages" caused by the wrongful attachment, yet in practice the bonds are ordinarily interpreted by the courts in such a way that only actual damages are recoverable. Indirect and consequential damages are almost never awarded, and vindictive or exemplary damages are recoverable only in certain jurisdictions, and then only upon proof that the attachment was sued out maliciously as well as wrongfully. Generally speaking, an underwriter who is satisfied that his principal is a real creditor and is acting in good faith need not fear that anything more than actually proved damages will be recoverable by the defendant in case the attachment is vacated.

What those damages may be will depend, of course, upon the circumstances of the given case. When the subject of the attachment is real estate that the defendant continues to use, hardly any damages would be assessable under ordinary conditions, because the real estate would presumably be worth as much at the end of the proceeding as it was when the levy was made, or if it were not worth as much, the depreciation could hardly be ascribed to the attachment. While the levy remained in force, however, the real estate would be effectually tied up and could not be sold, and if an advantageous sale were pending and about to be completed when the attachment was ordered, the defendant would be able to recover the actual damage resulting to him from the miscarriage of the negotiations.

While public knowledge of the fact that a man's property has been attached for a debt does not notably enhance his reputation or help him in a business way, yet in most jurisdictions no damages, or at least only nominal damages, would be awarded to a successful defendant, in the absence of malice, in a suit based on an attachment bond. Oftener perhaps than anything else money is attached, and in such cases the damages may be closely appraised, since they will amount only to the interest upon the sum attached during the time it is tied up. The decisions are discordant in different states, but in many jurisdictions a successful defendant may recover under an attachment bond fees of reasonable amount paid to an attorney for resisting the attachment.

The bond referred to in this section is a *plaintiff's* bond to secure an attachment—not the *defendant's* bond to release an attachment treated in the next section. From an underwriting point of view the risks are antipodal in character, and any confusion of them by an agent or underwriter might have heartbreaking consequences.

122. Defendant's Bond to Discharge an Attachment

When the property of a defendant has been attached, as described in the preceding section, the defendant will often desire to regain possession of the property. He will surely seek means to do that, if he disputes the claim underlying the attachment; and if he knows the same to be valid, as he frequently does, he may still deem it advantageous to get back his property, even though he can do so only by securing his creditor in some other way. The avenues of escape from his dilemma open to a defendant in attachment vary in different states, but he can usually repossess himself of his property by giving a forthcoming or delivery bond, conditioned for the production of the property in response to a judgment, or by giving a bond for the discharge of the attachment, conditioned for the payment of any judgment that may be recovered against him in the pending action.

Sometimes there are conflicting claims to the attached property—that is, after a levy has been made under a warrant of attachment, some third person will claim the property. The procedure thereafter is likely to be complicated, but in most jurisdictions the new claimant is

permitted to make himself a party to the original action
by giving a forthcoming or delivery bond to either the
sheriff or the attaching plaintiff.   The statutory requirement varies in different states.

It is clear that these defendants' attachment bonds
are highly hazardous instruments, since they guarantee,
in effect, the payment of an amount of money, if that
amount is found to be due, and since in fact and from the
nature of the circumstances the amount is commonly
found to be due.   For underwriting purposes, anyway,
it is quite necessary to assume that the amount is due.
Regardless, therefore, of the presumed financial responsibility of the principal, these bonds should be written
only upon full collateral security, since security is always
in order when it is known in advance that the condition
of the bond is pretty certain to be fulfilled.

Instead of attaching the property of a defendant that
is actually in the latter's possession, a plaintiff will
sometimes tie up or garnishee money owed to the defendant by third persons, or assets belonging to him in
their hands.   The bond that the defendant must give in
order to repossess such funds or property, known as a
"release-of-garnishment bond," has the same underwriting characteristics as bonds to release attachments.

123. Plaintiff's Replevin Bond

When a person's property has been wrongfully taken
from him or is wrongfully withheld from him, he may
usually have recourse to either of two remedies—he
may sue the wrongful possessor of it to recover damages
for conversion; or he may bring an action of replevin
against him in order to recover the property.   Not infrequently he elects to institute, as plaintiff, an action of
replevin against the wrongful possessor, as defendant;

and he is then permitted to take possession of the property, provided he gives a bond guaranteeing that he will proceed with the suit to try the title and will return the property to the defendant if the latter be found entitled thereto, and will otherwise respond to such judgment as the court may render.

Replevin bonds as a class are regarded as excellent business and are written freely, without collateral, for principals of good business and personal standing. It is a reassuring fact that in a normal case the principal is the plaintiff and is a creditor and takes the initiative, so that he would not naturally proceed unless advised by counsel and otherwise confident that no untoward developments would ensue. A large and profitable field for these bonds is furnished by instalment houses that find it necessary to replevy goods disposed of on a conditional-sale plan to buyers who pay a small amount down when the property is delivered, and are unable to keep their agreement to pay the remainder of the purchase-price in instalments at stated intervals.

These optional *plaintiffs'* replevin bonds are to be carefully distinguished from the compulsory counter-replevin bonds that *defendants* must give in order to regain possession of replevied property. These latter bonds, treated in the next section, are birds of quite another color.

124. Defendant's Counter-Replevin Bond

When a defendant has lost possession of property through replevin proceedings, as described in the preceding section, he may recover it by filing a bond conditioned for the return of the property "in like good order and condition as when taken," and for compliance with any judgment rendered in favor of the plaintiff. The bond that he thus provides is known as a "counter-replevin" or "redelivery" bond.

It is clear from the entire situation here that defendants' replevin bonds are financial-guarantee instruments pure and simple. In most cases the defendant owes the plaintiff money and the surety guarantees that the debt will be paid. Under such conditions, of course, the bond is not prudently issuable without full collateral security.

125. Removal Bonds

Sometimes the defendant in a suit, because he fears harm from local prejudice or for some other reason, wishes to remove the case to another court; and under certain conditions he is permitted to do that. The most common cases are removals from state to federal courts. The bond given by a defendant who petitions for a removal guarantees that he will enter in the court to which the case is to be removed, for the earliest available term, a copy of the record of the suit, and will pay all costs that may be awarded by the court, if the latter shall hold that the case was improperly removed. If the original court approves the petition for removal and the accompanying bond, it is divested of jurisdiction over the case.

When a case is removed from one state court to another state court, the condition of the bond is sometimes the same as before, but it may be (that is, in some states it will be) more serious—it may be conditioned for the payment of any judgment finally rendered. Under such conditions, of course, the "removal" bond is tantamount to an appeal bond (cf. section 128).

When the bond covers a removal from a state to a federal court the penalty is only $500, and it is similarly small when the removal is from one state court to another state court and only costs are guaranteed in the event of a remand. Since no serious damage will be sustained by a plaintiff if the new court finds that the case does not properly fall within its jurisdiction, and therefore remands it to the original court, these bonds are not deemed particularly hazardous, and are commonly written without security for substantial business concerns or well-to-do individuals. Whatever costs are awarded upon the remand will be the amount due under the removal bond in these cases. When, however, the amount of the bond and the statute under which it is given show that it is one of the other class referred to—one conditioned to pay any judgment finally handed down—collateral security will presumably be in order.

126. Security for Costs

In most jurisdictions a defendant may require his adversary under certain conditions (when the plaintiff is a non-resident, for example) to furnish security for the payment of all costs that may be adjudged against the plaintiff; and while a cash deposit with the clerk of the court is sometimes made in such cases, a corporate bond is the common and convenient way of caring for the situation. In most jurisdictions a plaintiff who fails to file security in some form consistent with the statutory requirement suffers a summary dismissal of his suit.

These bonds are not deemed particularly hazardous, and are written freely, without security, for established and substantial business houses—a common type of principal. The bonds are always written in behalf of plaintiffs, who are usually ordinary creditors, and who may naturally be expected to win their suits; and the surety is not liable for costs, generally speaking, when the plaintiff is successful. The costs in any event are not likely to be large, though under some statutes they include costs made on appeal as well as those accruing to the defendant in the court of primary jurisdiction. While the amount of the bond frequently exceeds the real liability, unless it is known in the given case that the bond will not cover costs awarded in the intermediate and final courts (as it frequently will not), the full penalty of the bond should be regarded as the liability thereunder.

127. Sheriff's Indemnity Bond

In attaching or replevying property, and in other official acts under some circumstances, sheriffs and marshals lay themselves open to damage suits on the part of persons against whom they proceed, as shown in section 111. Formerly, indeed, this liability was by no means a negligible factor in a candidate's consideration of the value of the office; but nowadays laws are pretty generally in force that enable the sheriff effectually to safeguard himself from loss of this nature by requiring an indemnity bond from the person in whose favor and upon whose initiative the doubtful procedure is taken.

These bonds vary vastly in hazard in accordance with the circumstances of the particular case and with the laws and practices of the given jurisdiction. Sometimes it is practicable for the surety company to obtain joint control of the seized property pending a determination of the title. If that cannot be arranged, and if the principal is not known to be abundantly responsible, collateral security is ordinarily required.

128. Appeal, Supersedeas, and Stay-of-Execution Bonds

A litigant who loses his case when it is first contested is allowed to try again—that is, to appeal to some higher tribunal—on his contention that some error fatally prejudicial to his cause has been made in the lower court. It would not be fair, however, to the successful litigant to permit this second trial, unless he were secured in some way as to the judgment which he has already obtained, and which, on general principles, he is entitled to collect at once. It is provided, therefore, that an initial loser who appeals in this way must give a bond to his successful adversary conditioned for the prompt prosecution of the appeal and for the payment of the judgment with interest and costs, if the case is lost again in the upper court. The bond so given is called an "appeal bond," and is one of the commonest and most important in the judicial class.

It is at once apparent to even a sluggish intellect that appeal bonds are worse than dynamite to handle. You pay (become bound to pay) if your principal loses, and he has lost, in a sense not altogether far-fetched, before he begins. The analogy of an endorsed note is often cited by way of illustrating the hazard of appeal bonds; and the comparison is apt. The only difference is that a regular note will mature in due season, as surely as death and taxes, while there is a chance that the analogous obligation endorsed by the surety will never fall due. Applicants for appeal bonds continually try to make it appear that *theirs* is such a case; they explain at much length, with eloquent emphasis and no doubt with sincerity, that they are bound to win in the appellate tribunal, though they lost through a singular mischance in the court below. They believe, with 'Rastus, that a court is a place "where dey dispenses wif justice." Their contention is, skeletonized, that a reversal of the first decision upon appeal may reasonably be *assumed* by the underwriter; whereas that is precisely what the underwriter should never dream of doing. On the contrary, it is imperatively necessary that he assume—invariably, instantaneously, and automatically—that his principal will *lose* in the higher court, just as he did below. How in the world can a judicial underwriter be expected to pass upon the legal merits of the multitudinous actions underlying his bonds? Obviously he cannot pay the slightest attention to any such aspect of the question. It is enough for him to know, superabundantly enough, in the case of an appeal bond, that a large majority of appealed cases (the precise percentage is variously stated) are lost in the appellate courts; and even if the statistics showed that appeals were oftener won than lost, it would still be known in the kindergarten grade of suretyship tuition that not a reversal, but an affirmance, of the first decision by the appellate court is the thing to be assumed by the underwriter.

Therefore, all that the simple-minded, stupidly obstinate underwriter can see, when he sits down with an appeal-bond application, is that he is invited to endorse his principal's note, usually for a large amount, falling due at some unknown date in the future; and the fact that this date is rarely less than one year distant, and may be anywhere from two to five years off, does not make the prospect any rosier. He cannot picture himself under such conditions as issuing the bond except in connection with gold bars or their equivalent as collateral security.

129. Security Particularly Appropriate Here

An attitude of that kind on the part of judicial underwriters is absolutely correct, and it is a pity that extreme competition for business makes it so hard at times to take such a position and hold it firmly to the end. There is nothing unfair to the principal in such an attitude—nothing whatever; because the surety company is *supposed* to be absolutely secured, and could not reasonably be expected to issue the bond unless so secured. The whole theory of judicial suretyship, and the whole basis upon which premium rates are made, assumes that the surety company, when it issues an appeal bond, is merely rendering a service to its principal, for a 'small fee, and is not providing credit insurance to its obligee for a vastly larger premium. The point is elaborated elsewhere (cf. section 3), with reference to surety bonds in general, but it has special applicability and force in connection with appeal bonds. Unquestionably judicial bonds of this class, the issuance of which by a surety company involves for all practical purposes an endorsement by the surety of the principal's note for the amount of the bond, should never be written unless the surety first receives security in the full penalty of the bond, or, in cases where the bond is double the amount of the judgment, security equal to the amount of the judgment plus costs and probable interest. In no other way can such business be safely written; and a group of companies that learned this too late now occupy a sadly spacious acreage in the potter's field of corporate suretyship.

The legal proceedings known respectively as "supersedeas" and "stay-of-execution" suspend the carrying out of judgments precisely as perfected appeals do, and the corresponding bonds given in connection with them involve the same hazards and are underwritten on the same basis as appeal bonds.

130. Release of Libel or Stipulation for Value

Creditors whose claims have to do with ships may frequently avail themselves, in collecting such claims, of what are known as "maritime liens." Materialmen and mechanics, for example, may assert liens for materials furnished and repairs made by them to a ship lying in a foreign port (they could not ordinarily do this if the ship were at its home port). In all the numerous cases where the conditions are such as to create maritime liens, the creditor may proceed against the ship and freight *in rem* or against the master or owner *in personam*. The United States District Courts, sitting in admiralty, have jurisdiction to enforce the liens, and the procedure is for the creditor to "libel" the ship, and thus automatically to effect the seizure and detention of it by the United States marshal. If the libel is sustained, a sale of the ship is ordered, and the proceeds of the sale are applied to the satisfaction of the lien first, and then to such distributees as the court may direct.

All this, obviously, is a decidedly high-handed proceeding, fraught with grave consequences to the master whose ship is tied up for an indefinite period and thus prevented from discharging its cargo or proceeding to sea. Almost always, therefore, the master or owner of the ship, if not prepared or willing to meet the demands of the libelant, will desire to release the libel; and he can do that ordinarily only by filing a bond conditioned for the payment of any judgment recovered by the libelant with interest and costs.

All that is said in section 122 regarding the hazardous nature of defendants' attachment bonds applies to the situation here—with added emphasis, perhaps, because these bonds are likely to be large (they are sometimes huge), and because the proportion of successful defenses in these cases is probably less even than in those of ordinary release-of-attachment bonds. The only principals in whose behalf such bonds in moderate amount might perhaps be issued without security (the great steamship companies) do not often require them; and in practice stipulation-for-value bonds ("release of attachment" and "stipulation for value" are convertible terms as regards these bonds) are rarely writable except upon full security.

No bond is required from libelants in admiralty practice corresponding to the bond that plaintiffs in attachment proceedings must give (cf. section 121). It would be illogical to require a bond in such cases, since a libelant who acts in good faith, even though he fails to establish a lien, is not liable in damages to the captain or owner of the vessel attached beyond the taxable costs of the suit.

131. Bond to Discharge a Mechanic's Lien

In many jurisdictions people who work upon a building, or furnish material for it, may by filing an appropriate notice secure a lien for the amount so due upon the building and the underlying land. This lien at once clouds the title to the property, so that it is usually deemed necessary either to pay the claim promptly or otherwise to discharge the lien. The latter way out of the difficulty is frequently sought, through a bond conditioned to satisfy the demand of the lienor provided his claim be found valid.

These bonds are pure financial guarantees and are not ordinarily written except upon full collateral. Usually the principal is a contractor whose financial condition is such that the lienor deems it necessary to make sure of his claim through the drastic course described; and he would hardly do this, in the face of strong business reasons opposing it, unless the need were urgent. For underwriting purposes anyway it seems necessary always to assume that the contractor against whom the lien is filed is not in a position to meet the claim, and that the surety will ultimately have to do so.

132. Petitioning Creditors' Bond

When a person or a business house is or is thought to be insolvent, creditors may petition the appropriate court that the person or concern be adjudicated a bankrupt, and that a receiver or trustee be appointed to take over the bankrupt's estate; and the creditors under such circumstances must give a bond conditioned for the payment to the alleged bankrupt, in case the petition is dismissed, of all costs, expenses, and damages sustained by him as a consequence of the unwarranted procedure.

While a person or business concern that is really solvent undeniably has a serious claim for damages against petitioners who unsuccessfully attempt to have him or it declared bankrupt, yet in practice these bonds are found to be writable upon a basis of exceptional freedom. In a large majority of cases the whole procedure is cut-and-dried, and the petition is filed with the prior knowledge and approval (or if not that exactly, with the acquiescence) of the debtor, who knows his real condition only too well, and who is resigned to this way out of it. Moreover, the indemnity is almost always excellent, since there are three or more principals on the bond, and since they are likely to be business concerns of known responsibility. Another favorable feature of these bonds is that liability runs off ordinarily within a few days.

133. Cancellation of Judicial Bonds

Court bonds, of course, are not insurance policies and are not cancellable at the will of the principal. When once entered on the surety company's books they remain there as live risks, upon which the company must carry a reserve, until such time as convincing evidence is received that, in fact, they are no longer alive. The mere statement of the local agents to that effect is not "convincing evidence"—at least not to the official Insurance Department examiner of the surety company's books. A letter from a reputable attorney who handles the case for the principal would sometimes serve the purpose, but the best kind of termination evidence in the case of judicial bonds is a copy, preferably a certified copy, of the judgment or order of the court in the given case. If such judgment or order requires the principal to do something, and if the bond guarantees that it will be done, of course there must be additional evidence that it has been done.

In many cases court bonds terminate soon after they are issued—and in a great many cases before a year has passed—and agents would save themselves and their companies a lot of trouble and expense by following up such bonds at regular intervals for cancellation inquiries, without waiting until they come up automatically at the anniversary date. If such a system is closely and intelligently carried out, the agent does less work in the long run than he would have to do otherwise, the home-office is enabled to mark off its liabilities and take down its reserve so much sooner, the expense and annoyance of preparing and forwarding subsequent-year bills is largely avoided, and everybody concerned is happier.

CHAPTER XI

CONTRACT BONDS

134. Most Important Field of Corporate Suretyship

Because contract bonds are written in vast volume, and because huge losses are an inevitable sequence of laxity, ignorance, or poor judgment in the underwriting of such bonds, all surety executives, I suppose, regard this division of their business as at once the most promising, the most dangerous, and the most difficult to handle with safety and success. On the one hand, no company can hope to become an important factor in the surety business unless it can maintain a well-equipped contract-bond division, capable of caring for all kinds of contract bonds, big and little, quickly and efficiently; because agents derive a large part of their income from contractors, and they cannot afford to offer the bonds of their clients to companies which are not in a position to provide the desired suretyship, if the clients are reasonably entitled to it, or which in any event (since *all* companies must sometimes decline bonds) are unable to handle such matters promptly and intelligently. On the other hand, no company can hope to become an important *and a permanent* factor in the business unless it can underwrite its contract bonds with skill and judgment and consistent conservatism; because otherwise, while it may be important for a while, it will sooner or later cease to be anything except a distant memory and a sad example. More companies have come to grief, I suppose, through contract-bond losses than from any other single cause.

When William Howard Taft was Governor-General

of the Philippine Islands, he fell sick in Manila and for several weeks had a serious time. While at his worst and almost in despair over his gigantic task of civilizing the Orient, he pulled out from under his pillow a volume of Kipling, opened it at random, and found himself reading this passage:

> And the end of the fight is a tombstone white
> With the name of the late deceased,
> And an epitaph drear, "a fellow lies here
> Who tried to hustle the East."

Every home-office underwriter of contract bonds, and every fieldman entrusted with authority to write such bonds, should cultivate the mulish immobility of the East if he would keep his company solvent, because a large proportion of contract-bond losses are due to the fact that somebody has not only tried to hustle the home-office or the agent into a premature acceptance of a risk, but has succeeded in doing so.

While the foregoing may seem sufficiently somber-hued, it is all consistent nevertheless with my earlier statement that the contract-bond department of the surety business is "most promising." Evidential of this is the fact that some companies maintain highly profitable contract divisions, and make money year after year in that branch of their business. That they should be able to do this, while other companies operating under essentially the same conditions are simultaneously slipping into bankruptcy, is a complex proposition to understand and explain; but it is chiefly a matter of agency organization, discipline, and character, of underwriting methods and standards, and of general capacity and judgment at the fountain-head of authority.

135. A Rare Chance for Agents

In hardly any other line of insurance can agents who really know their business be so useful to both the contracting parties—do as much to demonstrate their reason for being—as in the field of contract suretyship. While some contractors deal directly with the home-offices of surety companies, especially large contractors who desire to have a first-hand acquaintance with people whose good-will and business friendship mean so much to them, yet in most cases applications for contract bonds are made, in the first instance anyway, through some agent. The latter is then charged with a heavy responsibility. On the one hand, the contractor, who may be and probably is giving the agent considerable business in other lines, counts upon the agent not to fail him in this vital detail of the bond; while, on the other hand, the surety company expects the agent to give it every last shred of information about the contractor that has any bearing upon his desirability as a risk, even if, and indeed especially if, such information may cause the company to decline the business. It is greatly to the credit of agents generally —and it is a pleasure to record the fact—that the home-office is able to rely so largely upon the representations made to them by agents about bonds in which they have a potential commission interest. Because that interest is so important (contract-bond premiums sometimes amount to several thousand dollars), and because other lucrative business often hangs upon the fate of the bond, the average agent takes it very much to heart when the home-office is unable to agree with his optimistic views regarding some big contract bond; and his conduct upon those painful occasions reminds one of another great man, Talleyrand. A lady once asked the

French statesman the meaning of the word "non-intervention." "Madam," he replied, without the flicker of an eyelid, "non-intervention is a diplomatic term that means intervention." Similarly agents often seem to regard the home-office formula, "we reject this risk," as a diplomatic phrase meaning, "we accept this risk." The poor underwriter, cowering behind his desk at the home-office, sometimes feels as helpless as if he were the King of England. According to that astute publicist, Walter Bagehot, the English monarch has three constitutional rights and only three—the right to be consulted, the right to encourage, and the right to warn. If the bond is one exceeding their underwriting authority, agents concede to the home-office the right to be consulted—that is, they consult it by ordering the bond by return mail. The right to encourage is obviously a dead letter; for the home-office to encourage the agent in such a matter would be,

> To gild refined gold, to paint the lily,
> To throw a perfume on the violet.

The right to warn is grudgingly conceded, so that the home-office is not too long about it, and thus delays the execution of the bond.

136. Close Underwriting Ultimately Best for Contractors

If the circumstances of a given case are such that a prudent underwriter, keenly desirous of increasing his volume and making money for his company and having no means of doing so except by writing business, feels unable, nevertheless, after a thorough and sympathetic consideration of all the facts involved, to provide the requisite suretyship, then the ultimate interests of the contractor himself are often served and protected by a rejection of the risk. Surely every experienced contract underwriter would not have to go far below his care-creased brow to turn up plenty of border-line bonds, issued by him perhaps with some misgiving, where subsequent developments proved with grievous finality that he would have rendered a very distinct service to the contractor if he had turned down the risk instead of accepting it.

Even when the situation is not so bad as that, a contractor may well take to heart an underwriter's indisposition to back him up with suretyship in a given case. After all, the judgment of experienced contract underwriters is not to be altogether ignored, especially if it be the combined judgment of a committee of underwriters. Most contractors go to their bankers for advice as well as for loans, and attach importance to the bankers' opinion regarding the advisability of their undertaking a given piece of work. A contractor's relations with his surety company are a good deal like those with his banker; and he should value the counsel of his surety as he does that of his bank. Wise and experienced contractors understand all this and they do not resent, but rather welcome, conservative practices by the bonding companies. They realize that such an attitude on the part of underwriters tends to improve the general condition of the business and to lessen the competition of irresponsible contractors.

137. Experience and General Standing of the Contractor

While most kinds of surety bonds are affected by numerous elements of risk, the considerations bearing upon contract bonds are so many and diverse that one hardly knows where to begin a discussion of them. The average underwriter inquires first perhaps about the experience of the contractor and his general business reputation. It is reassuring, of course, to an underwriter to know that the applicant for a bond has been many years in business and has completed numerous similar contracts with satisfaction to his patrons and profit to himself. While some large contractors engage in a variety of undertakings, they commonly prefer to limit their activities to work of the same general nature and of such a character that they can utilize in all of it the same plant and equipment. It is important to ascertain whether or not the contractor has had experience in the same line of work as that concerned with the given contract. In recent years, for example, the vast amount of highway building undertaken in various states has caused a good many contractors without road-building experience to enter this untried field, with unfortunate results for their sureties.

Most forms of application blanks call for information regarding the previous experience of the contractor, but frequently what is stated on this point in the application needs amplifying or explaining by the agent or somebody else. All underwriters, for example, are unfavorably affected at the start if they find that the proposed principal is a concern recently organized. Often, however, in such cases the men composing the concern have had a long and successful experience in the same line of business—a fact that goes a long way (though not quite the entire distance) to offset the superficially adverse feature referred to. Whenever such a situation exists the agent should secure full information, and embody it in the application papers.

As for the general standing of the applicant, the agent in many cases can obtain trustworthy information from competitors, local bankers, materialmen, and others;

and while the home-office underwriter naturally makes his own inquiries and investigations upon this vitally important aspect of the case, his work will be greatly facilitated and expedited by skillful and thoroughgoing preliminary research on the part of the local agent. In consulting bankers care must be taken to make sure that the information furnished is disinterested. Sometimes a banker, already a heavy creditor of a contractor close to insolvency, is anxious to have the bond issued, because of the chance that the debtor will be able to pull himself out of the hole by means of the new contract; and under such conditions the banker's personal interest in the situation may color somewhat his representations regarding the contractor's financial condition and prospects.

Other things being equal, a partnership or a corporation is a better principal than an individual, because the death of the principal in the latter case before the contract is completed may have serious consequences to the surety.

138. Nature and Extent of Contract to be Performed

It goes without saying that one who guarantees the performance of a contract needs to know what it is that he is guaranteeing. Usually, therefore, and always in the case of large contracts, a copy of the contract should accompany the application papers.

Obviously some kinds of contracts are far more dangerous, from an underwriting point of view, than other kinds. Subways, tunnels, coffer-dam work, and similar underground contracts will be bonded, generally speaking, only for exceptionally strong and successfully experienced principals. Lighthouses, sea-walls, concrete river dams, and the like are naturally deemed dangerous contract risks. Bonds guaranteeing the performance of wrecking contracts, or of mail-carrying agreements, or of contracts . concerned with public-utility franchises—are all deemed undesirable risks except in connection with the strongest kind of principals.

139. Financial Condition of the Contractor

· He must be possessed of financial resources reasonably commensurate with the size and other capital requirements of the undertaking. Nothing will take the place of this prime requisite—not skill and experience, nor high personal character, nor good banking connections, nor anything else whatever; and when the principal is weak financially, either absolutely or in comparison with the magnitude of his contract, prudent underwriters will prefer not to bond him, however favorable the other aspects of the risk may be.

A principal's financial condition can most conveniently and dependably be shown by means of a statement fully itemized and recording all assets and every last item of liability. Financial statements should always be attested before a notary, because many people will balk at swearing to a "doctored" statement that they would not hesitate to give out unattested. All the important items in the statement should be verified by the underwriter as far as practicable. It is particularly important that the alleged bank balances be confirmed. In one case, for example, in my own experience we were asked to issue a large contract bond in behalf of a concern experienced in the given business, well rated by the commercial agencies, and apparently all right in every way. There was only one thing about the risk that did not look right, and that looked bad only because it looked too good. The bank balances shown in the contractor's statement were so large that they seemed suspicious, and we determined to verify them if we could. We found that we could not, for the excellent reason that they were false. The contractors had no such balances as their statement recorded. We declined to issue the bond, the contractors threw up their hands while a considerable part of the work remained to be done, and the two surety companies that rushed in where we had feared to tread (to put it with maximum politeness and modesty) completed the job at a cost to them over the contract price of many thousands of dollars.

Inadequacy of financial resources results in more declinations of contract bonds than any other one cause of rejections. It also exposes home-office executives to more criticism from the field than any of their other unnumbered shortcomings. Yet, to me at least, it seems as clear as noon-day and as undeniable as the tides that if a contractor is without capital (absolutely or relatively to the undertaking contemplated), there is absolutely *nothing* pleadable about the other aspects of the risk that can possibly offset this simply fatal weakness in the man's credentials. Under the conditions stipulated, anything and everything else is superfluous and irrelevant. It is as if an agent should urge the issuance of a $50,000 cashier's bond in this wise:

"The applicant has a wonderful mind—his encyclopedic knowledge and Napoleonic intellect are unequaled outside the bonding company home-offices. He can add an agent's monthly commissions completely before an ordinary man could cover the first $10,000. He knows all that there is to be known about accounting, and his books are models of neatness and accuracy—they are even income-tax-proof. His executive ability and general efficiency baffle description. In fact, there is only one thing that could possibly be said against him—

namely, that he is a notorious 'crook,' who would cheat his own mother out of her last limousine, and who will surely walk off with his employer's safe if they give him half a chance."

The analogy is not absolutely complete, but in essentials the situation in the two cases from an underwriting point of view seems to me substantially the same. Just as it matters not what the cashier's *other* qualities may be in view of the fact that he is an admitted rogue, so a contractor's successful experience, high character, and general capacity are all of no underwriting account when financial resources are wholly lacking or are relatively so in comparison with the magnitude of the contemplated work.

140. Competitive Bids

It is a good sign, of course, from an underwriting point of view, if a number of other contractors were willing, as shown by their bids, to perform the given contract for amounts not many per cent above the applicant's bid; just as it is a disquieting feature if most or all of the other bids are a long way off. Sometimes when the latter condition exists the contractor will try to suppress the information, especially if he has had experience with perverse underwriters, and thus knows their finical notions about such matters; and then the agent has a chance to render a *quid pro quo* for his commission. Frequently applications are received containing the statement that "the other bids were close"; such a disposition of this important point is quite unsatisfactory and should never be accepted, because too often the phrase is only a cloak designed to conceal the fact that the other bids were *not* close.

While, therefore, if a contractor's bid is far below the

other bids, the presumption arises that he has miscalculated or overlooked some important item, with resultant loss to the surety in case the latter has to relet the contract, this presumption is sometimes rebuttable. In a highway job, for example, the disproportionately low bidder may recently have completed a similar contract close to the location of the new work, and may be the only bidder who has a complete plant and equipment and sources of road-building material near at hand. Such a condition of things might give him so big an advantage over the other contractors as to explain the difference in the bids. In any case of this kind, however, the burden of proof rests decidely upon the proposed principal, and prudent underwriters will not issue a contract bond in behalf of an abnormally low bidder unless and until some satisfactory explanation of the difference in bids is forthcoming.

141. Amount and Nature of Other Work on Hand

The application should contain this information, and the agent or somebody else should see to it that the point is covered fully and upon an accurate percentage-of-completion basis. This detail is of prime importance, because a large proportion of contract failures and corresponding surety-company losses have been due to the fact that the contractors were too ambitious and undertook a greater quantity of work than their resources and facilities enabled them to handle. If it be true that much of the work on hand is nearly completed, the fact is reassuring in a way; but it is not conclusive, since defaults frequently culminate at the later stages of the work. This point must be considered, of course, with a sense of proportion. Most large and successful contracting concerns have a number of jobs on hand most of the time, in various stages of progress, and it would not do in the case of such a principal to decline a bond otherwise acceptable covering a new contract merely because of the simultaneous existence of a lot of other work. The whole question depends upon a principal's total resources, plant, and organization, in comparison with the volume of work on hand, considered in connection with the amount and nature of the new undertaking contemplated.

142. Retained Percentages

Most large contracts provide that as the work goes on the contractor shall receive less than a pro-rata part of the contract price; that is, the contractee is privileged to withhold a certain percentage (from 10 to 20, for example) of the price during the progress of the contract and for a time after the completion thereof, as a protection against liens, undiscovered defective work, etc. This feature of a contract is, of course, distinctly advantageous to the surety company, and many losses have been wholly or partly averted because of these retained percentages.

Not infrequently underwriters are asked to forego this advantage by consenting to premature payments of withheld percentages; and the circumstances are sometimes not a little embarrassing to the surety, since the alternative seems to be either to consent or to face the strong probability of a claim—that is, the contractor will go under, it is thought or represented, if this retained amount is not available to tide him over his troubles.

No hard-and-fast rule can well be formulated for the guidance of underwriters in such a contingency. Certain it is that they should not be expected to give their consent unless a full explanation of the emergency is made and found to indicate the safety or at least the ad-

13

visability of their giving such consent. They agreed to
provide the suretyship partly at least because of this
reassuring feature of the contract, and they should not
be expected (as they sometimes seem to be) to give up
the protection of this reserve fund merely because the
contractor's convenience will thus be somewhat served.
The "full explanation" referred to would include a
statement, confirmed through the obligee or otherwise,
of the amount of work already done on the contract and
amount already paid to the contractor; a close and
confirmed estimate of the cost of completing the contract;
a list of the unpaid bills concerned with the contract—
the principal's affidavit must be depended upon for that;
and a statement by the contractor of the reason why he
needs the money, and what he means to do with it.
Frequently it is in order to stipulate that the money
shall be used exclusively for the payment of bills incurred in connection with the bonded contract. If the
surety company finally decides to permit the payment of
the retained percentage or a part of it, care must be taken,
of course, to procure the approval of such a course by
co-insurers or reinsurers, if there be any.

143. Maintenance Guarantees

Too often for underwriting ease, bonded contracts include maintenance provisions—an agreement by the contractor that a roof, say, will be rain-tight, and will remain
so for ten years; that a highway will need no repairing
for five years; that a certain machine or plant will serve
satisfactorily a described purpose; and so on *ad infinitum*.
All contracts should be examined narrowly for such provisions, as they are usually important, and sometimes
have a crucial bearing upon the writability of the bond.

Performance and maintenance guarantees are reasonable, no doubt, in connection with the sale of machinery, patented devices, and the like; but they seem to be illogical and unjust to the contractor where the latter undertakes only to do a certain piece of work in exact conformity with specifications laid down by the contractee. Under these latter conditions, responsibility for results should seem to rest logically with the framer of the specifications rather than with the contractor who merely does exactly what the specifications call for. When, for example, a highway engineer representing the county or other contractee lays down the precise manner in which a certain road shall be constructed, including the quantity and nature of the material to be used, it would seem to be no affair of the contractor's whether the resultant highway stands up under the traffic for six months or six years. In the case of road contracts, maintenance provisions seem particularly unfair to the contractor both on general principles as indicated, and because a road normally used only for comparatively light traffic may from unexpected causes be subjected during the maintenance period to continuous heavy traffic. Many highway engineers have come to see the matter in this latter light, and no longer favor the inclusion of maintenance guarantees in their contracts with road-builders; but many others still ask contractors and the latters' sureties to bind themselves in this respect. The point is of particular importance with street-pavement contracts, where considerable losses have been sustained by surety companies in the past. The conditions there, however, seem to be improving gradually from year to year in several respects as follows:

> (a) There are numerous large and responsible concerns engaged in the paving business in behalf of which maintenance bonds may be written with comparative safety.

(b) By the joint efforts of the contractors and the surety companies, with the enlightened assistance of many city officials, the maintenance period is gradually being lowered.

(c) The specifications for paving contracts and bond forms are becoming standardized and made to set out more justly and accurately the rights and obligations of the respective parties to the contract.

(d) The premiums obtainable are considerably higher than they were formerly, and collateral security is frequently obtainable.

(e) Certain cities have wisely adopted the plan of retaining part of the contract price for repair work until the expiration of the maintenance period.

144. Penalty for Delayed Performance

It will often be found, in going over the agreements underlying contract bonds in a microscopic search for dangerous points, that the contractor binds himself, in case he fails to perform his part of the agreement within the stipulated time, to pay the contractee a certain amount of money for every day of delay. Such a feature of the contract is not, of course, attractive from the standpoint of the surety company, especially where the time of performance seems none too long anyway, and where a heavy penalty, $100 a day perhaps, for delayed performance is imposed upon the contractor.

Provisions of this kind in contracts are sometimes "penalties" and are sometimes "liquidated damages." The general rule of law is that where the agreement between the parties provides a "penalty" for delay, the contractor need not pay anything unless the contractee can prove that he has suffered actual damage by reason of the delay; and the contractor need pay then only the amount of such damage, irrespective of the amount named in the contract as a penalty. If, however, the contract calls for "liquidated damages," and if that view of the matter is sustained by the court, the contractee need not show any actual damage, but can collect from the contractor the full amount named in the agreement as a sort of anticipatory but final (as to amount) liquidation of the damage.

The subject is one of great practical difficulty in negotiating and completing agreements. The fact, for example, that the contracting parties use the words "penalty" or "liquidated damages" by no means settles the question in a suit at law. The court will consider, not the language of the agreement alone, but all the collateral and incidental features of the case, so as to ascertain, if possible, what it was in fact that the parties really agreed upon, whether or not they correctly named it. The point is one of endless confusion in the statutory law of the various states and in the recorded decisions of the courts.

There is no way, of course, in which the surety company can avoid liability for breaches of a penalty feature of a contract any more than for any other feature, and all that one can do is to weigh that aspect of the risk with the other underwriting considerations in determining one's final decision. In a very close case the penalty provision of the contract may be just enough to turn the scales against the bond.

145. Subletting of Parts of Contract

The primary contractor on a large job will often sublet parts of the work to other contractors. Such an arrangement causes the surety no disquietude when the main contractor is responsible and otherwise acceptable; but underwriters are sometimes urged to write a given bond offered by a contractor none too strong financially on the ground that he has sublet important parts of the work, and is abundantly able to care for the remainder himself. Prudent underwriters hesitate to provide suretyship in such cases. In the first place, the subcontractors should always be bonded in such cases in favor of the main contractor, and in practice such bonds are sometimes not obtainable. Finally, even if parts of the work are so bonded, the situation, though improved, is still unsatisfactory. The main contractee, of course, knows nothing officially of the subcontractors, and has no direct relations with them, and looks to the principal contractor and the latter's surety for full performance of the entire undertaking. In the event of trouble it will not infrequently be found that the subcontractors are not functioning in the way contemplated—they are not completing in every detail their parts of the contract; and it is then incumbent upon the main contractor to make good their deficiencies. Even when bonds are given by the subcontractors, this contingency will not be covered unless the bonds have been drawn with extreme care and with reference throughout to the obligations assumed by the main contractor. The only safe theory upon which the surety can proceed in these cases is to regard the main contractor as ultimately liable (as he is in fact), and to become his surety only if such a course would be in order without regard to the subletting of parts of the contract.

146. Consulting Engineers in Contract Departments

The underwriting methods of the surety companies seem to me to show slow but constant improvement, and the time will ultimately come, I have no doubt, when the big companies will have specialists and technical experts upon their underwriting and claim-adjusting staffs, and will thus be able to handle both ends of the business in a more efficient and scientific way than is possible with their present personnel and equipment. One comparatively recent development in the evolution referred to is the engagement by a number of companies of consulting engineers as permanent members of their contract-division staffs. Not all companies have taken this step, and the practicability of it may be doubted except in the case of companies doing a very large volume of contract-bond business.

While engineering talent is of obvious and high value when a company is confronted with an important contract-bond claim, and is likewise of undoubted use for *general* underwriting purposes, it is not so clear that the special knowledge and training of an engineer can be readily availed of in practical, every-day, contract underwriting. In the first place, an engineer could hardly find much play for his special talent in the case of the vast volume of contract bonds that are authorized prior to the receipt of either contracts or specifications, upon telegraphic information perhaps. Moreover, even in the more important cases, where contracts and specifications should (but do not always) accompany applications, the contracts are so big and complicated that the engineer, however expert he might be, could hardly form an opinion of much value as to the adequacy of the contract price without devoting a number of days to the task, securing additional information, etc.; and it is quite out of the question for a surety company to handle such matters in that deliberate fashion. A considerable proportion of the contract bonds written by surety companies are authorized within an hour or two of the time the application is received; and a large proportion of the remainder are authorized within twenty-four hours. This is so because the contractors are old patrons of the surety companies, and have been thoroughly investigated by them, or because the underwriters rely upon the commercial-agency ratings and general reputations of the contractors or for other similar reasons.

A large volume of contract-bond business consists in the first instance of bid bonds, and it seems more impracticable still to utilize a consulting engineer in such cases. Contractors wait until the last minute before putting in their bids (there are good reasons for that practice, and the surety companies could not hope to change it), and they need the essential papers up to the time when they decide what their bid will be. It would rarely be practicable, therefore, to make much use of engineering talent in the case of bid bonds.

It remains true, nevertheless, that a company writing a large volume of contract bonds would find it a great convenience to have upon its contract-bond underwriting committee a well-informed and widely-experienced engineer of keen and balanced judgment. While he could make but limited use of his professional attainments in a multitude of cases, as indicated, so far as initial acceptances are concerned, he could contribute most valuable assistance in the subsequent treatment of such risks, and could be of direct and original service in many other instances. Any proposal that makes for safe and scientific underwriting is surely worth prolonged consideration and adoption, if found at all practicable; and it seems probable that all progressive and growing surety companies will ultimately make arrangements for the employment of engineering and other professional talent in their Underwriting and Claim Departments.

147. Bid or Proposal Bonds

These are embryonic contract bonds, and are full of danger. Indeed, they would be more important and more dangerous than contract bonds themselves, except for the fact that only one out of all the bid bonds issued in connection with a given contract ever gets beyond the embryonic stage. Many agents seem not to realize this extremely important condition of things. Let us see whether this is not quite true.

When contracts are about to be let a frequent requirement is that each bidder shall file with his proposal a bond guaranteeing that he will furnish, in case the contract is given to him, a further bond conditioned for his execution of the contract in accordance with its terms. Sometimes the former instrument, known as a "bid" or a "proposal" bond, is written in a fixed amount, so that the surety company's maximum liability is known in advance. Oftener a bid bond is a bald guarantee that the final contract bond will be forthcoming upon demand; and the liability is then, of course, indefinite and unknown (except as the bid price, if known, indicates it), and may easily, in the case of large contracts, be a considerable amount.

How dangerous these proposal bonds are was shown some years ago when a large viaduct contract was awarded in Ohio. One of the contractors in that case made a stupendous error in his calculations, and put in a bid about $100,000 lower than that of his nearest competitor. The officials in charge of the letting saw that a mistake had been made—they were so informed, in fact, by the contractor—and they seem to have been disposed not to take advantage of the error; but they were advised by counsel that the proposal bond furnished by the unfortunate contractor must be forfeited in conformity with the law. This particular bond, as it happened, was one of the kind that contained a named penalty, $10,000 in the given case, and that amount was paid by the contractor. If the other form of bid bond had been used, the contractor or his surety would have lost about $100,000.

In considering proposal bonds the surety underwriter must always keep in mind the fact that he will really be writing, if he accepts the business, and if his principal's bid is accepted, the final contract bond; but he is without the important advantage, existent under ordinary contract-bond conditions, of being able to compare the bid of his principal with the amounts for which other contractors are willing to undertake the same work.

Sometimes fieldmen think that the bid bond may be considered on its sole merits, without regard to the resultant contract bond that must be filed if the bid is accepted. That is a dangerous misconception of the real situation, since, as stated, the condition of the bid bond is that a final contract bond will be filed; and in practice the surety company on the bid bond would almost invariably be forced to write the final bond, since it would be hard, if not quite impossible, to obtain a new surety on the final bond if the conditions were such that the surety on the bid bond preferred not to go on with the risk.

The foregoing description of bid bonds explains another point that agents sometimes fail to grasp—namely, the fact that it is deemed quite inconsistent with inter-company comity, and highly dangerous besides, for one company to execute a final contract bond when another company has executed the bid bond concerned with the same contract. The reason why the second company will not execute the final bond is, of course, that the first company has already assumed liability on the final bond in executing the bid bond, and has incurred all the expense, trouble, and risk involved in the execution of the final bond by executing the bid bond; and it would obviously be unfair to the surety company executing for a trifling premium the bid bond, if a second company could step in and avail itself of all the work and expenditure and judgment of the first company by writing the final bond and obtaining the vastly larger premium payable thereon.

148. Supply Bonds

These, also, are a species of contract bond, and not a particularly difficult or dangerous member of the genus. The federal government usually, other civic bodies sometimes, and private buyers increasingly, require from sellers bonds guaranteeing the fulfillment of contracts for the furnishing of staple supplies. These bonds are thus nothing but contract bonds in principle—that is, they both guarantee the due fulfillment of a contract. In surety practice, however, the terms have distinct meanings. In speaking of "contract bonds" a surety man has in mind bonds guaranteeing the fulfillment of contracts involving complicated operations and the possession of capital and a plant by the principal on the bond. The term "supply bonds," on the other hand, means in surety parlance bonds guaranteeing the fulfillment of contracts for the furnishing of ordinary supplies—stationery for a federal department at Washington, say, or grain for a city, or coal for a railroad. The line of demarcation between supply bonds and contract bonds is sometimes obscure, and several pages of the Towner Manual are devoted to the clearing up of doubtful points and the prevention of misquotations by agents because of the erroneous classification of business.

While supply bonds involve some hazard in a period of inflation and rising prices, and in connection with certain kinds of supplies at all times, ordinarily they may be written freely in reasonable amounts for business concerns of good standing.

149. Annual-Guarantee Bonds

These constitute a special class of supply bonds. They are of limited applicability, but are of sufficient importance perhaps to justify separate consideration.

In its business of buying supplies for certain federal departments the government has found it convenient to permit contractors who are constantly bidding for federal contracts to furnish blanket supply bonds instead of separate bonds with each bid or contract. These blanket bonds are known as "annual guarantees," and are of two kinds—one covering bids and another covering contracts that may be awarded as a result of bids. The annual bid bond contains no stated penalty, and guarantees that all the principal's bids submitted during the year and accepted by the department will be duly effectuated by the principal. The annual contract bond guarantees the performance by the principal of his contracts with the department during the year, and states a penal amount of liability, which is arbitrarily fixed by the government at a sum deemed sufficient to cover its probable risk on the basis of the amount of business that the principal is expected to transact with it during the year.

These bonds must be handled with much more circumspection than may be necessary in passing upon supply business of a definitely known amount for the same principal. Under an annual bid bond a principal may, of course, file any number of bids, and as the surety loses all control of the situation when once its bond is filed, it is quite possible for a reckless principal to involve the surety very heavily by wildcat bidding. As for annual contract bonds, since the government permits a person to have outstanding at any one time under such bonds contracts aggregating five times the amount of the bond, the underwriter must assume when considering one of these bonds that it will cover a contract liability five times greater than its amount.

While annual guarantee bonds obviously present some special points of hazard, they are not as a class hard to underwrite and they constitute on the whole desirable business. This is so partly because they relate in most cases only to ordinary supplies that may be readily obtained in normal times upon a close competitive basis, and especially because the principals are likely to be large and well-known manufacturers, jobbers, or other business concerns which have been dealing with the government for years, and which are altogether unlikely to undertake contracts that they cannot fulfill. When the conditions are not of this usual type—when the principals are small or new or inexperienced in the given line of business—the bonds, of course, are *prima facie* unacceptable.

CHAPTER XII

DEPOSITORY BONDS

150. Reason for Bond

Depository bonds are conditioned for the payment by banks upon proper demand of money deposited with them. They are required increasingly by governmental bodies to protect public moneys deposited in banks. New York, Pennsylvania, and Ohio are conspicuous examples of commonwealths that safeguard state funds in this way. Similarly a good many counties and numerous cities, as well as minor political units, require the banks in which their funds are deposited to furnish bonds conditioned for the safekeeping of such money. This practice has not been followed in New England—somewhat strangely, perhaps, in view of the prudent and thrifty habits of the good people there. In connection, for example, with the recent Ponzi performances in Boston, seven or eight banks failed containing hundreds of thousands of dollars of the Boston taxpayers' money; and in no case, it is thought, had the banks been required to furnish depository bonds as a condition precedent to the receipt of such funds. While the bonding companies were sorry for the Boston taxpayers, supersaturated as many of the latter are with dividends and coupons, yet they were not without hope that the unhappy experience might lead to the enactment in Massachusetts and contiguous states of depository legislation similar to that already in force in most other parts of the country.

151. Private or "Individual" Depository Bonds

Most of the depository bonds issued by surety companies run in favor of governmental bodies. There is no reason, of course, so far as the surety company is concerned, why that should be so—the risk is the same whoever the obligee may be. In fact, at least one company has made strenuous efforts on several occasions to build up a business in private depository bonds, but it has met with indifferent success. There is, however, some demand for the insurance from the general public, especially after an important bank failure. Large fraternal orders, corporations with branches or manufacturing plants in small cities or country towns, insurance companies lending money to small banks upon certificates of deposit, and a few other special classes of depositors are the chief buyers of these "individual" bonds. The business is so small that it will not be further discussed, and it may be understood that everything in this chapter outside of this section refers to public depository bonds. The underwriting considerations, however, are substantially the same in both cases with two exceptions: (a) In the case of private bonds the form is determined by the surety company, and contains a cancellation provision, so that the surety has a considerable advantage in this respect over the ordinary public depository risk (cf. section 169). (b) Since public depository bonds are usually taken out because they must be (some provision of law requires it), while an individual acts under no such compulsion when he buys the protection, the fact that a bond is called for at all may under some circumstances constitute a good reason for not writing it—the mere fact that the prospective obligee deems a bond necessary or desirable may be a suspicious circumstance. When, for example, as occasionally happens, one bank asks a surety company to issue in its favor a depository bond covering some other bank, the fact does not constitute exactly what one would call, if one were at all punctilious in his use of the mother tongue, a flattering endorsement of that other bank. In most cases, however, when private depository bonds are called for it is easy to see that no reflection upon the given bank is involved.

152. Private Banks and Bankers

Surety companies are frequently requested to guarantee deposits made with, or credit accounts carried with, private bankers. A large business, for instance, could probably be built up by any company that would issue bonds, even at rates considerably higher than the current depository rate, in favor of investors and speculators having marginal accounts with bankers and brokers. Similarly public officials occasionally desire to deposit public funds with private bankers and request corresponding depository bonds. Generally speaking, at least, and perhaps unqualifiedly speaking, no surety company issues these bonds. While it may be freely conceded that some private banks are stronger than some incorporated banks, the fact remains that the latter as a class are vastly safer depository risks for a surety than are the former as a class. Organization under time-tested laws, national or state supervision, periodic official examinations, and other safeguards protect the surety in the one case, and are wholly or largely absent in the other. Many private banks, of course, are managed with scrupulous care and integrity, and serve a highly useful purpose in commercial and social life, but others remind one of the plight of the Arkansas darkey who deposited $5 in a fellow-countryman's private bank. Having decided in a profligate moment to withdraw the entire deposit, he was enlightened as to modern financial methods in this way:

"Five dollars, nigger," expostulated the Ethiopian banker, "five dollars! Well, if you ain't de most unreasonablest coon dat ever cum down de pike. You ain't got no five dollars here now. Don't you know, nigger, dat de interest done et up dat five dollars long ago?"

153. A Desirable Line of Business

Since depository bonds are usually given as a matter of law, and must thus be furnished without regard to the responsibility of the bank—that is to say, it is not a case where the selection is against the surety company—and since, like kissing, depository bonds go by favor, and political considerations often determine what banks shall be designated as public depositories, so that the largest and most powerful banks are frequently selected, this business as a class is deemed highly desirable by most underwriters and has proved a profitable line.

154. General Financial Conditions Extremely Important

It is true, however, that in certain years the business has developed heavy losses, and has been a source of much worriment to surety executives. In a period of prolonged industrial depression culminating in an acute crisis a surety company that has overextended itself in this field, and thus has outstanding a large line of depository bonds, may easily be forced into a precarious situation. In the fall of 1907, for example, when the financial troubles of that year came to a disastrous head, many surety executives were distracted with anxiety over their depository risks; and well they might have been, since there can be slight doubt that, if the panic then raging had gone a little further, so many more banks would have closed their doors that a number of surety companies would have been unable, for a time at least, to meet their obligations.

14

In the opinion of most economists and bankers, the Federal Reserve Law has removed for all time the menace of any such distressful experience as the country went through in 1907. Bank failures enough and to spare we shall have, no doubt, as in the past, because some bankers will permit their portfolios to become congested with slow credits and other unliquid and unmarketable assets; but simultaneous and numerous runs on banks in the same city or locality, currency shortages and hoardings, and the similar agonizing incidents of the old-style "panic" seem to be highly improbable hereafter. These phenomena would almost surely, indeed, have formed a painful part of the financial record of the last few months, had it not been for the existence of the Federal Reserve Law; and even so, bank failures in this period have been sufficiently numerous to cause the depository loss ratio of most surety companies to mount much higher than it has since 1907. Almost all the companies doing much depository business, it is thought, have paid out in losses in the last year or so far more than they have received in premiums from this class of bonds.

155. Recoveries Gratifyingly Large

The last statement, however, does not necessarily mean that the companies referred to will finally lose money on their 1921 depository business. They *may* do so, but it is at least certain that their final losses will be much less than those indicated by the account as it now stands, because it is certain that the failed banks will pay substantial dividends upon their unpaid deposits, with corresponding benefit to the surety companies. Some insolvent banks will presumably be able, in the final liquidation, to pay their depositors in full, however little their stockholders may receive; and all the rest of the banks will probably pay substantial percentages of their deposits. Since the National Bank Act was passed, February 25, 1863, the percentage of deposits ultimately paid by insolvent national banks, up to October 31, 1920, is 83.71. No doubt the percentage would be higher if the period covered began, say, twenty-five years ago, since it seems reasonable to assume that bank failures were more numerous, comparatively, and more serious in the first thirty years after the Civil War than they have been since then. Corresponding insolvency statistics for state banks and trust companies have never been published, it is thought. They would probably be far less favorable than the figures covering national banks. In 1921 only 34 national banks failed, while 528 state and private banks were closed. As state banks vastly outnumber national banks, and as surety companies issue a large number of depository bonds in behalf of state banks and trust companies, the national-bank salvage figures cited above cannot, of course, be applied to all the depository losses of the companies. There are about 8,200 national banks in the country, about 22,500 state banks and trust companies, and about 1,200 private banks.

156. Depository Underwriting in General

The underwriting of depository bonds is not particularly difficult, generally speaking—it is, indeed, about the easiest of the major lines of suretyship. In some cases banks whose solvency the surety company is guaranteeing could drop the "guarantor" and all its belongings into some remote corner of their assets without knowing that they were there at all. When a surety company with a capital of $500,000, say, bulwarks with its depository bond a bank with a capital of $50,000,000 perhaps—well, to call it a case of the tail's wagging the dog would be to magnify unduly the tail. While that is an extreme example, surety companies are all the time receiving applications for depository bonds from long-established and highly responsible banks and trust companies where the underwriting problems involved are small and simple—as simple, indeed, as those of the ordinary kindergarten lines of insurance.

On the other hand, the conditions are sometimes such that serious trouble is likely to result unless the surety company involved brings to bear upon the particular problem all the gray matter at the command of its under-writing staff—if any reader is able faintly to sense that inconceivably stupendous conception. This is particu-larly true in the case of small banks; and the companies receive in the course of the year thousands of applica-tions for depository bonds from small banks located in the West and South and less important towns in the East. When, for example, an underwriter is confronted with a summary demand from a valued agent to write a $100,000 depository bond in behalf of a bank which gives all its business to the company, and confidently counts upon procuring its depository suretyship likewise from the company, but which has a capital of only $50,-000, and presents a financial statement not particularly reassuring, one indicating perhaps that its resources are pretty well tied up in frozen cotton, sugar, or grain loans—then one has a chance to do some scientific under-writing.

157. The Underwriter's Open-Sesame—Perhaps

After ascertaining whether or not he has any out-standing liability on the given bank, the first thing that the underwriter does, when requested to issue a depository bond, is to examine minutely the latest financial statement of the bank that he can obtain—the latest published statement will usually, and should always, accompany the application for the bond. This statement, of course, is the underwriter's chief resource, and if it seems to him to show conditions that would cause the bank to go under in the event of such mischances as are likely enough to befall any bank, then almost nothing that the agent or the bank president or anybody else can say will make the risk acceptable. "Tell me what you want to prove," said the statesman, "and I'll manage the statistics." Figures may be manipulated in many cases, as everybody knows, so that the real situation is largely concealed, but that is not true, generally speaking, in the case of bank statements. Those are made up under oath, and may be confidently regarded as setting out the real condition of the bank at the given date; and if, after the bank officials have done their best to make the statement as favorable as possible, it still looks bad to an experienced and expert appraiser, not much can be said by anybody that will dissipate the underwriter's misgivings.

Sometimes under such conditions, when the explanation lies in past mismanagement, and there has been a thoroughgoing housecleaning, it may seem practicable to provide the desired suretyship upon the strength of an agreement of counter-indemnity executed by a number of responsible directors of the bank. They should not object to furnishing such indemnity under the circumstances described; and in fact they do furnish it not infrequently. Occasionally, however, they object on the two-fold ground that they should not be expected to become surety for a corporation, supposed to stand on its own feet, and that it is distinctly the surety company's province to assume whatever risk there may be in the situation.   This argument, as I have tried to show elsewhere (section 3), will not bear close examination; it is really on a par in its logic with the position of the man who insisted that his freight be shipped via the B. & O. because the scenery was so fine.

Careful underwriters do not limit their examination of statements to the current one—they go back a number of years (such information being available in trustworthy banking publications), and make up a table showing the trend of the more important items in the statement. Such a table under some conditions is extremely significant, and gives one a line upon the bank's growth or decadence and its general development such as could hardly be obtained more dependably in any other way. Suppose, for example, to take an easy and common instance, successive statements show capital stock of the same amount and a constantly dwindling surplus, with deposits amounting to a smaller aggregate each time— would not such a state of facts stand a lot of explaining on somebody's part?   Can you think at the moment of any explanation that would be likely to cause a nervous, sour-livered, constitutionally pessimistic underwriter to issue a large depository bond for the bank in an ecstasy of joy?

158. Loans and Discounts

A bank statement shows on one side what the bank owes (to depositors, general creditors, and stockholders), and on the other side what resources it has with which to meet the indebtedness.   By far the most important item in the statement, from the underwriting point of view, is the first one on the "Resources" side, entitled

"Loans and Discounts." The bulk of the stockholders' investment in the bank and the depositors' money is tied up in this item, and the whole position of the bank pivots upon the soundness and liquidity of its loans and discounts. It is not enough, of course, that the people to whom the bank has loaned its resources be *ultimately* good for their loans, or that the security with which such borrowers buttressed their loans be liquidatable at some indefinite future date at a value approximating the amount of the loan. The bank must pay *its* creditors (depositors) on demand, and it cannot do that, of course, with its borrowers' promises to pay or with their pledged cotton, sugar, or grain.

After all is said and done, and however expertly one may analyze a bank statement, it seems impossible, from the nature of the case, to be *certain* of a bank's soundness without full knowledge of the composition of this "loans and discounts" item. It may consist largely of loans to planters secured by cotton valued at 20 cents a pound when the staple is selling at 12 cents, though it may have been selling at 30 cents when the loan was made; or of advances to sugar brokers or to wheat-growers upon the security of commodities taken at similarly inflated (judged by existing standards) valuations; or of loans made for plant-extension purposes to oversanguine manufacturers—really a long-time investment that should not be even considered by a commercial bank. In any of these or numerous similar conditions of "slow credits," "frozen inventories," and the like, it is clear that the bank would be in no position to weather the gales of depression and maladjustments that occasionally sweep the financial seas.

Since it is rarely possible for an underwriter to have first-hand and detailed knowledge of this "loans and discounts" item, vitally important as that knowledge is, he must estimate the quality of the loans as well as he can from the general character of the management. Other parts of the statement, too, throw some light upon the loans of the bank, and show, to some extent at least, how far they are readily liquidatable, and whether or not the bank is overextended. The proportion of loans and discounts to deposits, for example, may be so high as to suggest the inference that the bank has been forced to renew loans to an unsafe extent. The latest statement contained in the last annual report of the Comptroller of the Currency (1920) shows that the loans and discounts of all national banks upon the given date amounted to 74.1 per cent of the deposits of all national banks on the same date.

159. Real Estate, Furniture, and Fixtures

This item, found on the assets side of the statement, is not outstandingly important, but may deserve brief mention. Although many banks have felt it worth while for their own convenience and for advertising purposes to house themselves in buildings of architectural pretension and of corresponding cost, yet it is not a good sign, generally speaking, to find a bank crediting itself under this head with a relatively large amount. As for "furniture and fixtures," many banks carry the item at $1 only; but it is sometimes suspiciously large, and subject to severe shrinkage in the underwriter's recast statement, in the case of banks which are able to show only a small surplus, and which have presumably availed themselves of every resource to bolster up their assets side. The Bank of England, by the way, owns a site that is worth something like $40,000,000, but no such asset is included by the bank in its statement. It has completely written off its books such fixed assets as its own premises and furniture, and it takes credit in its statement for only such liquid assets as securities, loans, discounts, and cash.

160. Cash and Cash Items

The proportion of reserve that banks belonging to the Federal Reserve system must carry against deposits is much less now (13 per cent in central reserve cities, 10 per cent in reserve cities, and 7 per cent elsewhere) than it was before the enactment of the Federal Reserve Law, because of the fact that really solvent banks need never fail under the new system. Before the Federal Reserve banks opened their doors, however (on November 16, 1914), this part of the bank statement (cash and cash items) was regarded as extremely important, and banks that habitually carried larger reserves than those required by law were thought to be exceptionally safe, while those continually skirting the edge of the reserve line and occasionally slipping off below it were looked upon as rather too insistent upon keeping their money at work. The point seems far less important now, since any bank that has a proper loan account can replenish its reserve at will by the simple process of rediscounting a *quantum sufficit* of paper with its Federal Reserve bank.

161. Capital Stock and Surplus

The first thing that an underwriter looks at in a statement is the stockholders' investment—the capital, surplus, and undivided profits. While no national bank may be organized with a capital stock of less than $25,000, banks and trust companies organized under state laws frequently have much less capital. The point is obviously of vast importance, since even if some loans have been made injudiciously, the capital and surplus of the bank may be large enough to absorb the loss and keep the bank solvent. The point is of special importance in the case of national banks and of banking institutions organized under the laws of states that prescribe a double liability for stockholders (cf. section 164), because in all such cases the real capital at the risk of the business and available to creditors in the event of trouble is twice the amount paid in and shown in the statement (twice the amount theoretically, somewhat less in practice).

If the surplus is large compared with the capital, the fact is gratifying as indicative of a determination on the part of the management to subordinate the distribution of profits to the upbuilding of the bank. National banks, indeed, are required to set aside at each dividend period for surplus purposes one-tenth of the net profits until the surplus amounts to 20 per cent of the capital. Prudently managed and conservatively inclined banks do more than that. Almost any bank will occasionally suffer losses, and the existence of a good surplus is highly convenient upon any such unpleasant occasion. The surplus, however, should not be availed of as a receptacle for loans and other assets of doubtful character, because so far as that is done the surplus belies its name.

Bonding companies commonly base their depository lines on the combined capital and surplus of the given bank; that is to say, they adopt the principle of writing, in behalf of any bank, depository bonds aggregating a certain percentage (fifteen, for example) of the bank's capital and surplus. This rough rule of thumb varies with the character of the bank, its location, the nature of the bonded deposit, and other considerations, but all companies doubtless follow some such principle in their underwriting. The practice of the companies varies markedly as regards maximum depository lines. Some underwriters are able to issue enormous bonds in behalf of certain big banks and slumber peacefully thereafter, while other underwriters under the same conditions would have continuous and horrible nightmares. Similarly the companies follow divergent paths in the matter of writing depository bonds for small banks. Some underwriters prefer to hold aloof altogether from banks having a capital of less than $40,000 or $50,000, while other more adventurous spirits write bonds freely, though in reduced amounts, for banks of much smaller size.

162. Amount of Deposits

The profits and general welfare of a bank depend, of course, upon its deposits, and large and increasing deposits indicate a safe and desirable state of affairs. It is necessary, however, to consider deposits from several points of view. As we saw in discussing the "loans and discounts" feature of the statement, the ratio of that item to deposits has some bearing upon the soundness of the bank's loan account. The proportion of *public* deposits to total deposits is likewise worth considering. If the proportion is large, the fact has a number of unfavorable implications: it may mean that the bank is paying a dangerously high rate of interest in its zeal for deposits; it may mean that the bank has political affiliations of an undesirable nature—indeed, a strong admixture of politics in the management of a bank should give any underwriter pause; it may mean that the bank is subjecting itself to the possibility of abrupt withdrawals of public funds, with consequent embarrassment in meeting the drain. The ratio of the stockholders' investment in the bank (capital, surplus, and undivided profits) to the deposits affords an indication of the margin of protection to depositors; a ratio of between 20 and 25 per cent, for example, would be high, and would constitute, in itself, a reassuring feature of the statement.

163. Borrowed Money

Bills payable, notes rediscounted, and borrowed securities result from a bank's reversal of its normal functions—when it becomes a borrower instead of a lender. The item of borrowed securities is usually not especially significant, since securities are frequently borrowed by the strongest banks and for reasons not indicative of weakness. Under the Federal Reserve Law notes are rediscounted as a matter of course by almost all banks in any period of active business, and the fact is not regarded as reflecting upon the bank. "Bills payable," however, used to be deemed more or less of an ill omen in a bank statement—something for a critical underwriter to think about. The frequency of the item nowadays, even in the statements of strong banks, has materially abated its unfavorable significance, but, even so, bankers are glad to see it go down, and are more pleased still when it fades out of focus altogether. It is also worth while to consider, in connection with the bills-payable item of the statement, the amount due from the bank to holders of its certificates of deposit, because some banks, especially in the West and South, try to keep down the bills-payable item by borrowing upon certificates. Commercial paper, to be rediscountable with the Federal Reserve banks, must be of choice quality as to promptness of maturity and presumed liquidity; and when a bank must list among its borrowings not only a considerable item representing rediscounts, but also a lot of bills payable, the explanation may be that it resorted to the latter shift because its stock of prime paper gave out. All things are relative, however, and it would not do to condemn a bank out of hand merely because a particular statement showed heavy borrowings. Successive statements should be examined, and the whole industrial situation in the bank's territory reviewed, to see whether it is always knocking at the lenders' doors; perhaps it was merely taking good care of its patrons during the crop-moving season or performing some other legitimate function.

Here, as elsewhere, the parts of a statement are closely inter-related, and it is desirable to consider a bank's borrowings in connection with other items—with its capital and surplus, for example. If the latter amount to considerably less than the aggregate borrowings, the fact is disquieting; the ratio of borrowings to capital and surplus was 90 per cent only, instead of more than 100, in the case of all the national banks of the country at the date of the universal statement cited by the Comptroller of the Currency in his last annual report. It may also be useful to note the ratio of accommodation at the Federal Reserve bank to total loans and investments: in the first few weeks of 1922 the average amount of accommodation, in the case of all reporting member banks, was about 3 per cent.

164. Stockholders' Liability

Underwriters are more likely, other things being equal, to accept depository-bond applications tendered by national banks than those submitted by state banks or trust companies. That is so partly because national banks must be conducted in accordance with the rigid requirements of the federal law, tested by nearly sixty years' experience, but especially because the stockholders of national banks may always be called upon, in the event of the bank's insolvency, to pay over to creditors, to the extent of the par value of their stock, any amount needed to enable a bank to pay its depositors and other creditors. The same favorable considerations, it is true, apply to banks and trust companies organized under state laws—the former feature (official supervision) to some extent in all states, and the latter (double liability) to the same extent in many states. The laws of the several states, however, and the practices under those laws, vary greatly, while the similar laws and practices applicable to national banks are uniformly favorable.

This double liability of stockholders (called "double" because stockholders by becoming such subject themselves to liability to creditors of the bank not only for the full amount, par, paid for their stock, but also for the same amount in addition, if needed to pay claims) accounts largely for the fine showing that insolvent national banks as a class have ultimately made. Creditors cannot safely assume, however, that the full amount of the capital stock is available for them. On the contrary, it is found in practice that a large deduction must be made from the salvage theoretically obtainable, because of the inability of some stockholders to meet the obligation imposed upon them by law. From February 25, 1865, when the National Bank Act was passed, up to October 31, 1920, slightly less than half the amount of the assessments levied upon the stockholders of insolvent national banks had been paid (48.4 per cent). The final result will be somewhat better than this, since legal proceedings are still pending to enforce the stockholders' liability in the case of failures in recent years. These figures are taken from the latest report of the Comptroller of the Currency—as the frenzied Cockney orator put it, "These ain't my own figures I'm quoting. They're the figures of a man 'oo knows wot 'e's talkin' about.''

Some years ago the Comptroller of the Currency took steps to insure the responsibility of the initial stockholders at any rate, by requiring each subscriber to the stock of a national bank in process of organization to be worth at least twice the amount of his subscription. Too many banks have been organized by promoters like the gentleman, who, when asked how he got into the banking business, frankly explained, "Well, I had a little place and I hung up a sign 'Bank.' Pretty soon an old lady came along and deposited $200. The next day a man happened in and deposited $300. With this $500 I considered it a good risk and put in $500 of my own money." The Comptroller logically and properly takes the view that the liability of a stockholder to respond to an assessment is an asset of the bank created by law for the benefit of the bank's creditors, and that it is the Comptroller's duty to see to it that the presumed asset exists when the bank is organized at least. It is thought that this new rule will stop an old practice of promoters, who have frequently taken large blocks of stock in a new bank, whether able to pay for it or not, and have then peddled it out to more or less irresponsible buyers.

In England bank failures are very rare, and when they occur the liability of shareholders becomes a matter of much importance to creditors. They have no double liability law over there like ours, but in place of it they follow a custom that usually results in greater benefit to creditors than our liability law confers. Holders of English bank shares are liable, in case of the insolvency of the bank, up to the amount of the unpaid portion of their stock; and this unpaid portion is commonly far greater than the amount paid in. Generally speaking, therefore, bank stockholders in England are under a greater proportionate liability than are the owners of American bank stock.

Many states, as indicated, have wisely followed the federal statute as to the double liability of stockholders in banking institutions organized under state laws. That is so as to commercial banks (the rule is occasionally different as to savings banks and trust companies) in the case of the following states: Arizona, Arkansas, Colorado, the District of Columbia, Florida, Georgia, Idaho, Illinois, Indiana, Iowa, Kansas, Kentucky, Maine, Maryland, Massachusetts, Michigan, Minnesota, Mississippi, Montana, Nebraska, Nevada, New Hampshire, New Mexico, New York, North Carolina, North Dakota, Oklahoma, Oregon, Pennsylvania, South Carolina, South Dakota, Texas, Utah, Vermont, Washington, West Virginia, Wisconsin, and Wyoming.

In California there is a constitutional provision that "each stockholder of a corporation or joint stock association shall be individually liable for such proportion of all its debts and liabilities contracted or incurred during the time he was a stockholder as the amount of stock or shares owned by him bears to the whole of the subscribed capital stock or shares of the corporation or association." In practice, however, this unlimited liability of bank stockholders has not been found to yield to creditors the salvage that would theoretically seem to be available.

165. Clearing-House Examinations

In the case of banks in large cities, it is desirable to know whether or not they are members of the local clearing-house association; if they are not, the fact is *prima facie* unfavorable. These clearing-house associations frequently exercise close and rigid supervision over their members, and constitute a more valuable safeguard perhaps even than the periodic examinations of the Comptroller of the Currency.

166. Preferred Deposits

Sometimes the deposits carried by the bond are "preferred"—that is, they are payable, in case the bank closes its doors, ahead of ordinary deposits and the claims of general creditors. This is so, for example, in the case of funds deposited by the state of New York in a bank or trust company organized under the laws of the state of New York. Wherever such a condition of things exists, the depository risk is materially lessened, of course, and may, indeed, vanish almost to the zero point. It is hardly conceivable that a large New York trust company, for example, whose preferred deposits would never constitute more than a very small part of its total deposits, would fail so disastrously as to be unable to pay even its preferred creditors.

167. "One-Man Banks"

This term is commonly used by surety men in connection with fidelity bonds, as elsewhere explained and discussed (cf. section 36), but it also has significance— sinister significance—in the plural number, to depository underwriters, because every little while some bold financial operator gets control of a chain of banks, uses them recklessly in the exploitation of his personal outside ventures, and finally ties them all up in a knot requiring numerous receivers to undo. Some time ago, for example, a man of this type, operating in a western city, got control of a large national bank, an incorporated savings bank, and a trust company. He simultaneously

15

carried on immense operations in stone quarries, coal mines, and railroads. These various enterprises dovetailed together nicely, the banks receiving the deposits of the industrial concerns and the latter procuring loans from the banks on the strength of their securities. The trouble was that this strength ultimately became weakness, and the banks collapsed under the weight of the quarries, mines, and railroads. Another notable example occurred in Chicago a few years ago, when a large trust company and a train of affiliated institutions closed their doors, and brought numerous surety companies face to face with depository claims of disastrous amount. The aggregate depository liability carried in that case by the various companies involved, as reported at the time, was $1,600,000. While somewhat less than that amount was presumably paid by the companies, because the deposits at the time of the failure were probably less in some cases than the amounts of the bonds, yet it is known that the net liability of the companies was enormous in the aggregate. Their final loss, too, in this case seems likely to be heavy, as depositors have recovered from the wreckage up to date (May 1, 1922) only 35 per cent in dividends.

It is not so easy now as it used to be to form chains of banks in the large cities, because of the numerous mergers going on all the time and the increased difficulty of effecting control of the larger resultant organizations; but in the smaller cities and in the country generally the ease with which banks may be organized and made to promote and sustain external financial and industrial schemes involves grave danger to the banks and their sureties, to depositors, and to general creditors. Prudent underwriters will steer clear of banks that are dominated by one man or one small group of men who are known or suspected to be using their banks in outside operations.

168. Determining General Character of Management

While all the considerations heretofore discussed are important, and will not be overlooked by a forehanded underwriter, the most useful thing by far that he can do is to run down in the most thoroughgoing way the character and ability and business or political connections of the men who are operating the bank. If the directors and active executive officers of the bank are men of high character and good business judgment and are well informed, as they naturally would be, regarding the industrial life and personnel of the community, little apprehension need be felt over any depository bonds issued in behalf of the bank. How can such knowledge regarding the management be obtained? In various ways as follows:

(a) The officers of the bank will often be bonded by the company that provides the depository suretyship. If so, the company's files will contain abundant and presumably satisfactory information about them; and if not, they can be investigated through the usual channels.

We noted in section 162 the fact that banks strongly impregnated with political virus are not looked upon with favor by depository underwriters. When the president of the bank or some other active executive simultaneously holds an important political position, especially one that involves the handling and disposition of large amounts of public funds, well-advised underwriters will be most circumspect in their acceptance of depository risks. The danger is, of course, that the banker will be merged in the politician and will do things in the latter capacity that are forbidden in the former.

He will be eager to help out his bank with more deposits perhaps than are allowed by law or than can be properly secured; and his political associates will aid and abet him in any such ambition, because they will have a much better chance to make use of the money when it forms part of the bank's loanable funds. A case in point became citable some time ago from one of the middle states, when a savings bank failed with deposits of about $600,000 belonging to the state. The president of the insolvent bank was also the treasurer of the state—a coincidence having a causal connection with the preceding statement. The wisdom of keeping out of situations of that kind was appreciated by one underwriter, who cancelled a depository bond that he had written in behalf of the savings bank, explaining that low-down proceeding as follows: "Having learned of the treasurer's dual capacity and of his tendency to play both bank ends against the commonwealth middle, we concluded that selective discretion was the better part of underwriting valor, and one dark night, when the moon was low and nobody was looking, we stealthily tiptoed off the risk."

(b) The directors of the bank will usually be shown in the application papers, and they can be identified readily anyway. It is quite important to do this, ascertaining their business connections, looking up the commercial ratings of such connections, and considering whether or not any director is likely to demand and receive more loan accommodation from the bank than his business standing and financial responsibility will justify. Commercial agency reports may advantageously be procured and studied of all the concerns in which any director is actively interested. Whether or not the board is likely to give the bank close and wise and conservative supervision is a question that the underwriter must always ask himself and answer correctly ninety-odd times out of a hundred.

(c) Highly useful and trustworthy information about distant banks may often be obtained from the correspondent bank located in the home-office city of the surety company.   Banks must be guarded in giving out credit information to the public, but they are frank with each other; and if a big New York bank, for example, writes to its correspondent bank in Chicago about some institution with which the Chicago correspondent is in close touch all the time, the New York bank will soon be in a position to give its surety-company patron first-hand and authoritative information.

(d) When the bank requesting the bond is located in a town or one of the smaller cities of the country, it is a good plan to procure information about it from a local attorney of good standing (readily found in a legal directory).   I have long used for that purpose with excellent results the following stock letter:

> We have been requested to issue a bond guaranteeing the safety of a deposit to be made in the bank named below. We desire to have your opinion as to the standing and responsibility, of the bank.
>
> Are the directors solid, reputable business men?   Are any of them politicians who might be able to obtain public deposits for their bank by reason of their political influence, and who might conceivably use such funds for their private purposes without giving the bank adequate security?. Are any of the directors promoters of private enterprises requiring unusual financial support?
>
> We will pay you a fee of ....dollars for your information, if that will be satisfactory.
>
> As we may hold up the matter pending the receipt of your advices, we hope that you can make it convenient to answer by an early mail.

169. Cancellability of the Bond

Depository bonds, generally speaking, contain no provision giving the surety the right to terminate liability. This is regrettable, from the standpoint of a surety, for a number of reasons: (a) In practice it is often necessary to write bonds at short notice, upon only a general underwriting survey of the situation and without an opportunity to investigate the bank thoroughly, and afterward unfavorable information about the bank may be received. (b) Even if the bank seems all right when the bond is written, its management may change or for some other reason it may become during the life of the bond an undesirable principal. (c) Frequently the term of the bond is a long one—four years, say—and on general principles one would prefer not to issue any bond that is imperatively in force for a long period. Such bonds are an inevitable incident of the surety business, but in most cases there are palliating circumstances (joint control in the case of fiduciary bonds, for example), whereas with depository bonds there is little or nothing that an underwriter can do when he has written in haste and must afterward repent at leisure. In the old ailroading days when single tracks were almost universal and automatic signals were unknown, they used to have what they called "telegraphic collisions"—some operator would make a ghastly blunder by ordering two trains going in opposite directions to meet at overlapping points, and would discover the error too late to stop either train and in time only to dispatch a wrecking train with surgeons to the scene of the foreordained disaster. Similarly a surety company has sometimes learned after wiring its agent authority to issue some depository bond that a "telegraphic claim" would probably result from its premature decision.

There seems to be no good reason, in the nature of things, why the obligees of depository bonds should object to a fair cancellation condition—one requiring thirty days' notice, say, of the termination of liability. That would give the depositor plenty of time in which to transfer the funds to another bank. In fact, some depository bonds do permit the surety to serve a notice of cancellation upon the obligee. Bonds running in favor of the federal government, for example, covering Indian funds (Department of the Interior, Form 5020) run for a designated period (usually one year) and indefinitely thereafter, with the proviso that either the surety or the Commissioner of Indian affairs may terminate liability by giving thirty days' notice in writing.

170. Some Depository Losses Inevitable

Even when all the underwriting precautions discussed above (and others as well) are thoroughly tried out in every case, losses are bound to occur. That is so partly because the status of the bank sometimes changes for the worse while the bond remains in force, and partly because the real condition of the bank is so cleverly concealed that even a searching investigation fails to reveal it. A case of bank insolvency occurring in the Middle West not long ago gives painful point to this general statement. Out of a clear sky there, and with not a single premonitory rumble (so far as the public was concerned at all events), a flash of confessed insolvency annihilated a large national bank. The bank was supposed to have intact a capital of $1,000,000 and a surplus even larger. This capital and surplus was wiped out, and in addition the stockholders were assessed to the full limit of the law, or 100 per cent. So closely guarded was the secret of the bank's real condition, even among local investors, that a short time before the collapse, the stock of the bank sold for $250 a share, so that an investor who had bought one hundred shares, say, on that basis would have been obliged a month later to charge off his fancied asset of $25,000, and to debit himself in place of it with an immediate and inescapable liability of $10,000.

Lord Curzon defined enterprising journalism as "an intelligent anticipation of events that never occur"; successful depository underwriting demands an intelligent anticipation of improbable events that may nevertheless occur.

CHAPTER XIII

FIDUCIARY BONDS

171. Primarily Fidelity Risks

This chapter has to do with an extremely important branch of corporate suretyship—with the bonds given by administrators, executors, guardians, conservators, testamentary trustees, and other like fiduciaries. These bonds are primarily fidelity instruments—that is to say, the chief element of risk to the trust estate and to the surety company lies in the possible dishonesty of the executor, guardian, or other fiduciary. The bonds, however, involve vastly more than a mere fidelity hazard; and it is entirely true that a fiduciary may default, and his surety may suffer a heavy loss, when there has been absolutely no dishonesty or even bad faith of any kind or degree on the part of the fiduciary. An executor, for example, may invest his trust fund or a part of it in a way not authorized by law, with resultant loss to the estate; he must make good such loss to the estate, however well-intentioned he may have been, however innocent of any purpose to be false to his trust.

A fiduciary, therefore, must be much more than merely honest. He must show diligence and zeal in assembling the assets of the trust estate; he must be vigilant in protecting such assets after they have been collected; he must disburse them only as valid debts, court orders, or the will or trust deed may require; he must do everything in rigid accordance with the law governing the administration of estates, and ignorance of the law will not in the least absolve him from liability; and if he default as to any part of these comprehensive

233

and unmodifiable obligations, whether or not such default is due to dishonesty, he or his surety must make good to the estate any resultant loss.

172. A Fundamental Underwriting Classification

All fiduciary bonds fall within one or the other of two classes that present somewhat different underwriting problems. The first class embraces all those fiduciaries, such as administrators, executors, receivers and trustees in bankruptcy, and guardians *ad litem*, who merely liquidate the trust estate, assembling and distributing the net assets thereof, if any. The second class embraces those fiduciaries, such as committees of incompetents, guardians of minors and others under disability, and trustees under wills or deeds of trust, who not only assemble (or at least receive) the assets, but who also preserve and invest them in connection with current partial distribution. Bonds issued in behalf of these latter fiduciaries are more hazardous as a rule than bonds covering the first class, not only because the duties and obligations of the fiduciaries are likely to be more onerous in the latter case, but also and especially because the period of liability and consequent chance of adverse developments is usually much longer. The first class of bonds ordinarily remain in force for comparatively short terms. Administrators and executors, for example, commonly complete their work in a year or so. Fiduciaries of the second class, however, may obviously be years in discharging their trust. Sections 173–185 treat of fiduciaries of the first class, 186–188 of second class.

173. Appointment of Administrator

When one possessing personal property dies without leaving a will disposing of such property, the court.

upon the application of some person concerned with the estate, names someone, usually one of the decedent's next of kin, to care for the interests thus left unguarded. This appointee, called an "administrator," upon filing a bond and taking an oath that he will faithfully execute the trust about to be committed to him, is vested with authority to take possession of the decedent's personal estate, to pay all lawful debts of the decedent, and to distribute among the next of kin the residue of the estate. In most jurisdictions the administrator is required by law to give a bond conditioned for the faithful performance of the duties of the trust. The "next of kin" are the persons who, under the statutes governing the distribution of personal property, share in the unbequeathed assets of a decedent after the payment of debts and expenses, other than a surviving husband or wife. The "heirs-at-law" are the relatives who succeed to the real property of a person who leaves no will. The next of kin and the heirs-at-law are commonly the same persons.

As a general rule an administrator has nothing to do with the decedent's real estate. He has, by virtue of his office, no implied power to continue a business in which his decedent was engaged, beyond a period reasonably necessary for its liquidation. Moreover, it is unwise for him to continue a business, because he cannot charge the estate with losses incurred in the business (the beneficiaries of the estate being entitled to whatever assets there were when the decedent died), and yet he must account to the estate for any profits. Partly for that reason, and partly because a fiduciary has exceptional opportunity for wrongful acts and irregularities when conducting a business, underwriters very much prefer not to have principals go on with a decedent's business longer than is absolutely necessary for the proper administration of the estate.

174. Duties of Administrator

He must assemble with diligence all the assets left by his decedent and convert them, by public or private sale as the court may direct, into money. He must file, generally within thirty days after his appointment, an inventory made by competent and disinterested appraisers. He must publish, in the manner required by law, a notice requiring all persons having claims against the decedent to exhibit the same, with the. vouchers therefor; and he must be careful, in such notification to creditors, to follow the statute rigidly, if he would clear himself of liability for valid unpaid-because-unknown claims. *After*, but not before, the statutory time for the presentation of claims has expired, he must pay all lawful debts owed by the decedent or incurred in the administration of the estate; but he must be careful to pay only valid debts, since no others will be chargeable by him to the estate; and he must be careful, also, especially if there be any question as to the solvency of the estate, to pay debts only in the order of their priority, since if he pays a claim of inferior degree and afterward lacks funds with which to meet a demand of superior merit (funeral expenses, for example), he must make good the resultant loss to the prior creditor. Finally, the administrator must file an account of all his proceedings, simultaneously notifying all persons interested of its filing and of his application for its allowance and settlement. This notice must be given to all persons interested in the estate, in order that, if any of them object to anything done or proposed to be done by the administrator, such objections may be adjudicated by the court.

When the account has been settled by the court, a final decree or order of distribution is made and entered, directing the administrator to distribute the residue of the estate remaining in his hands among the persons named in the decree. When distribution has been made as ordered by the court, and when proper receipts from the distributees have been filed, an order or decree is usually made discharging the fiduciary from further duty and cancelling the surety's bond. While this final decree is regarded as the equivalent of a judgment, yet in practice, as all experienced fiduciary underwriters know, such settlements are not absolutely final, and may be set aside under conditions that occasionally, though rarely, arise.

175. Appointment and Duties of Executor

An executor is one to whom another commits by his last will and testament the execution of that instrument. While administrators must usually file a bond as a necessary incident of their qualifying for the office, executors are frequently permitted to serve without bond, especially when the testator expressly provides in the will that no bond need be given. The laws of the various states differ markedly on this point. In some jurisdictions even when a general law requires bonds, it is held that the court may waive the requirement in its discretion—if, for example, all those interested in the estate consent to such a course. On the other hand, in jurisdictions where no bond is required by law (in New York State, for example) the courts will nevertheless under some conditions withhold the appointment of the executor named in the will unless and until a suitable bond is filed; if, for example, someone interested in the estate demands that a bond be filed upon the ground that the financial responsibility of the proposed appointee is inadequate, that he is not a resident of the state, etc.

The amount of the bond, in the case of both executors and administrators, varies in different jurisdictions. Sometimes the amount is determined by statute, while in some states the amount is left to the discretion of the court. A common rule is to make the amount double the estimated value of the personal property. In some states, as in New York, the surrogate may allow the securities of the estate or a part of them to be deposited with him, with the county treasurer, or with some trust company, and made withdrawable from such depository only upon the order of the fiduciary countersigned by the surrogate; and when that is done, the bond otherwise appropriate will be reduced by the amount of the securities thus deposited.

Executors must look to the will for their powers, while administrators must look to the statutes and decisions of the court. If a man dies without leaving a will, he is said to die intestate; when he leaves a will, he is said to die testate. The duties of an executor, generally speaking, are substantially the same as those of an administrator (cf. section 174), with the exception that, after the payment of the decedent's debts and all taxes due from the estate, the residue remaining in the executor's hands is distributed to the legatees named in the will. Unless the will otherwise directs, an executor, like an administrator, has no implied power by virtue of his office to continue a business in which the decedent was formerly engaged; and should he do so and lose money in the venture, he and his surety will be liable for the resultant loss, be his motives ever so praiseworthy.

176. Administrator de Bonis Non

When an administrator has performed a part of his duties, but for some reason does not complete the administration (dies, perhaps, resigns, or is removed), the court will appoint a successor, who is termed an "administrator de bonis non," commonly written "administrator d.b.n." (administrator of the property not yet administered). The duties of an administrator d.b.n. are the same, in essentials, as those of a general administrator.

177. Administrator cum Testamento Annexo

When there is a will, but no executor is named therein, or when an executor named by a testator for some reason does not qualify, the court will appoint an "administrator cum testamento annexo," commonly written "administrator c.t.a." (administrator with the will annexed). The duties of an administrator c.t.a. are the same, in essentials, as those of a general administrator. If, however, the will contains provisions indicating that the testator gave certain powers to the executor named in the will (for example, discretionary authority of some kind or special authority regarding the real estate) because of the testator's special confidence and trust in such nominee, the administrator c.t.a. will not be permitted to function as to such special authorizations.

178. Administrator cum Testamento Annexo de Bonis Non

When an executor, or an administrator c.t.a., has performed a part of his duty, but for some reason does not complete the administration (dies, perhaps, resigns, or is removed), the court will appoint a successor, who is termed an "administrator cum testamento annexo de bonis non,". commonly written "administrator c.t.a.d.

b.n." (an administrator with the will annexed of the property not yet administered). The duties of an administrator c.t.a.d.b.n. are the same, in essentials, as those of a general administrator, though under certain conditions the limitations referred to in the preceding section will apply likewise here.

179. Ancillary Administrator

When a will disposing of personal property has been admitted to probate in a foreign country or a state where the will was executed or where the testator lived at the time of his death, and when for some reason it becomes necessary to administer the estate or a part of it in some other jurisdiction, the surrogate or similar official in such other jurisdiction will, upon the presentation of proper papers, record the will and the foreign letters and issue ancillary letters testamentary, or ancillary letters of administration with the will annexed, as the circumstances may require. Such an appointee is called an "ancillary executor" or "ancillary administrator." His powers are in general the same as those of ordinary executors or administrators.

180. Temporary and Special Administrators

When the validity of a will is questioned, or when for any reason a permanent administrator cannot be appointed, a temporary or special administrator, or an administrator *pendente lite* (during the period of litigation), is appointed. His chief and paramount duty is to preserve the estate pending the judicial determination of the controversy or the failure for other reasons of the permanent administrator to qualify; and he should make no disposition or distribution of the estate except under the order of the court that appointed him.

181. Assignee of Insolvent Estate

An assignee is one to whom another, called the "assignor," transfers all his property, with directions to convert it into money and to distribute the proceeds among the assignor's creditors. Assignees are appointed in connection with bankruptcy proceedings conducted under state laws. Assignees' bonds are looked upon with disfavor by many underwriters because the making of an assignment is itself an act of bankruptcy and facilitates the adjudication of the assignor as a bankrupt under federal law; that is, if, after an assignment has been made under state law, a creditor institutes the necessary proceedings under the federal Bankruptcy Law and has the assignor adjudicated a bankrupt, and if it then develops that the assignee has made some disposition of the assets inconsistent with the federal Bankruptcy Law, the assignee and his surety will very likely be held liable. Such unhappy developments are not improbable, because these assignments are frequently made for the purpose of preferring some creditor or of procuring some advantage that could not be obtained if the insolvent estate were administered under the federal law.

182. Receivers and Trustees in Bankruptcy

A receiver in bankruptcy is a mere custodian of the bankrupt estate, and ordinarily his powers continue only until a trustee in bankruptcy qualifies. Trustees in bankruptcy are usually appointed at the first meeting of the creditors after an adjudication of bankruptcy. It is their duty properly and efficiently to liquidate the bankrupt estate, and to distribute any resultant cash proportionately among all the creditors. Trustees in bankruptcy must deposit all funds in banks designated by the bankruptcy court; and the funds are disbursed under the supervision of the referee in bankruptcy, who countersigns all checks drawn by the trustee. Because of these safeguards and of the fact that receivers and trustees are likely to be lawyers of good standing, or business men well and favorably known, underwriters deem these bonds excellent risks.

183. Receivers in Litigation

A receiver is an officer appointed by the court to take possession of property involved in litigation, in order to preserve such property from waste, and, when the interests of the litigants have been judicially determined, to dispose of the property in such manner as the court may direct. Such appointees are naturally as a rule men of character and responsibility, and their bonds are deemed desirable.

184. Referees and Like Officers for Sale of Property

Referees, trustees, and commissioners are appointed by the court to sell property at public or private sale in foreclosure actions, partition actions, and in other proceedings under decree of the court, in order that such officers may distribute the proceeds of such sales in accordance with the order of the court. While these sales and the distribution of the proceeds thereof are usually completed within a year, in some jurisdictions the law requires the officer, not only to make the sale, but also to invest and preserve the funds so obtained; and in such cases the surety's liability will continue for an indefinite time, and the bonds are correspondingly hazardous.

In order that one danger common to all bonds of this class may be obviated, fiduciaries should see to it that everybody having an interest in the property to be sold, however small that interest may be, is made a party to the litigation; because if for any reason a person so interested is not made a party, and consequently fails to participate in the proceeds of the sale, such person can reopen the whole proceeding, and under conditions easily realizable in practice the surety may be called upon to compensate the claimant.

185. Guardian ad Litem

A guardian *ad litem* is appointed to represent an infant who is interested as a party to an action pending in a court of law. The guardian *ad litem* must file a bond in an amount usually not less than twice the value of the money or property that he is expected to receive as a result of the action. The bond is usually conditioned for the application of such money in accordance with the directions of the court. No disposition of the funds received by such a guardian, should, therefore, be made except in pursuance of the order of the court.

186. Committees, Guardians, and Conservators, of Incompetents

People unable to take proper care of themselves or their affairs by reason of idiocy, lunacy, habitual drunkenness, imbecility, or other cause, can legally act only by a duly appointed committee, as he (or she) is usually called, though in some states the term "guardian" or "conservator" is used. His duties are principally to keep the estate productive and legally invested, to attend to the personal wants and comforts of his ward, and to take all reasonable means to restore his ward's health. He should as a rule procure a court order covering the investment of the estate and an application of the income therefrom for the maintenance of the ward;

and he should never encroach upon the principal fund except under order of the court.

187. Guardians and Tutors of Minors

A minor is one who has not attained an age, usually twenty-one, at which the law presumes that he (or she) has sufficient understanding to manage his own affairs and property. During his non-age or period of disability, if he has property, a guardian is appointed to manage and preserve it until he attains his majority. The duties of a guardian may be summarized as follows:

(a) He should file with the court an accurate inventory of the ward's property as soon as it comes into his possession.

(b) He should keep an account-book concerned exclusively with guardianship affairs, in which there should be recorded at the time of its occurrence every transaction relating to the estate; and he should take and preserve a receipt for every expenditure.

(c) If the ward's estate as received consists of un-invested funds, the guardian should at once invest them in such securities as the law of the particular jurisdiction authorizes a trustee to hold. If the ward's estate comes to the guardian in the form of securities that the guardian could not lawfully invest in, he should hold the securities until he has a reasonable opportunity to sell them without loss; and if the estate should suffer loss as a result of his neglectful failure to sell such unauthorized securities and reinvest the proceeds properly, he and his surety would be liable therefor. A guardian should never lend a ward's money upon unsecured notes, second mortgages, mortgages on leasehold security, or in business ventures. The courts have quite commonly held that trust funds may be invested in loans secured by first mortgages on real estate, provided the loan is not more than half the value of the land securing it; and bonds of the United States and of the several states are also generally held to be proper and legal investments.

(d) Under no circumstances should a guardian commingle the trust funds with his own funds; he should always deposit them in an account entitled "John Doe, as guardian of Richard Roe, a minor." If he holds securities or depositable assets of any kind, they should be placed in a safe-deposit box leased under the same designation.

(e) A guardian must exercise towards his ward the highest good faith in all his dealings with the trust estate, and should never knowingly place himself in a position where it may even be charged that he has used his office for his personal advantage. It goes without saying that a guardian should never, whatever the palliating circumstances may be, appropriate his ward's property to his own use.

(f) The guardian should file with the court, at such time as may be required by law, statements of account, and obtain, if practicable, judicial approval of such accounts.

(g) When the ward attains his majority the guardian should render a final account of his stewardship to the court that appointed him, and have the account judicially settled and allowed by the court.

188. Trustees under Will or Deed of Trust

All fiduciaries, in a broad sense, are trustees; but the trustees referred to in this section are those appointed by a testator in his last will (sometimes called "testamentary trustees") and those named by the creator of a trust in a deed of trust. The title to specific property is given to these fiduciaries, as such, to hold during the life of certain persons, or for a certain specified time, with directions to apply the income in accordance with the terms of the given will or deed.   Trusts so created usually continue during the lives of one or more beneficiaries.

Trustees, like guardians of minors and incompetents, are bound to exercise the utmost good faith, and to derive no benefit from the trust aside from the statutory or otherwise lawful compensation.   As regards investments, unless the will or deed of trust gives the trustee a wider latitude, the funds of the estate must be invested only in such securities as are sanctioned by law.   Trustees should file with the court annual settlements of accounts; and even where the law does not require them to do so they should annually render to the beneficiaries an accurate account of all transactions and get their approval thereof.

189. Joint Control Explained

An administrator or other fiduciary holds the legal title to securities and other assets, and so far as third parties are concerned he is the absolute owner thereof. If, therefore, he is permitted to have sole control of the assets, he may do with them what he will, and his surety will be helpless. A dishonest fiduciary, or even an honest but ignorant and incapable one, may easily under such conditions dissipate the trust estate. Experience has abundantly shown that under circumstances continually arising in practice fiduciary bonds cannot prudently be written unless the fiduciary will permit the surety to have joint control over the assets of the trust estate.

When joint control is exercised all moneys that the fiduciary is to handle are deposited in a bank, in the fiduciary's official capacity, under an arrangement with the bank whereby the fiduciary's checks or drafts against the account are honored only when they bear the countersignature of the surety's representative. Similarly all other depositable assets, such as stocks, bonds, notes, mortgages, and jewelry, are placed in a safe-deposit box leased by the fiduciary in his official capacity and unopenable by him unless accompanied by the surety company's duly authorized representative. Both of these joint-control arrangements are perfected by serving upon the bank and safe-deposit company a notice signed by the surety and the fiduciary containing the substance of the agreement between them, and by taking from the bank or depository an acknowledgment evidencing their agreement to be governed by such notice.

There are certain classes of property, such as livestock, household furniture, farming implements, and the like, over which it is seldom practicable to exercise joint control; but, since it is usually the duty of a fiduciary holding such property to sell and convert it into money, the proceeds of such sale may and should be subjected to joint control. In a situation of this kind the surety's representative must be vigilant to see that such proceeds are promptly and wholly deposited in a joint-control account.

Joint control, to be effective, must be perfected over *all* the depositable assets, for if some of them are left in the sole control of the fiduciary, the safeguard is correspondingly weakened. How is the surety company's representative to know that all the assets are under his joint control? In the first place, the written application for the bond should contain a complete statement of the assets, so far as known. While this statement is extremely important and will commonly be the primary source of the company's information, it is sometimes not practicable to embody in the application a full record of the assets of the estate. Fortunately a fiduciary is required by law to file in the court having jurisdiction of the estate, usually within ninety days, a sworn inventory and appraisal; and careful surety practice requires that a copy of this inventory and appraisal be procured as soon as it has been filed, and that the assets under joint control be then checked up with the inventory, so as to establish the fact that all depositable assets are actually under the company's joint control.

190. Thoroughgoing Exercise of the Function Essential

The securing of joint control is more or less a futile procedure unless such control be *exercised* vigilantly and continuously. Strange as it may seem, surety companies not infrequently suffer substantial losses because their joint-control representatives do their work in a careless, half-hearted manner, and consent to the unlawful and improper disposition of the trust funds. Since a surety is responsible not only for a fiduciary's intentional wrongdoing, but also for his errors and mistakes, regardless of his worthy motives, the extreme importance of this aspect of the matter is obvious. Where, for example, a will gives a legacy of $1,000 to John Brown, and the executor pays that amount, with the surety's consent, to someone who is actually not John Brown at all, but who, with intent to defraud, represents that he is, the fiduciary, as well as his surety (their liability being coextensive), will be liable to the real John Brown for the legacy that ought to have been paid to him. The agent should, therefore, before countersigning a check invariably inform himself thoroughly concerning the purpose for which the payment is to be made.

In the case of administration bonds, the undertaker's

bill, reasonable legal expenses incurred in the appointment of the administrator and in the settlement of the estate, and the family allowance, are preferred charges against the estate, and may, therefore, be safely paid out of the first money coming into the fiduciary's hands. Where a father is the guardian of his minor children, and is of sufficient financial ability to support and maintain them adequately without having recourse to his children's estate, he should do so, since he is under a legal obligation to care for them properly under such conditions. Where, however, a mother is the guardian of her minor children, the same rule does not generally obtain, and she will be permitted to use her children's estate for their proper maintenance.

No check should ever be countersigned that is not drawn to the order of the person to whom the payment is to be made.

191. Uniform Attitude of Companies toward Joint Control

While joint control is always acceptable, in many cases highly desirable, and under certain conditions absolutely essential, the circumstances are frequently such that joint control will be waived if the business cannot otherwise be secured. Where the fiduciary is a woman, however, or a mechanic, perhaps, presumably unaccustomed to business and legal affairs, or where the bond is a large one, or where the term of the bond is likely to continue beyond two or three years, most underwriters rarely feel able to write the bond without joint control. The attitude of all the important surety companies is substantially the same as regards this point; and agents should not too lightly accept as accurate statements that some other company is willing to issue without joint control a bond that cannot prudently be so written.

Agents sometimes prefer not to request joint control, partly because they fear that the principal will resent such a request, and partly because they begrudge the loss of time required for the exercise of joint control. On both counts this attitude seems a mistaken one—the principal will take no offense, if the matter is properly presented to him; and the time devoted by agents to these cases is far from wasted. Many fieldmen, indeed, regard their joint-control cases as a valuable advertising and business-producing adjunct of their business. There are many advantages to a principal, especially one not familiar with business and legal matters, in the joint-control arrangement, and there is no real disadvantage.

192. Three Fundamental Underwriting Considerations

Points concerned with the underwriting of the various bonds discussed in this chapter were taken up specifically in connection with the given bonds. In this section I should like to point out three general considerations upon which the underwriting of almost *all* fiduciary bonds more or less pivots:

(a) CHARACTER OF THE FIDUCIARY. Since fiduciary bonds are primarily fidelity instruments, it follows that the character of the fiduciary is an underwriting factor of high importance. If, accordingly, the investigation of a proposed principal's character and career discloses unfavorable features, the bond will be rejected as a matter of course and without regard to other considerations. This point, however, is of theoretical rather than practical importance, because fiduciaries are altogether likely to be persons of excellent character. A testator selects his executor, and the probate court appoints the administrator, largely in both cases because the fiduciary is known to be a person of high character; and for like reasons other classes of fiduciaries are almost always desirable principals so far as their character is concerned. In practice fiduciary bonds are rarely rejected because of flaws in the personal credentials of the applicants.

A plurality of principals is a favorable underwriting feature, generally speaking, of a fiduciary bond. This is so for the obvious reason that they will usually act together in all important matters, with a lessened chance of wrongful or mistaken steps; and for the reason not obvious, but in most jurisdictions equally valid, that each fiduciary will be responsible for all the acts of the others. The law is in some states, however, that fiduciaries of this character on a joint bond are liable for each other only in the case of their joint acts.

(b) CHARACTER OF THE PRINCIPAL'S ATTORNEY. Underwriters attach great importance to the character and professional attainments of the attorney who is to act for the principal in the administration of the trust estate. That is so, of course, because of the fact that legal questions, sometimes of a rather complex and difficult nature, are all the time coming up in the course of the administration of the trust estate, and must be answered correctly at the peril of the fiduciary and his surety. So important is this underwriting factor in the judgment of many underwriters that they would much rather write a bond for a somewhat weak principal represented by a lawyer famous for his expert and careful probate practice than one for a strong principal represented by an attorney of mediocre talent. Hardly any underwriter, I suppose, would care to provide fiduciary suretyship for a principal represented by an attorney of dubious reputation, however good the principal's own credentials might be. Fortunately there are legal directories that show with remarkable accuracy the standing of about all the attorneys in active practice in the country, except in the largest cities.

If the estate proves to be insolvent, or insufficient to pay all the legacies, the advice of competent counsel is particularly important. Under such conditions the fiduciary, if he should pay particular claimants or distributees in full, might easily store up trouble for himself and for his surety.

(c) JOINT CONTROL. Since the condition of the obligation in the case of most fiduciary bonds is that the principal shall assemble, preserve, and distribute properly the assets of the trust estate, it is clear that the risk of the surety will be very much lessened if it can itself exercise control over the assets for which it is secondarily responsible. Under many conditions, therefore, an underwriter prefers not to write a given bond unless the principal will concede either sole or joint control of the cash and securities of the trust estate. This point is discussed in detail in sections 189–191, and is mentioned here only as one of the three important factors that are taken into account by an underwriter in considering whether a given bond may prudently be issued. If joint control is conceded, the question is vastly simplified.

193. Cancellation Evidence

A fiduciary bond is a continuing obligation until discharged in one of two ways—by performance or by operation of law. Moreover, the contract embodied in the bond is one not only between the parties directly named in the instrument, but also in a sense with the state in that the prime object of the contract is the due administration of justice. That is why in many states the obligee is "the People of the State," or "the Governor of the State," or perhaps "the Judge of the Probate Court." The bond cannot be cancelled merely because the principal desires cancellation or fails to pay the premium; if the bond could be cancelled for any such reason, the obligee would be deprived of the protection that the law deems essential to him and to the state. Before a surety company, under the regulations of the various state insurance departments, may terminate liability on its books as to a given bond, and take down the reserve that it is required to carry for the benefit of the obligee named in such bond, it must receive from some source (its principal perhaps, or the latter's atrorney, or its own agent) one of the three following:

(a) A certified copy of a final judgment, order, or decree of the court in which the bond was filed, settling and approving the fiduciary's final account and discharging the surety on his official bond.

(b) A certificate issued by the judge or clerk of the judge, under the seal of the court, certifying to the discharge of the fiduciary and the release of his surety.

(c) A statement or certificate from the agent or attorney of the surety company showing that he has personally examined the records of the court in which the matter was pending, and found such records to evidence the discharge and release of the fiduciary and his surety. In every case this statement should give the date, page, and book number of the official entry, and embody an exact copy of the record relied upon as of discharging effect.

194. Explanation of Fiduciary Application Form

While most application forms for bonds require no special explanation, the fiduciary form is rather complicated, and a brief description of it may be worth while. About all companies use forms calling for:

(a) PRELIMINARY DATA. The amount of the bond is essential for two reasons—for premium-computing purposes and for comparison with the amount fixed by the court. The date of the fiduciary's birth is essential, because most underwriters prefer not to bond minors and to bond aged persons only under exceptional circumstances. The "exact official title" must be known in order that the underwriter may properly classify the risk, and may understand what the duties of the principal are. The financial responsibility of the applicant is, of course, an important underwriting consideration, especially in the case of certain kinds of fiduciary bonds. References are essential because of the desirability of investigating the applicant thoroughly.

The question about possible prior bonds is also very important; if a bond was formerly given in connection with the same estate the surety may have become insolvent and there may have been a loss while the applicant was bonded by the first sureties, with retroactive liability falling upon the new bond. The query concerning business operations is important because, as emphasized elsewhere (cf. sections 173 and 175), a fiduciary risk is deemed abnormally hazardous where a business is to be continued for any period longer than that necessary to liquidate it. The information called for about the expected duration of the risk is much desired, and the answer should be made as nearly accurate as possible. The attorney for the principal will usually know about how long the bond will probably remain in force.

(b) INDEBTEDNESS OF FIDUCIARY TO ESTATE. The question as to whether the fiduciary is indebted to the estate is extremely important, because if he is, the fact may seriously impair his bondability. In some jurisdictions the debt of the fiduciary will be regarded as in the same class with all other debts, and its non-payment may not constitute a claim against the surety (if, for example, the fiduciary throughout the administration is insolvent); but in other jurisdictions even under such conditions the surety will be liable. Everywhere the debt would be charged against the fiduciary and his surety if at any time during the administration the fiduciary was able to pay the debt. In practice, therefore, under almost all conditions a debt of the fiduciary to the estate must be regarded in law as the equivalent of cash in the hands of the fiduciary, to be correspondingly accounted for; and under such circumstances most underwriters would deem it imprudent to issue the bond unless the debt were paid at once.

(c) VALUE OF THE ESTATE. The questions about the value of the estate are, of course, essential, and pains should be taken to obtain full and accurate information. When the debts of the estate exceed the assets, the bond is often highly hazardous. The question regarding investments is obviously of outstanding importance, since only certain kinds of investments are lawful, and since the surety will be responsible if the estate sustains loss because of illegal investing by the fiduciary. The tables concerning the assets and liabilities of the estate should be completed with the utmost care and particularity. The question about the annual income is important because the underwriter uses the information in various ways in checking the operations of the principal.

(d) INFORMATION ABOUT REAL ESTATE ESSENTIAL. It will be noted that information regarding real estate is called for. While it is true that real estate upon the death of the owner vests at once in the heir or devisee, and that administrators under all conditions, and executors in the absence of express authority under the will, have nothing to do with real estate, yet the existence of realty among the assets of a decedent so far affects the administration of the estate under some circumstances that an underwriter needs to know what real estate the decedent owned at the date of his death. Any rents due, for example, at that time must be collected by the representative of the estate and are chargeable to him. If the personal property of the estate is insufficient to satisfy the debts thereof, the realty may often be applied to the payment of such debts; and when such a condition of things exists, highly technical legal proceedings are in order. Sometimes a special bond is required from the fiduciary covering such a sale. Under other circumstances frequently arising in practice an administrator or executor may have much to do with the realty formerly owned by the decedent. It is thus desirable on all accounts that a complete statement of such holdings be included in the application form.

(e) MINOR POINTS OF INTEREST. The query regarding the title of the case should be answered with precise and legal accuracy, as the surety-company indexes are made in accordance with this item. The date of death is particularly important, because periods of legal limitation sometimes begin then. The names of the persons interested in the estate should be given in full. The ages called for are essential because if there are minors, the appointment of a guardian before the estate is distributed is necessary. Moreover, when the court finally authorizes the fiduciary to distribute the funds of the estate, this information is essential to check up the distributees, and to see that none of them are omitted in the distribution. The information called for about the relationship of the persons interested in the estate is exceedingly helpful in the underwriting. The item about maintenance is important because courts have different ideas regarding maintenance allowances; and the amounts shown in the application are carefully considered by the underwriter with a view to possible trouble with the courts later over the allowance proposed. The name of the fiduciary's attorney is called for because underwriters attach great importance to his character and standing (cf. section 192). Fiduciaries ought not to take any important action (indeed any action) except upon the advice of counsel; and the disposition and ability of counsel to advise him wisely thus becomes a matter of primary importance.

195. Termination of Liability upon Initiative of Surety

For various reasons that become operative not infrequently in practice, surety companies, after having accepted a fiduciary risk and issued a corresponding bond, desire to terminate liability under such bond as to future acts of the principal. Perhaps the bond was authorized in haste, upon the urgent representation of some misinformed agent that everything was all right, when in fact hardly anything was right, and when the glowing reports about the risk made to the agent merely illustrated the poet's words:

> All were but syllabled air,
> Fancies that fluttered and flew.

Perhaps the principal tires of paying premiums year after year and procures personal sureties and refuses to pay premiums thereafter, upon the ground that the personal suretyship has superseded the corporate bond. He may really believe that, and instances are not wanting where local probate authorities have erroneously supported such contentions on the part of principals.

When a situation of this kind arises, and a surety company deems it advisable to get off a fiduciary risk,

17

the statutes and recorded decisions and probate practice of the given jurisdiction must be studied minutely and followed rigidly. In some places, as in New York State, no particular difficulty is encountered by the surety, and releases as to future acts of the principal may be obtained by surety companies as a matter of course by merely applying the statutory provision to the given case. In other jurisdictions, however, the process of terminating liability upon an undesirable risk or one for which it is impracticable to receive compensation is not so easy. Compelling reasons justifying such a course on the part of the surety company must be adduced and made to satisfy and convince an official who may not realize the importance to the surety company of an authoritative clearance, or who may feel indisposed anyway to assist in the plan of the distant corporation at the possible inconvenience or cost of some local principal. Fiduciary underwriters should equip themselves with complete information as to this point in the case of all the states in which their companies operate, because it has a direct and important bearing upon the acceptability of a considerable part of a company's fiduciary business. In the case of small bonds likely to run only a year or so, an underwriter will hardly take this consideration into account; but the point is of distinct importance in connection with large bonds, and especially in connection with bonds that are likely to remain in force for a long period. If, for example, it is known in advance that the company can, if such a course seems advisable, terminate its liability almost surely and with no great expense or trouble, an underwriter will sometimes accept a given piece of business when it would seem to him imprudent to do so if the situation as to terminability were less favorable.

CHAPTER XIV

THE CUSTODY OF COLLATERAL SECURITY

196. Importance of the Subject

Not many people realize, I imagine, to what a large extent the surety companies are the custodians of other people's cash and securities. They are entrusted with stocks, bonds, and large amounts of money for two purposes: (a) for their own indemnification, in cases where they feel unable to issue a given bond unless secured in this way; (b) for their own and their principals' protection, in cases where the principals are charged with the custody and proper distribution of funds and securities, and where the bonding companies deem it necessary, in order to ensure such distribution, to take physical possession of the trust estates. Deposits with the surety companies of cash and securities on these two accounts occur every hour in the day, and in the aggregate the companies must hold in this way all the time scores of millions of dollars.

The safeguarding of all this property, belonging to other people and held by the surety companies in trust, is obviously a feature of the business of extreme importance. Considerable amounts have been lost by the companies through the dishonesty or ignorance or carelessness of employees and agents. In one case, for example, an officer of a company permitted a principal to take away from a safe-deposit box over $100,000 worth of securities for the alleged purpose of having them registered. In fact, he sold them immediately, pocketed the proceeds, and disappeared into Mexico with the fatal finality of a fadeaway film. He never came back himself, but the lady of light-opera fame who helped him spend the money in Mexico doubtless reappeared on the Rialto, after twenty years or so, as an ingénue. In another notable case, a much larger loss was sustained by a surety company through the defalcation of a branch-office manager. Both these losses occurred years ago, and neither could easily happen under the safer systems of safeguarding securities that most companies now follow; but minor losses are not uncommon even now, and big losses are inevitable in the absence of eternal vigilance.

197. Rules for the Care of Collateral

On the chance that the information may be of use to some readers and of interest to others, I reproduce the rules adopted by one company for securing itself against loss and protecting its depositors.

(a) DEFINITIONS. Security received by the Company for its indemnification is herein called *Collateral Security*, and must be either cash or its equivalent. By the equivalent of cash is meant a security or asset that can be readily converted into the amount of cash represented to be its value at the time of its acceptance. The legal title to collateral security must at all times be in the Company. Securities or assets that are held by the Company to insure proper distribution are herein called *Estates' Security*. The title to estates' security need not be in the Company. Both forms of security described above when deposited with the Company are held in *Sole Control*, and are collectively referred to herein as *Security*.

(b) RECEIPT FOR SECURITY. All *Collateral Security* must be received and held under the terms and conditions set forth in Form 639, "Receipt for Collateral Security," which must be properly drawn and executed in duplicate on receipt of the security, one copy being retained by the depositor of the security, and the other sent to the home office. The security received must be minutely described in the said Receipt. The same rule applies when the security received is *Estates' Security*, except that Form 1241, "Receipt for Fiduciary Securities," is the form of receipt then used.

These rules regarding receipts are more important than they might seem to be at first to one inexperienced in fiduciary underwriting, since in practice rival claimants for security sometimes turn up, and since not infrequently doubt arises concerning the propriety or the safety of surrendering security to a given claimant even when nobody else at the time is demanding it.

(c) RECORD OF SECURITY. All security accepted must immediately upon its receipt be recorded in the book provided for that purpose called the *Security Book*, wherein it must be described with minute accuracy. This record will be supplemented by a card index. When the security has been duly recorded it must be forwarded to the home office at once, or in any event on the same day it is received, by express or by registered mail, fully insured in either case, unless under general or special authorization it is to remain in the custody of the branch office accepting it. In the latter case the rules hereinafter set forth will be applicable.

(d) SURRENDER OF COLLATERAL. Collateral Security held by the Company will not be surrendered to a depositor until legal evidence has been received at the home office that all liability on the bond in connection with which it was deposited has terminated. The security in all cases is to be returned, except as provided in the next paragraph, only to the depositor, who must acknowledge its return by endorsement to that effect on his copy of the collateral receipt given therefor; and the receipt must then be sent to the home office.

Security may be surrendered to a person other than the depositor only under the following circumstances:

(1) When it has been assigned by a duly executed instrument based on an express consideration;

(2) When a duly executed power of attorney is presented authorizing the holder of such power to receive the security;

(3) When the depositor is dead, and his duly appointed legal representative demands the security.

(e) CERTIFICATES OF STOCK. When certificates of corporate stock are accepted as collateral security, the following rules as to the form of the certificates must be observed:

(1) They are acceptable if made out by the transfer office in the name of the Company;

(2) If the certificates were originally made out by the transfer office in the name of the indemnitor, they must be endorsed by him in blank and the endorsement must be duly witnessed, or they must be accompanied by an irrevocable Power of Attorney, duly executed, in favor of the Company.

(3) If the certificates were originally made out by the transfer office in the name of an owner other than the Company or of the indemnitor, they must be what is known as "Street Certificates"—that is to say, they must be duly endorsed in blank by the original owner, and the endorsement must be guaranteed by a national bank, or a stock-exchange house of good standing.

(f) BONDS. Bonds accepted as collateral security should be payable to bearer. If registered in the name of the indemnitor, they must be accompanied by a duly executed power of attorney in favor of the Company.

(g) SAVINGS-BANK ACCOUNTS. When a savings-bank account is accepted as collateral security, the pass-book must be in the possession of the Company and Form 1325, Assignment of Bank Account, must be executed by the indemnitor, assigning to the Company all funds represented by the pass-book as standing to his credit. Only accounts standing in the individual name of the indemnitor will be accepted as collateral security: accounts in the name of an indemnitor in a representative capacity such as Trustee, Guardian, or Administrator, will be declined.

(h) CHECKS, CERTIFICATES OF DEPOSIT, ETC. All checks, certified or uncertified, accepted as collateral security, will be cashed at once; and the Company reserves the right in its discretion to cash any certificates of deposit, irrespective of the bank of issuance, or the rate of interest promised. No certificate of Deposit in the sum of $10,000 or over is to be accepted as collateral security without the authority of the home office.

(i) CASH. All cash (currency, checks, etc.) will be deposited in an account opened by the Company for that purpose, and the indemnitor will be allowed whatever rate of interest is received on the deposit.

(j) COUPONS. The surrender of coupons attached to bonds deposited as collateral security is in the discretion of the Company. Those attached to bonds forming part of Estates' Security will be deposited, when due, to the credit of the estate's account over which the Company exercises joint control; but no coupons will be detached for any purpose until a specific request therefor has been received by the Company from a source deemed by it authoritative.

(k) THE SAFEGUARDING OF SECURITY RETAINED IN BRANCH OFFICES.

(1) *Safe-Deposit Box.* The Company will rent a safe-deposit box in its own name in a local safe-deposit vault, in which all Bonding Department security held in sole control, other than cash, shall be deposited under the joint control of the Resident Manager or General Agent and such other representative of the Company as may be appointed for the purpose by the home office.

(2) *Bank Account.* An account in a local bank or trust company will be opened by the Company in its own name, in which all cash security received by the local office will be deposited. The account shall be used for no other purpose, and money shall be withdrawn therefrom only by check or draft signed by two persons appointed for the purpose by the home office. Whatever rate of interest is received on a deposit will be allowed to the depositor of the cash security.

(3) *Deposit of Security.* When a complete record of the security has been made in the Security Book, the security, of whatever nature, will be turned over to the Resident Manager or General Agent, and the local Examiner or other person appointed for the purpose by the home office, who will initial the entry in the security book as evidence of their receipt of the security, and will promptly deposit it in the Company's safe-deposit box or bank account (as the case may be) kept for that purpose. Such deposit must be made as soon as possible after the security is received, and in any event on the same day it is received in the local office.

(4) *Withdrawal of Security.* The Resident Manager or General Agent, and the local Examiner or other person ap-

pointed for the purpose by the home office, will have charge
of all security in the branch office from the time it leaves the
custody of the underwriter or other person originally receiving
it. They will release security only upon the written request
of the local bonding department (Form 1375) signed by the
head or assistant head of that department. This request must
include a statement to the effect that he deems such release
proper, and that the evidence of termination, release, or discharge of liability on the bond in question has been submitted
to and approved by the home office, or that the home office has
authorized the surrender of the security. Whenever security
is withdrawn from the safe-deposit box for surrender, renewal,
or exchange, the purpose of the withdrawal must be accom-.
plished on the day the security is so withdrawn, or it must be
redeposited in the Company's safe-deposit box.

(5) *Surrender of Security*. The head or assistant head of
the local bonding department will have charge of all security
released for surrender, and will surrender it only in accordance
with the provisions of paragraph (d). He will initial an
entry in the Security Book acknowledging the receipt of the
security from the Resident Manager or General Agent and
the local Examiner or other person appointed for the purpose
by the home office for surrender.

(6) *Savings-Bank Accounts as Collateral Security*. The assignment of the bank account (Form 1325) must be placed
with the pass-book in the safe-deposit box, and the depository
immediately notified of the assignment on Form 1344. When
a savings-bank account is to be released, the pass-book should
be returned to the indemnitor and the depository advised of the
release on Form 1343. The signature of officers or agents
authorized to draw upon the assigned account will not be filed
with the depository unless a specific request therefor is made
by the bank, or it becomes necessary to draw upon the account.

(7) *Certificate of Deposit*. Where the certificate of deposit
accepted is made out to the order of the Company as payee, the
bank or trust company issuing the certificate must be notified
of its deposit with the Company as collateral security on our
Form 1343; while if the certificate is made payable to the
order of the Company by endorsement, Form 1344 must be
used for this purpose. The due date of all certificates of de-

posit must be noted and they must be renewed at the proper time. To effect a renewal, the certificate must be endorsed to the order of the bank of issuance and sent direct with Form 1346.

(8) *Defective Security.* When collateral security on its receipt is not in satisfactory condition for final acceptance, but is held pending an effort to put it in such condition, a memorandum stating the defects and the steps that are being taken to remedy them must be attached to the security when it is placed in the safe-deposit box. All such defects, of course, must be remedied with the least possible delay.

(9) *Changes in Security.* No substitution of collateral security by other security, or changes in the form of the security accepted, are to be made without the authority of the home office.

(10) *Auditing.* The Company's auditors will audit the Bonding Department Security Record and the security account at convenient intervals, and at least semi-annually, at all branch offices where collateral is held. The auditor in each instance must verify by an actual examination and count the security reported on, and must submit in every case a certificate (Form 1307) duly executed by the person charged with the custody of the security and by the auditor.

198. Laxity of Agents Regarding Collateral Security

While surety agents as a class compare favorably, I am confident, with other business men as to the care and efficiency with which they conduct their affairs, the regrettable fact remains that all bonding companies find it hard to procure complete compliance with rules like the foregoing by their fieldmen. All home offices, I doubt not, have occasionally found it necessary to send to their agents letters more Chesterfieldian in style than, but of the same general purport as, the following characteristically hydrophobic concoction emitted by me not long ago to a long-suffering field force:

Recent audits of our branch offices show that the rules of the Bonding Department for the safeguarding of securities

are sometimes violated by our fieldmen through either ignorance or carelessness. Such irregularities are deemed by us
serious breaches of duty—under some conditions extremely
serious; and we cannot overlook them or fail to take whatever steps may be necessary to ensure correction.

The procedure followed by us in these matters as outlined in
Bulletin 89, and the rules embodied therein, are the result of
much study and consideration of all the points involved from
every angle; and we must ask you to familiarize yourselves
thoroughly with our rules and practices and to follow them
absolutely in every case. This material is not to be read cur-
sorily and then laid aside and forgotten. On the contrary,
it must be *studied*, and completely comprehended by you, and so
filed in your office that it may be readilyr eferred to in any
case of doubt regarding Company rules. These rules are set
out with particularity and entire clearness, as we suppose, and
we cannot easily imagine conditions that would justify failure
to follow them, in the absence of prior and contrary home-
office instructions.

We know that this detail is more or less troublesome, but
there is no other way in which to transact the business safely.
We admonish you, therefore, with firmness and finality, to
follow our rules and instructions in all respects and in every
case, and thus avert unnecessary correspondence, delays, and
misunderstandings, as well as actual loss.

CHAPTER XV

PROHIBITION BONDS

199. General Considerations

The enactment of the Eighteenth Amendment to the federal Constitution, effective January 16, 1920, not only spoiled the fishing, as some astute philosopher laments, but also annihilated the large business of the surety companies in the field of state liquor-tax bonds, as well as a vast volume of brewers', distillers', and other federal bonds concerned with the liquor industry. Simultaneously, however, it created a great mass of surety business of similar character—namely, the prohibition bonds treated in this chapter. Under the new order of things every one, generally speaking, who desires to make or to handle any kind of intoxicating liquor or alcoholic compound containing half of 1 per cent or more of alcohol by volume must first obtain a permit to do so from the Federal Prohibition Director of the state in which operations are to be conducted; and applications for such permits (with few exceptions) must be accompanied by bonds. These bonds guarantee compliance with the provisions of the National Prohibition Act (passed October 28, 1919) and with the corresponding "Regulations" of the Internal Revenue Bureau, and also guarantee the payment of any taxes and penalties imposed under the Internal Revenue laws. The bonds are, therefore, to some extent financial-guarantee instruments, and they must be underwritten with that detail of the risk prominently in mind. The moral hazard, however, is frequently and perhaps usually—in the case of small bonds anyway—more important still, since a principal who really means to live up to the law, and to comply in good faith with all the rules of the Federal Prohibition Director, is not likely to cause trouble to his surety.

200. Non-Beverage Alcohol Bonds

The permits referred to above authorize the use of intoxicating liquors, of course, only for non-beverage purposes. They may be so used in a variety of ways, almost all of which require the filing by the permittee of a "non-beverage alcohol bond." The bond, indeed, must be filed before the applicant becomes a permittee, and whether or not he ever becomes one; that is, it must be filed before or simultaneously with the filing of the application for the permit, and it guarantees, in addition to the things mentioned above, that no false statements are contained in the application. The bond is numbered 1408 and is by far the most common and important prohibition bond with which surety companies are concerned. The amount of the bond varies with the magnitude of the operations conducted thereunder, from a minimum of $1,000 to a maximum of $100,000. It is given in connection with various lines of business, which are treated separately in sections 202–204 and 206–212.

201. Brewers of Beer, Ale, or Porter

These beverages may be furnished only to industrial-alcohol or to dealcoholizing plants, for conversion into beverages containing less than half of 1 per cent of alcohol by volume. Brewers must file in connection with their permit the old Internal Revenue bond Form 20 (not 1408). This is a highly hazardous bond, because of the limited legitimate and unlimited illegitimate outlet for the product, and prudent underwriters will issue the bond only in behalf of principals of high financial as well as unexceptionable personal credentials. When collateral security is not available, the principal's net worth should greatly exceed the amount of the bond; and the moral hazard should at least *seem* to be small.

202. Manufacturers of Cider and Vinegar

Anyone desiring to manufacture or to use cider or other intoxicating liquors for conversion into vinegar must file a 1408 bond with the application for a permit. When intended for use as a beverage, cider must be marketed in sterile, closed containers, or be so treated as to prevent fermentation and keep the alcoholic content below half of 1 per cent of alcohol by volume. If it gets by that dead line, it will not seem "sweet" to the Prohibition Director, and the maker will be presumed to have made and sold without authority an intoxicating liquor.

Persons holding permits to manufacture cider for conversion into vinegar may, of course, make sweet cider, as anyone else may, regardless of permits, and do with it what they will, as anyone else may; but such permittees in practice sometimes run out of sugar and sell as "sweet" cider a liquid of which the alcoholic content refuses to remain below half of 1 per cent. Carelessness of that nature on the part of a permittee constitutes a violation of the law and a breach of the bond.

While there are doubtless many legitimate manufacturers of vinegar and cider, on the whole these bonds must be deemed abnormally dangerous, and collateral security should be required of applicants not possessed of substantial financial resources. It goes without saying, of course, that in addition their standing in the community should be thoroughly investigated, if not already known.

203. Dealcoholizing Plants

Persons who produce beverages of a permissible alcoholic content by the process by which beer, ale, porter, or wine is produced must file a 1408 bond with the usual application for a permit. The premises where these "soft drinks" are manufactured are designated as "dealcoholizing plants." The permittee of such a plant may develop liquids, in manufacturing his beverages, containing more than the maximum permissible quantity of alcohol, but such liquids must be removed to another plant for the purpose of having the alcohol extracted, before they are placed upon the market, or their alcoholic content must be reduced in the original plant to less than half of 1 per cent by volume. Permittees of these plants must make, in quadruplicate, complete and precise daily records of their operations, retaining one copy and filing three with designated officials.

As might be surmised, these bonds vary vastly in acceptability. They are excellent in the case of long-established and highly reputable manufacturers of well-known beverages; they are open to dark suspicion when the principals are persons of slight financial responsibility, of an unknown or dubious past, and of no prior experience in the business; and many intermediate grades of risks diversify the day's work. No hard-and-fast underwriting rule can well be formulated for these bonds—some of them are receivable with open arms, others are instantaneously rejectable, and many are writable only after prolonged investigation and perhaps only with collateral security.

204. Druggists and Pharmacists

Non-beverage alcohol bonds are required in large numbers by the wholesale and retail drug trade. Pharmacists may medicate alcohol in accordance with any one of seven listed formulae; they may use it in the manufacture of lotions, hair tonics, antiseptic solutions, etc.; and they may sell it in quantities and under conditions narrowly defined by the law.

The bond for wholesale druggists presents a more difficult underwriting problem than that for retailers, not only because it is likely to be much larger, but also because it has to do with conditions oftener leading to violations of the law. Many people who could not distinguish a drug from a dragon apply for permits as wholesale druggists, in order that they may specialize in the alcoholic department of the business. On the other hand, these bonds are highly acceptable when the principal is one of the numerous large concerns long and favorably known in the drug trade.

As for the multitude of bonds procurable from retail druggists everywhere, the liability involved commonly ranges from $1,000 to $5,000 only, entire regularity of operations may usually be assumed, and the bonds may be written freely for legitimate and reputable dealers. To this line of business underwriters may well apply the inscription on the gates of an ancient city: "Be bold; ever be more bold; be not *too* bold."

205. Exporters

Intoxicating liquors lawfully manufactured, including wines for sacramental use, but excluding liquids produced for conversion into non-alcoholic beverages, may, upon the issuance of a permit, be exported for non-beverage purposes. The exporter must keep in his files correspondence and other evidence tending to prove the legitimacy of all operations under the permit; and the liquor must be consigned in the first instance to some collector of customs, who thereafter controls it. Exporters are not required to file a 1408 bond covering their general operations, but they must file before each exportation a bond in a penal sum sufficient to cover the tax on the spirits then to be exported. Various bond forms are used for this purpose in accordance with the circumstances of the given case—547, 548, 643, 657, 658, 1459, 1460, and 1495–1498.

These bonds are desirable, generally speaking, since the business is largely in the hands of established and responsible exporting concerns and since in any other case investigation of the essential conditions is not difficult.

206. Importers

Similarly, persons who desire to import intoxicating liquors for sacramental or other permissible purposes were formerly able to do so under the National Prohibition Act by securing a permit and filing a 1408 bond. The liquors were entrusted on arrival to some collector of customs; and no one was permitted to enter them at any custom house or possess himself of them without first filing with the collector an appropriate permit. Under authority of the Willis-Campbell Act, approved November 23, 1921, the Commissioner of Internal Revenue is at present (May, 1922) permitting no importations of liquors or wines.

207. Hospitals, Sanitariums, and First-Aid Stations

Distilled spirits, wines, and certain alcoholic preparations fit for beverage purposes may be administered in bona fide hospitals or sanitariums upon prescriptions of resident physicians, when the latter believe that the use of liquor as a medicine is necessary and will afford relief.

Sanitariums devoted to the treatment of chronic

alcoholism may likewise have recourse to these beverages, "but only where the tapering-off method is used or where the dosage is steadily reduced until the patient within a reasonable time, such as four weeks, has lost the craving for alcoholic stimulants" (Regulations 60, Internal Revenue Bureau).

Industrial establishments of such magnitude as to warrant the maintenance of first-aid stations for their employees may similarly use alcohol for medicinal purposes in case of accident or other emergency.

No bonds are required in the first and the last of the foregoing cases, but sanitariums that receive alcoholic patients must file a 1408 bond. Such bonds are written freely for reputable institutions.

208. Rectifiers

Persons desiring to rectify distilled spirits or wines for any legitimate purpose may apply for a corresponding permit, stating such purpose and filing a 1408 bond. If the application is approved, the permittee may then engage in the business of rectification, paying special taxes and otherwise complying with all the requirements of Internal-Revenue law and regulations governing rectifiers. While permittees of this class may either use or sell their product, most of them handle it in a wholesale way, having authority to sell it to anyone possessed of a permit to purchase. Under present conditions collateral security or assured financial responsibility commensurate with the amount of the bond, and unexceptionable personal credentials, are underwriting essentials.

209. Transportation

Any person who legally possesses intoxicating liquor in his private dwelling and changes his permanent resi-

18

dence may have the liquor taken to his new home; and any person entitled to possess intoxicating liquor for non-beverage purposes may have any liquor so possessed taken from one place of business to another; but in all such cases the transportation must be entrusted only to carriers who have received a permit covering such transportation. These permits are granted as a matter of course to railroad, express, and steamboat carriers; and they are necessarily granted as well, though with due circumspection, to operators of trucks. The Federal Prohibition Directors reserve the right to approve the method of transportation proposed by the shipper, and they designate, as far as practicable, because of the increased security, railroads and similar carriers rather than truckmen. On the other hand, shipment by truck is permitted when the distances to be covered are short and the usual means of conveyance are deemed inadequate.

Bonds are not required from railroads, express companies, or steamship companies; but citizens holding permits to transport liquors by other means must file 1408 bonds. When small truckmen apply for such bonds—or even large ones, if not long established and known to conduct a legitimate business—an underwriter may well make haste slowly. Liquor once loaded upon a truck may or may not reach its local destination. Roads radiate in all directions, and nothing but the conscience of the truckman compels him to take the right one. The moral risk must, therefore, be good in every case; and in the absence of collateral security, there must be, also, an excellent, verified, financial statement, showing a net worth largely in excess of the amount of the bond, exclusive of the confiscatable truck.

210. Wine Manufacturers

Wines for sacramental and other specified purposes may be produced on bonded winery premises, provided a corresponding permit, accompanied by a 1408 bond, is first issued. All such wines, when removed from bonded wineries or bonded storerooms, must be tax-paid (except when withdrawn free of tax under special, specified conditions).

These bonds are required from owners of bonded wineries, and they frequently present difficult underwriting problems. In the first place, a financial hazard is clearly involved in the requirement that the taxes must be paid, with a few exceptions, when the product is removed from the bonded premises; and in the second and more important place there is an obvious and considerable moral hazard. Collateral security is frequently appropriate in the case of this class of non-beverage bonds, and thoroughgoing investigations are always in order.

211. Wine Dealers

Rabbis, ministers of the gospel, and other like persons connected with religious orders may procure wine for sacramental purposes without obtaining permits; but persons who desire to handle wine for religious use must first procure permits and furnish 1408 bonds. These bonds are quite acceptable when the applications come from persons or concerns of good standing in the community, and with an established business in this line.

212. Flavoring Extracts and Syrups

Alcohol is sometimes an ingredient of flavoring extracts and syrups, and in such cases manufacturers must procure a permit to conduct the business and file a 1408 bond. These bonds are desirable, of course, when, as frequently happens, the principal is a well-known and long-established concern; and they are likewise good when the principal, though not long established, is a concern of evident responsibility and legitimacy. Applicants for these bonds, however, who are just starting in the business requiring the bond obviously require investigation.

213. Industrial-Alcohol Bonds

Persons who desire to operate an industrial-alcohol plant must procure a permit to do so, filing with their application for the same a bond known as Internal Revenue Form 1432. This bond is conditioned for faithful compliance with all laws and Bureau regulations relating to the operation of such plants, and is written in a penal sum varying from a minimum of $1,000 to a maximum of $100,000, and sufficient within those limits to cover the tax at the rate of $2.20 per proof gallon on the quantity of alcohol producible by the plant in fifteen days' time at top speed. Rigid supervision is exercised by the Internal Revenue Bureau over industrial-alcohol plants through inspectors who watch and check operations at every stage. Where, however, a plant is so small as to make inadvisable the assignment of an officer to it for continuous duty, a meter is installed, securely enclosed and locked, to measure the output and prevent fraud.

Under the foregoing conditions industrial-alcohol bonds are deemed acceptable from principals of good business character and possessed of financial resources reasonably proportionate to the amount of business contemplated.

214. Bonded Warehouses for Industrial Alcohol

The National Prohibition Act provides that warehouses for the storage and distribution of alcohol to be used exclusively for other-than-beverage purposes may be established upon the filing of an application and bond and the issuance of a corresponding permit, at such places as the Commissioner of Internal Revenue may determine and subject to such conditions of operation as the Commissioner may by regulation prescribe. The bond referred to is issued on departmental Form 1435 in an amount not exceeding $100,000, but otherwise sufficient to cover the tax at the non-beverage rate on all alcohol produced or received during a period of thirty days. Permits are not issued for a definite term, but remain in force until voluntarily surrendered or revoked by the Commissioner; and the bond likewise contains no stated term, but continues in force "until duly cancelled."

In the case of distillery bonded warehouses established under the old Internal-Revenue laws, as well as in that of general and special bonded warehouses similarly established, the original operating bonds are not disturbed. So, too, the original warehousing bonds (Forms 80, 235, 351, and 359) covering the Internal-Revenue tax on the spirits stored in such warehouses are not disturbed, but remain in force as a rule until the expiration of the eight-year bonded period. Sometimes, however, the original warehousing bonds are cancelled and replaced with new Forms 779, 780, or 781, as the case may be, such new bonds in that event remaining in force until the spirits are removed from the warehouse.

Thefts of liquor from bonded warehouses have been numerous, and the proprietors of such warehouses were formerly held rigidly responsible for the tax on all such stolen liquor. The Willis-Campbell Act, however, approved November 23, 1921, affords relief in such cases provided that the loss occurs without the negligence, connivance, collusion, or fraud of the owner or person legally accountable for the spirits, and provided further that the claimant is not indemnified against or recompensed for the loss. This provision, of course, as well as the statutes granting relief in case of loss by leakage, casualty, etc., materially lessens the hazard involved in these bonds.

Since the operation of bonded warehouses is rigidly and comprehensively supervised by the Federal Prohibition Commissioner the opportunities for violation of the law are thought to be small. Because of this fact, and because warehouses are commonly conducted by persons or concerns of noteworthy responsibility, these bonds are regarded with favor by most underwriters.

A considerable volume of new business based upon bonded distilled spirits will soon be available for the surety companies, because the Act of Congress approved February 17, 1922, contains a provision under which the Commissioner of Internal Revenue has authority to concentrate the distilled spirits in warehouses throughout the country into a small number of secure warehouses. Regulations pursuant to this provision of law have been prepared by the Internal Revenue Bureau, and when approved by the Department the Commissioner will proceed to bring about such concentration. The proprietors of the warehouses designated will doubtless be required to give bonds as warehousemen, and in addition the persons responsible for the tax will be required to give bonds covering the Internal-Revenue tax.

215. Plants for Denatured Alcohol

Ethyl alcohol to which something has been added that makes it unfit for internal administration is known as "denatured alcohol." It is used only in the arts and industries. Alcohol may be withdrawn free of tax for denaturation in an approved plant; but before a plant can be approved its operator must qualify by filing a bond on Internal Revenue Form 1462 and procuring a permit. Denaturing plants are supervised rigidly by the Internal-Revenue authorities. Each plant is under the joint control of the owner and the Internal-Revenue officer assigned to it, and no one is permitted to enter any plant building unless the officer is present. The buildings are kept securely locked except when the plant is in operation and the revenue officer is present. The safeguards against any misuse of the alcohol received at the plant or other violation of law are numerous and elaborate.

The amount of the bond covering a denaturing plant is based upon the quantity of alcohol withdrawn for use in the business during a period of thirty days plus the quantity remaining on hand and unused. The bonds may never be less than $10,000, and they are often much more (though never more than $100,000), because the plants covered are frequently operated by persons engaged in manufacturing industrial alcohol upon a big scale. If the principals bonded are reputable business houses, and if their financial statement shows a net worth reasonably commensurate with their scale of operations, the bonds may be deemed desirable.

216. Specially Denatured Alcohol

Alcohol that has been denatured in accordance with certain fixed formulae prescribed by the Internal Revenue Bureau is known as "completely denatured alcohol." It is injurious to the human system, and every package of it containing less than five gallons sold or offered for sale must carry a label showing the word "POISON" in large letters and in red ink, under the skull-and-bones symbol. No bond is required from persons who handle

completely denatured alcohol, nor need they render any
account of alcohol bought, sold, or used. If, however,
they recover any alcohol for reuse, a 1480 bond must be
filed. When alcohol is not *completely* denatured, it is
known as "specially denatured alcohol," and may be
obtained and used only upon the filing of a bond and the
issuance of a permit. Dealers in specially denatured
alcohol must file bonds, ranging in amount from $10,000
to $100,000, in accordance with the quantity of dena-
tured alcohol handled, written on Internal Revenue Form
1475. Manufacturers who use specially denatured alcohol—manufacturers of toilet articles, for example—must
file bonds ranging in amount from $500 up to $100,000
written on Internal Revenue Form 1480.

These bonds guarantee compliance with the National
Prohibition Law and Regulations made pursuant thereto,
and are also conditioned for the payment, by the principals, at the rate of $4.50 per wine gallon, of any de-
natured alcohol unlawfully used or unaccounted for, as
well as for the payment of all penalties and fines. Bonds
executed on Form 1480 have no stated term, but remain
in force "until cancelled or revoked."

These bonds are deemed comparatively good business
because of the non-beverage character of the product
handled, and they are written rather freely for principals
of fair financial and good personal standing.

217. Use of Alcohol by Hospitals, Colleges, etc.

Alcohol may be withdrawn, under regulations, from
any industrial plant or bonded warehouse, tax-free, for
the use of hospitals or sanitariums, institutions of learning, laboratories engaged exclusively in scientific research, and the like. In all such cases, however, the
privileged licensees must first file bonds on Internal

Revenue Form 1448 and procure permits. These bonds are naturally deemed highly desirable. Unless, however, as would usually be the case, the principal is a well-known institution, care must be taken to verify the presumed regularity of the proceeding.

218. Duration of Liability

Hardly any prohibition bonds have a stated term of liability, and in order to ascertain when a bond will terminate it is necessary to consider the duration of the permit with which the bond is concerned. Sometimes permits are granted for an indefinite period—they continue to be valid unless and until revoked; and in such cases apparently the bond will follow the permit as regards the term of liability. In other cases a permit is granted for a definite term—three years, say—and at the end of such period the bond automatically terminates as to future acts of the permittee. The latter, presumably, if he remains in a business requiring a bond, will obtain a new permit and file a fresh bond at the end of the period. Where the accompanying bond is written on Internal Revenue Form 1408, permits issued on and prior to August 31 of any year expire at the end of such year, while permits issued between August 31 and the beginning of the following year remain valid until the end of the following year. Permittees must apply for renewals of their permits before October 1 of the year in which their permits expire; but they may continue operations under the old permit until a decision is reached regarding a renewal, in case such decision is delayed beyond the end of the year. No new bond need be filed with the application for renewal, if a satisfactory bond, still in force, has already been filed and approved. Although Form 1408 makes no mention of any term, by regulation such bonds "remain in force and effect three years from the date of execution." They would, however, necessarily terminate as to future acts of the permittee upon revocation of the latter's permit. All permits are, of course, non-transferable; and any permit may be revoked in whole or in part by the Commissioner at any time, if the latter, "after proper hearing," concludes that the terms of the permit have been violated. While none of these prohibition bonds contains a provision under which the surety has a right to cancel, the Commissioner would presumably revoke a permit, and thus automatically cancel the bond as to future breaches, if the surety should submit to the Commissioner, at a hearing, reasonable proof of violations of the law on the part of the permittee.

219. Liens on Plants and Warehouses

The proprietor of an industrial-alcohol plant or of a bonded warehouse not included in such plant must either own in fee, unincumbered by any mortgage, judgment, or other lien, the tract of land on which the plant or warehouse is situated; or must file with the Collector the written consent of the owner of the fee and of any mortgagee, judgment creditor, or other lienor that the premises may be used in the way contemplated, that the lien of the United States for taxes and penalties shall have priority over any such mortgage, judgment, or other incumbrance, and that in case of forfeiture the title to the premises shall vest in the United States, unclouded by any such mortgage, judgment, or other incumbrance. Since in some cases (under circumstances easily foreseeable) the proprietor of a plant cannot obtain the written consents referred to, there is a further provision of law under which the Commissioner, if convinced of the impracticability of the proprietor's procuring such consents, may waive them and accept in lieu thereof an indemnity bond in a penal sum equal to the value of the property involved.

This bond is obviously one not to be lightly regarded. Complete information regarding all the circumstances that make the bond necessary, financial statements, and sometimes collateral security are in order.

CHAPTER XVI

LICENSE AND PERMIT BONDS

220. When Required in General

The federal government and the several states to some extent, and towns and cities to a large extent, require persons who wish to engage in certain kinds of business (auctioneers, junk-dealers, and pawnbrokers, for example), or to do certain things (e.g., to excavate a street, place building material on sidewalks, install a swinging sign), first to file a license bond covering the given business or a permit bond authorizing the given act. This is an interesting and somewhat important field of suretyship, as a multitude of standard bonds of this class have long been in existence, and as new varieties are all the time appearing. To list them all would be like cataloguing the Homeric ships. They range from grave to gay, from lively to severe. Embalmers, for example, and handlers of unclaimed dead bodies must give bond in certain jurisdictions. So, in other places, must collectors of birds, nests, and eggs; oyster- and clam-dredgers; manufacturers and vendors of lightning rods; carriers of concealed weapons; dealers in hog-cholera serum; practicers of the "art, business or profession of Fortune Telling," the bond in the last instance indemnifying patrons for losses due to "theft or other unfair dealing" upon the part of the licensee. In some states ministers must be bonded before they can lawfully solemnize marriages (as if the subjects were not taking chances enough anyway!). In one place at least hat-cleaners must give a bond conditioned that they will "faithfully observe the provisions of the charter and ordinances" of the city (and Tony, no doubt, sits up nights pondering the said provisions, lest he inadvertently breach his bond).

Many kinds of license and permit bonds are written upon an insurance basis, with little or no investigation of the persons bonded; but other kinds are highly hazardous. A bond covering a licensed pilot, for example, may be completely forfeited through a collision resulting from the pilot's negligence. Claims have been numerous under auctioneers' bonds. The bond required by many cities from contractors who use in their work powder, dynamite, nitroglycerine, and similar erratic substances might be said, by a person not fit to be trusted with words, to have explosive qualities.

Most kinds of license and permit bonds commonly called for are cited in the Appendix; and a few of the more important and difficult classes are treated in the following sections (221–229).

221. Jitney Bonds

Many cities have passed regulatory ordinances prescribing the conditions under which jitney cars may be operated, and requiring drivers of such vehicles to file a surety bond with some designated public official before beginning business. The terms of these bonds vary in different places, but usually they are conditioned for compliance with traffic regulations and for the indemnification of the city and the payment of damages for injury to persons or property. The bonds are required in the interest of the public, and they are really nothing but accident policies furnished by benevolent surety companies to everybody luckless enough to get in the way of the Juggernaut jitneys.

Many thousands of jitney cars are now in operation,

and agents receive numerous applications for these bonds. While it is obvious that the bonds are highly hazardous, and that they could never be issued upon the usual basis of suretyship—that is, at a low service-charge premium and upon the assumption that the principal will be able to satisfy any claims—yet at the exceedingly high rates now charged (20 per cent, for example, in some cases for a single car), it would seem that careful underwriters ought to be able to write the business at a profit. Evidently the Rating Bureau has made up its tariff for these bonds upon the theory that all losses must be paid out of premium earnings. The surety, however, will still have a claim against its principal for the full amount of any losses sustained under the bond; and prudent underwriters, notwithstanding the high premium obtained, will hardly deem these bonds acceptable unless the principal is of excellent personal, and of at least fair financial, standing.

The Manual authorizes an alternative and much lower rate for these bonds when the principal protects its surety with collateral security to the full amount of the bond. The charge in such cases is only 1 per cent per annum upon the penalty of the bond, regardless of the number of cars covered. Jitney-car owners who are in a position to deposit security in this way will save a large amount of money. Conservative underwriters much prefer to issue the bond upon this basis, even in the case of presumably responsible principals, and urge their agents so to arrange the matter when that is at all possible.

The 1 per cent rate obtainable when full security is deposited with the surety is deemed to be in order likewise (by a ruling of the Rating Bureau) when a principal, instead of depositing collateral, protects his surety by taking out liability insurance. This latter protection, however, seems hardly the equivalent of security, and some companies are unwilling to write jitney bonds upon this basis unless the other incidents of the risk are especially favorable.

222. Permit Bonds for Oil and Gas Prospectors

Under the Federal Act of February 25, 1920 (Public No. 146), permittees may prospect for oil and gas on allotments of government land for a period of two years following the date of the permit. The application for such a permit must be accompanied by a bond of $1,000 guaranteeing that the prospecting operations will be conducted in accordance with approved methods; that all proper precautions will be exercised to prevent the waste of any oil or gas developed; and that water will not be allowed to enter the wells drilled by the prospector to such an extent that the oil, sand, or oil-bearing strata will be injured.

These bonds are less dangerous than they might at first blush seem to be, because drilling operations have been pretty well standardized, and only in an exceptional instance could damage be done to the oil strata. In something like 999 cases out of 1,000, of course, the only oil that the test well will even remotely approach will be that contained in the engine operating the drill. These bonds, therefore, are issued pretty freely by most underwriters for applicants experienced in oil prospecting and of reasonable financial responsibility.

223. Boxing Licenses

In some places athletic clubs and similar bodies desirous of holding boxing contests must first obtain permits to do so and file bonds conditioned for the payment to the state of some percentage of the gross receipts and for compliance in other respects with the law governing such exhibitions. While these bonds seem not particularly hazardous when given in behalf of reputable organizations, it is necessary, nevertheless, to have either full collateral security or unexceptionable indemnity. The latter will serve the purpose in the case of the high-grade clubs that frequently sponser these affairs; and there is ordinarily no difficulty in obtaining the indemnity of business men of character and responsibility connected with the clubs. Sometimes the laws are rather drastic, providing for forfeitures to the state of substantial amounts for each case of violation; and the licenses may run for a year, the bond then covering all such contests held within the twelvemonth. It is quite essential, therefore, that absolutely good indemnity be procured in the absence of collateral.

224. Commission Merchants

Some states require commission merchants to give a bond as a condition precedent to their conducting their business. The bond virtually runs in favor of the public and in effect guarantees that the commission merchant will deal honestly with his patrons. Though these bonds are largely credit risks, the experience of the companies with them has been better than antecedent reasoning might lead one to expect; and most underwriters issue them without security in moderate amounts for concerns of good business standing.

225. "Blue-Sky Law" Bonds

Thirty-seven states have passed laws intended to protect investors by stopping the sale of stock in "fly-by-night concerns, visionary oil wells, distant gold mines, and other like fraudulent exploitations"; and many of the states require dealers in securities to give bonds conditioned for compliance with such laws. While the laws vary greatly in the several states, with corresponding gradations of risk in the bonds, yet the hazard is abnormally high in almost all cases. Full collateral security is frequently deemed a condition precedent to the issuance of these bonds, though they are sometimes given without security in behalf of long-established and highly responsible bankers.

226. Steamship Agents

Many states have enacted salutary laws requiring people who sell tickets to foreign countries to give a bond that virtually guarantees honest dealings with the public on the part of such people. These steamship agents commonly act as bankers, also, and receive large sums of money from foreigners here for transmission to relatives in the fatherland; and the bonds referred to are usually broad enough to cover the agents in these latter transactions. The bonds are dangerous, because they run in favor of the public and may be sued upon by "anyone aggrieved," and particularly because, while theoretically only fidelity instruments, they amount in practice to much more than that. Most underwriters deem these bonds issuable only in connection with full collateral security.

227. Insurance-Company State-License Bonds

Some states require insurance companies desiring to do business therein to give a bond conditioned for the payment of taxes, assessments, and so forth. These bonds are not deemed particularly hazardous, and they are issued by most underwriters in behalf of any company of good repute and fair financial standing.

19

Some states, however, go a long step beyond this, and require insurance companies to give a bond conditioned sometimes for the payment of all claims, whenever made, based upon their policies issued within the given state during the term of the bond (one year, say) and sometimes for the payment of claims arising within such term. These bonds thus in effect guarantee the solvency of the bonding companies, in the one case as to all policies issued within the state during the term of the bond, and in the other case as to all claims accruing upon such policies within such period. While the latter form of bond is perhaps less formidable than the other, both are obviously financial guarantees with highly disquieting possibilities. In a few cases, indeed, the bond embraces both kinds of liability. Even if the active term of the bond be short (and in some cases no term is stated in the prescribed form of bond), *liability* may not be terminated for many years (cf. compensation claims resulting in losses represented by annual payments to a minor for a long term of years). Underwriting guidance is hard to give because so much depends upon the form of bond required in the given case, upon the nature of the business transacted by the bonded company (fire, life, accident, compensation, etc.), and particularly, of course, upon the experience, management, and general responsibility of the principal. In numerous cases the conditions are such that most underwriters are unwilling to provide the suretyship without full security.

228. Cigarette Dealers

Cigarettes were manufactured in the United States in 1921 in the aggregate quantity of 51,844,378,478. This was nearly fifty-two billion too many in the confident judgment of many people, and a considerable number of states have enacted laws requiring persons who wish to sell cigarettes to procure permits to do so and furnish bonds conditioned for compliance with the said laws and for the payment of the taxes, fines, penalties, and costs provided for therein.   The bond usually reads like this:

> Know all men by these presents: That we, Dopeful Drugsmith, as principal, and the Straightlaced Surety Company, as surety, are held and firmly bound unto the People of the State of Elysium in the sum of five hundred dollars, for the payment of which well and truly to be made and performed, we and each of us do hereby bind ourselves, jointly and severally, by these presents.
>
> The condition of this obligation is such that whereas Dopeful Drugsmith has obtained from the City of Bluelaws permission to keep and sell cigarettes, cheroots, and small cigars at No. 23 Whitelight Avenue:
>
> Now, if the said Dopeful Drugsmith shall well and truly pay to all persons all damages which they may sustain, either in person or property or means of support, by reason of the said Dopeful Drugsmith's selling or giving away cigarettes, cheroots, and small cigars, then and in that case this obligation to be void; otherwise to remain in full force, virtue, and effect. .

Names and locations have been disguised above (you would never have guessed it), but otherwise the text follows the official bond form, word for word.

Cigarette bonds are commonly of small amount, and they are written pretty freely by most companies in behalf of druggists, variety stores, and the like.   While the condition of the bond seems easily breachable (selling to minors, for example), it is thought that the experience of the companies in this line has so far been favorable.

229. Milk-Handlers' License Bonds

Extensive distributors of milk, and those who use it in large quantities for canning and manufacturing purposes, commonly settle their bills with farmers for milk on a monthly basis.   In some states, notably New York and Vermont, these milk-handlers must obtain a license to conduct their business, and must file a bond guaranteeing prompt payment of the farmers' monthly bills.   The amount of the bond is fixed by state authorities in accordance with the applicant's preceding year's business. It seems probable that more states will ultimately enact legislation of this character.

This bond amounts, of course, to a direct financial guarantee, and is thus writable, without security, only where the conditions are such that a bank would lend the principal, upon the latter's long-term note, without collateral, the sum represented by the penalty of the bond.   Not even that, indeed, is quite true, because a bank would not ordinarily lend the milk dealer any such amount unless he kept a substantial deposit with it, and because in various ways a bank is always in a better position than a surety company to protect itself, to some extent at least, when a borrower gets into trouble. Full collateral security is without doubt quite essential when the principals are unseasoned and unrated or inadequately rated; and at least partial security would seem to be in order even in the case of large concerns long established and well rated by the commercial agencies.   The bonds are frequently big and the premium fund is small (that is, comparatively few bonds are called for), and a single large loss would absorb a company's entire revenue from this source for a long period.

230. Custom-House Bonds

While an interesting and informative chapter might be written about the bonds that importers must give in connection with the entry at custom houses of merchandise received from foreign countries, I refrain from attempting to write the chapter, partly because other subjects seem more entitled to my limited space, and especially because the average surety agent rarely in practice has anything to do with customs bonds. They are almost always cared for by the brokers whom importers employ to attend to all the intricate and highly technical details of custom-house practice. These brokers, though they commonly have nothing otherwise to do with the surety or insurance business, are sometimes empowered by surety companies to issue themselves the custom-house bonds required by their clients; and in other cases they have close relations with bonding companies that enable them to procure promptly, and without the aid of regular surety agents, such bonds as they need in their business.

Only a minute fraction of the numerous custom-house bonds issued daily present underwriting difficulties, the vast bulk of the business being exceptionally safe. This is so partly because the rigid rules of the customs service make the risk of loss or trouble almost negligible, and partly because the principals upon the bonds are usually business concerns of ample responsibility. A few classes of bonds, however, must be handled with circumspection.

Warehouse bonds, for example, catalogue number 7555, have frequently caused annoyance and sometimes loss to the surety companies. The collector's indemnity bond, catalogue number 7581, has cost the companies a lot of money in the last two or three years, particularly in the Puget Sound region, where fraudulent manipulation of bills of lading has been rife. Similarly bond number 7563, Temporary Importation, has proved troublesome in practice: I once had a herd of performing elephants on my hands because of that bond, my other duties making it inconvenient for me at the moment to drive them across the border and thus satisfy the condition of the bond.

In the Appendix, under appropriate headings, I include most of the custom-house bonds commonly called for, and indicate roughly in each case my appraisement of the underwriting questions involved.

CHAPTER XVII

SPECIAL CLASSES OF SURETY BONDS

231. Financial Guarantees

When I told an agent one day that I felt unable to issue a certain bond without collateral security because it was a "financial guarantee," he asked me what I meant by that and said that every bond in his opinion was a financial guarantee. The agent was right—agents are always right, you know (except, of course, when they are wrong) —and it is true that in a certain sense virtually all surety bonds (as distinguished from fidelity bonds) are conditioned upon the ability of the principal to meet his financial obligations in connection with a given trust or contract or action at law. What surety underwriters mean, however, when they talk about a financial guarantee, is an instrument that binds the bonding company to pay out immediately in cash, upon proper demand, a definite and known sum of money in case the principal, upon whom demand is first or simultaneously made, fails to pay it. A contract bond, for example, is not in this sense a financial guarantee, because if the principal defaults in such a case the surety company is not required to pay anything to the obligee, but only to complete the contract (unless, indeed, it prefers to pay the full penalty of the bond).

Surety underwriting is far from an exact science, and I have never been able any way to do more than sense, as through a glass darkly, a faint image of the outer edge of a few isolated facts; but I venture the opinion nevertheless that one of the laws of the science, when it comes to be fully developed, will read, "No bond amount-

ing to a pure financial guarantee should be written without full collateral security." Such a law ought to be,
and more and more it is coming to be, of universal and
invariable validity; but one must take the surety world
as one finds it, namely, full of vigorous competitors, and
in practice it is sometimes not possible to procure collateral security.

232. Lenders' or Mechanics' Lien Bonds

In many states a lien for labor or material is superior
to the lien of a mortgage, even though the latter has been
recorded before the labor and material has been furnished,
and of course before the mechanics' lien has been filed.
In such jurisdictions one who lends money to be used in
realty improvements will naturally seek protection
against the endangering of his security by mechanics'
liens. As loans are invariably based upon the value of
the completed project, lenders' bonds commonly guarantee, also, the completion of the work. While such
bonds were not often required in the days of private
lending and close personal relationship between borrower
and lender, they are becoming increasingly common now
that lending is to a large extent centralized in financial
institutions. The bonds are so clearly warranted and
even necessitated by the situation described that agents
will find it easy to educate lenders into the habitual use
of the bond. The premiums are frequently large.

The interest of the applicant in the proposed improvement is of prime importance from the underwriting
point of view. A person building a home for himself is
usually a desirable risk, because as a rule he has his heart
as well as his accumulated savings in the project, and
will exhaust every resource to protect his equity. Speculative builders, on the other hand, whose only interest in

the work is the possible profit to be made from a quick sale, have been a prolific source of loss to the underwriters of these bonds. Such builders rarely have more than the smallest permissible equity in the property, are much given to overtrading, and are likely to decamp if a turn in the market indicates a probable loss.

An applicant for one of these bonds must, of course, be of excellent personal reputation; one whose statement of his affairs may be relied upon; and one who may be trusted to use the proceeds of the loan only for the project on which the loan is made. He must furnish convincing evidence that the work can be completed for a stipulated sum, either in the form of a contract with a reputable contractor for the whole job, or of estimates for various parts of the work that collectively will cover the finished building. He must then show that he has on hand, already available for the project, or surely to be available before needed, a sum which, together with the proceeds of the loan, will equal about 110 per cent of the contemplated cost of the work. This extra 10 per cent is only a reasonably safe margin for the amount by which the actual cost of building is likely to exceed preliminary estimates.

In the case of large risks and border-line cases underwriters will sometimes make acceptable an otherwise rejectable bond by assuming control over the entire building fund and having the contractor who is to do the work bonded in favor of the applicant and themselves as interests may appear. As a rule, however, a risk requiring these safeguards is of doubtful acceptability at best.

233. Open-Estate Bonds

If the personal property left by a decedent is insufficient to pay his debts, his real estate (if there be any) must be used for that purpose; and in most jurisdictions until all the debts are paid they constitute a lien against the real estate. When, therefore, it is desired to sell or to mortgage the realty of a decedent before the estate has been fully administered, and before the expiration of the period within which creditors may prove their claims against the estate, the prospective buyer or mortgagee may reasonably demand a bond guaranteeing that his title to or lien upon the real estate will not be impaired by subsequently proven debts against the decedent unpayable out of the personalty. .

In this as in many other surety problems the underwriter considers first and foremost the responsibility of his principal, and after that the chance that the principal will ever be called upon to pay a claim provable under the bond. If the latter seems likely, full collateral security is in order, even in the case of strong principals; while if the chance of loss seems remote, the bond may be written without security in behalf of a principal sufficiently responsible to take care of any unexpected loss. In dealing with open-estate bonds, accordingly, the underwriter considers first the financial responsibility and general credit standing of his principal, and then he tries to ascertain what the likelihood is that the personal property of the decedent will not suffice to pay the debts of the estate.

The principal will generally be someone interested in the estate—some legatee, heir, or next of kin—who is anxious to anticipate the slow settlement of the estate, or who desires to take advantage of a favorable opportunity to sell the realty. If he is financially responsible in an amount greatly exceeding the amount of the bond, irrespective of any interest that he may have in the estate (because it must be assumed for underwriting purposes, at this stage of the question, that the realty will be needed for debt-paying purposes, and that the principal's interest in the estate may turn out to be of slight value), the bond may be written without security, provided the situation seems favorable from the other point of view considered in the next paragraph. If, however, the principal is not possessed of financial resources to the extent described, collateral security is in order whether or not the risk seems acceptable in the other respect.

As for this second, highly important point, it is necessary, of course, to know, with as much particularity as possible, what the condition of the decedent's estate is when the application for the bond is made—how far debts have already been filed and proved, what personal property is available to meet them, whether or not any additional debts are known or suspected, how far, if at all, publication of notice to creditors has been made in newspapers, and so on; and full information must likewise be obtained regarding the decedent's character, mode of living, general station in life, and financial and personal reputation. All these considerations clearly have a bearing upon the question of whether or not unexpected debts are likely to turn up and perhaps precipitate a breach of the bond. If it seems at all likely that the estate will prove to be insolvent, or if the character of the decedent and the circumstances of his life do not exclude the idea of unexpected and unpleasant developments in the administration of the estate, collateral security should be made a condition precedent to the execution of the bond, whether or not the principal is presumed to be a person of responsibility.

In practice open-estate bonds are frequently writable without security, because both the prime underwriting factors described frequently present, upon investigation,

only favorable aspects; that is to say, the principal is
often a man of high personal and financial standing, and
the decedent has often led a worthy and well-ordered
life and has left an estate correspondingly valuable and
stable.

234. Guarantee of Quality of Merchandise

Many manufacturers, in their advertising matter and
elsewhere, make clear-cut statements about the quality
and serviceability of their products, and agree to replace
any defective merchandise or otherwise satisfy buyers;
and in recent years the practice has grown up of bulwark-
ing such statements and guarantees with corporate
surety bonds. A manufacturer of roofing material, for
example, will give to every patron a bond guaranteeing
that the material will last so many years; a manufacturer
of automobile tires will furnish to every purchaser a bond
guaranteeing that the tire will run 8,000 or some other
number of miles; and so on. These bonds serve a useful
purpose in the marketing of dependable merchandise,
and it seems probable that they will become increasingly
common.

Where such a bond is unlimited in time or in liability
few underwriters would write it except perhaps in behalf
of extraordinarily responsible principals. In most cases
fortunately a time limit of liability may easily be stipulated and is indeed consistent with the principal's own
representations regarding his product. The limitation
as to maximum liability is not so easy to handle, since
the value of the bond is greatly impaired, from the public
point of view, if a lump sum is named that must care for
all the demands of all possible claimants. Sometimes
such a bond will be accepted, one clause in the instrument providing that claims shall be paid in accordance

with the priority of their filing with the surety company and another one providing that the aggregate maximum liability of the surety shall be only so many thousand dollars (cf. section 42). Such a bond is obviously far less attractive to a prospective principal than one holding out an unqualified guarantee in a named amount, even if that amount be comparatively small, to all buyers of the product in question. In practice surety companies not infrequently find themselves able to write this latter unlimited form of bond, partly because the prospect of serious claims seems remote, and especially because the principals are concerns of high standing and responsibility in the business world.

235. Aliens' Admission Bonds

Under certain conditions aliens desiring to enter the United States must file bonds before they will be released at the port of entry. These bonds are of various kinds. If the alien is permanently defective, mentally or physically, he is not permitted to enter the country at all; but if the defect is judged to be temporary, he is sometimes permitted to enter upon his filing a bond guaranteeing that he will receive specified treatment and will not become a public charge during his stay in the country. In the case of alien minors, bonds must almost invariably be filed guaranteeing that they will not become public charges, and that they will be kept at school until they are sixteen years of age. Sometimes an alien is admitted temporarily for some special purpose, and a bond required guaranteeing that he will depart from the country within a stipulated period. Alien bonds customarily run from $500 to $2,000.

That these bonds are dangerous and generally unattractive seems reasonably clear from a mere description of them; but it may not be equally apparent that they are also, in practice, expensively troublesome and vexatious. A little experience with them, however, wonderfully clarifies an underwriter's vision; and after he has received a few official communications from the authorities in Washington, couched in terms more summary than diplomatic, and demanding information and explanations, with ominous implications between the lines, he has clear-cut ideas as to what he will do with the next application for an alien bond. The government rightly insists that the conditions under which the alien is permitted to reside here be fulfilled rigidly, and that it receive frequent and satisfactory assurances of such fulfillment; and if, as often happens, the relatives or friends of the alien fail to file proper reports, the surety company must procure in some way, if it can, the necessary information and see to it that the information is what it ought to be.

While the circumstances are occasionally such that alien bonds can be written upon indemnity alone, in a large majority of cases full collateral security is deemed by most underwriters a *sine qua non*. Each case is a law unto itself, and a good deal depends upon the age and apparent prospects of the alien and upon the character, responsibility, and station in life of his or her sponsors. In practice, as stated, the conditions ordinarily indicate (in medical parlance) full collateral.

236. Freight-Charge Bonds

As a convenience to both the railroads and their patrons, shippers and receivers of merchandise in large quantities are permitted to settle freight bills on a monthly basis, provided a bond is filed with the transportation company guaranteeing prompt payment of

such bills. These bonds amount, of course, to a direct
financial guarantee, and in strict underwriting theory
they would be issuable only upon full security. As a
matter of fact they are continually written without
security. This comes about partly from the circumstance that large shippers are ordinarily long-established
and highly rated concerns, partly because there is a big
volume of the business, and partly because the bonds are
relatively small—are not often so large as to give an im-
aginative underwriter cold shivers of apprehension.
New concerns, however, as well as old ones of moderate-
or-less financial weight, cannot ordinarily obtain this
suretyship without putting up full security.

237. Tax-Abatement Bonds

The amount due from a tax-payer upon a given year's
income or as an excess-profits tax is sometimes made by
the Treasury Department altogether too high in the
judgment of the tax-payer; and under such conditions
the latter is permitted to follow either of two courses—
he may pay the tax as assessed, and simultaneously file
a claim for a refund; or he may pay only the part, if any,
of the tax assessed that he deems just, and may file a
bond as to the remainder conditioned that he will pay
such remainder in case it is ultimately found to be due.
In deciding how to exercise his option the tax-payer must
do some close figuring, because if he pays in full and his
claim is afterward sustained, he loses all interest on the
money so tied up during the long period (several years
perhaps) of adjudication, while if he loses his contention,
he must pay the government interest at the rate of 1
per cent a month on the amount finally found to be
proper, from the date when the tax was originally levied
up to the date of payment. It behooves the tax-payer,

therefore, to compare the cost of the bond with the possible loss of interest, and especially to consider what his chances are of defeating the government's claim. In practice, in numerous cases, the solution of this intricate combination of mathematical and judicial puzzles is found in the filing of a bond.

These risks are obviously hazardous in a marked degree, since they are financial guarantees pure and simple, amounting in substance to an endorsement by the surety of the principal's note for the amount of the bond. It is not a case, moreover, where the underwriter can give much weight to the possibility that the note may never mature. Although the principal and the agent frequently have great confidence in the soundness of the tax-payer's contention and expect a correspondingly happy result of the adjudication, the underwriter cannot prudently be anything but darkly pessimistic in that respect; and instead of assuming, as the light-hearted agent urges, that the tax will be abated, he will assume, if he knows his business, exactly the reverse.

One important underwriting point concerned with these risks is that Sections 3466 and 3468 of the Revised Statutes apparently give the United States and sureties priority over ordinary creditors in the event of a tax-payer's insolvency.

It is a regrettable feature of these bonds that an early termination of liability cannot be expected. While some of the smaller cases are disposed of quickly, the government is years behind in its tax-abatement claim work, and in many cases liability under these bonds is certain to continue for several years. Such a state of things is, of course, highly undesirable from the viewpoint of the surety, since a principal abundantly responsible when the bond is issued may be quite unable to pay the tax when it is ultimately found valid years afterward.

While some tax-abatement bonds are deemed by most companies writable without security for long-established, highly rated, and thoroughly responsible concerns, in general full collateral security is thought to be necessary when this suretyship is provided.

Section 250 (f) of the Revenue Act of 1921 gives a taxpayer under certain conditions additional time (eighteen months at most) in which to pay a part of the amount due, and a bond may be required conditioned for such payment. This bond should be distinguished from the tax-abatement bond proper considered above, because it is decidedly more hazardous than that. In this latter case there is no chance that the principal on the bond will *never* have to pay any amount—he will always have to pay, the indebtedness being admitted at the start; and it is not a good sign, of course, that the principal is willing or forced to pay the heavy interest charged by the government (8 per cent) in addition to the bond premium, for the sake of postponing for a few months the inevitable outlay.

238. Refunding Bonds

The heirs, legatees, and next of kin of a decedent may share in such decedent's estate, of course, only if the estate proves to be solvent. All valid debts, duly proved, rank ahead of their claims, naturally, and must be paid, out of the personal property first, and, when that is exhausted, out of the real estate. It follows that an executor or an administrator cannot properly pay one of these presumptive beneficiaries his or her share of the estate until all claims against the estate have been received and proved (or at least until all creditors have had

20

an opportunity to prove their claims) and found not to exceed in the aggregate such an amount as will still permit the contemplated distribution. Pending the settlement of an estate, and before the executor or administrator is ready to make a distribution of the net assets thereof, someone presumably entitled to a share of such assets may desire to anticipate the slow administration of the estate and obtain such share or some part of it before it is absolutely certain that the debts of the estate will not render impracticable any such distribution, and at all events before the executor or administrator is under any sort of obligation, legal or moral, to pay the share.

It continually happens that such payments are known in advance to involve only slight risk of injury to the interests of creditors and other beneficiaries, because in a multitude of cases the decedents' lives have been so well ordered, and everything about the estate looks so satisfactory and normal, as to make it highly improbable, some time before the distribution of net assets is strictly permissible, that any untoward results would follow an anticipatory distribution in some given case. When, therefore, the entire situation indicates the safety and propriety of doing so, the court will permit a beneficiary to receive early recognition, provided a bond is filed conditioned for the return by the recipient of any such advance in case unexpected subsequent developments show the amount, or some part of it, not to be due. These "refunding bonds," as they are called, are quite common, and are well regarded as a class by surety companies.

The foregoing description of the risk shows pretty clearly, perhaps, the points of hazard that an underwriter must keep in mind in handling these bonds. Here, as almost everywhere, the character and financial responsibility of the principal are the first things to be thought of; and while, of the two, character may be more important than the other, it is certain that these risks cannot be safely underwritten upon the basis of character only. Unless the principal is possessed of financial resources, outside of the windfall from the estate, such as will enable him to refund the advance in case of need, the bonds should be written only upon collateral security or excellent indemnity, or upon condition that the amount paid be made subject to the joint control of the surety. This last expedient is sometimes not practicable, because the principal, if he cannot use the money, may prefer to let it rest and bide his time. Occasionally, however, the principal is willing to use the money in a way that is satisfactory to the surety company. One thing in favor of the joint-control device is the fact that the fund usually will not be tied up long—it can be released as soon as the claim-filing period has terminated, and the estate is otherwise ready for distribution.

In no case, of course, even in that of an exceptionally responsible principal, would an underwriter care to issue a refunding bond without collateral security, if the solvency of the estate seemed at all open to doubt. It is necessary to have the fullest possible information regarding that aspect of the risk—what the assets of the estate are, on the one hand, and, on the other, what its liabilities are as developed to date. This latter side of the account must be investigated with the utmost care, and searching inquiry must be made as to how far debts have already been filed and proved, what personal property is available to meet them, whether or not any additional debts are known or suspected, how far, if at all, publication of notice to creditors has been made in newspapers, etc.

Although in some cases, as indicated, refunding bonds are not prudently writable without collateral security or an equivalent indemnity agreement (though the latter is never *quite* the equivalent of security), yet in practice favorable conditions so largely preponderate that these bonds are continually issued upon the responsibility of the principal alone.

239. Bankers' Trust-Receipt Bonds

Banks are all the time making loans upon the security of warehouse receipts and similar documents evidencing the title to merchandise. The borrowers have frequent occasion to change such collateral and to substitute for the goods originally pledged and sold merchandise freshly purchased. Since it sometimes greatly serves the convenience of the borrower to receive from his bank the pledged receipt before the document representing the new collateral is in hand, a custom has grown up in many cities whereby the bank delivers to its borrowers of this class every day such receipts as may be called for by them, upon trust that either equivalent collateral or the proceeds of the sold merchandise will be promptly delivered to the bank. To meet the situation thus arising a bond of indemnity against a breach of the trust described is procurable from some companies. The bond covers loans made to any of the bank's regular borrowers as listed in a schedule forming a part of the bond, and is written at the outset in a penalty of one-tenth of the bank's annual aggregate collateral loans to all such scheduled borrowers, with a provision for an additional premium in case the actual loans exceed the estimated amount.

While these bonds have been written for some years now by a number of companies with fair results, the hazard involved seems considerable, and the chance of startling losses under conditions readily conceivable seems not altogether remote. It is true that theoretically only a fidelity hazard is involved, and it is likewise true that no harm can come to the surety, unless the principal is guilty of the grossest bad faith. In practice, however, risks of this character are likely to degenerate into something closely akin to credit risks; and these bankers' indemnity bonds particularly bear in certain aspects disquieting resemblance to assigned-accounts bonds (cf. section 47). Notwithstanding, therefore, the normally preponderant fidelity content of the risk, principals upon these bonds are hardly acceptable unless, in addition to high personal character and business reputation, they are possessed of financial resources bearing a reasonable relation to the amount of suretyship expected; and in practice, as might be expected, bankers make loans freely, upon the basis of the full security provided, to borrowers unable to qualify as surety principals in accordance with the foregoing financial requirement.

240. Lost-Instrument Bonds

When savings-bank books, certified checks, stock certificates, and the like are lost, destroyed, or stolen, the embarrassing situation so created may often be relieved by the giving of a bond conditioned to indemnify the bank or other obligee against any damage that it may sustain by reason of the reissuance of the lost instrument. Bonds of this type were rather unusual not so long ago, and because of their conditionless form and unlimited term were looked upon with deep respect by most companies; but the enormous increase in recent years in the number of losable instruments and resultant demand for bonds has familiarized underwriters with the hazard and put them less in awe of it. Not all of us are so careless as was the passenger who could not find his ticket, and who, when the conductor impatiently suggested that he could not have lost it, protested, "Ugh! You don't know me. I could lose a bass drum"; but all of us who handle securities habitually have occasion sooner or later to secure lost-instrument bonds. They are much in demand now and are written in considerable volume by all important companies. When the "Titanic" went down, for example, hundreds of lost-instrument bonds were issued in behalf of the owners of securities carried on the fated ship.

Lost-instrument bonds present several aspects of such importance as to warrant separate treatment.

(a) BONDS OF THE UNITED STATES. The rules of the Treasury Department, based upon Section 3702 of the Revised Statutes, concerning the replacement of lost United States Bonds may be summarized as follows:

(1) No relief is granted under any circumstances in the case of *coupon* bonds that have been *lost* or *stolen*.

(2) Coupon bonds that have been *destroyed* or *defaced* will be reissued, if suitable proof of such destruction or defacement has been adduced, upon the filing of an indemnity bond of twice the amount of the destroyed or defaced bond, plus the interest that would accrue upon such bond up to the time when the principal sum becomes due.

(3) The duplicate bonds referred to in the preceding paragraph are issuable only after six months have elapsed from the date of the alleged destruction or defacement.

(4) In the case of registered bonds duplicates are issuable, after appropriate proof, not only when such bonds have been destroyed or defaced, but also when lost or stolen.

(5) Such duplicates of registered bonds are issuable only after six months have elapsed from the date of the alleged destruction, defacement, loss, or theft.

(6) In the case of duplicated registered bonds there must be filed in the Treasury Department an indemnity bond in a

sum equal to the amount of the missing bond, plus the interest that would accrue thereon up to the date when the principal sum becomes due (not *twice* the amount, as in the case of coupon bonds).

(b) PREMIUM CHARGE. The standard rate for lost-instrument bonds, subject to partial refund under certain conditions, has long been, and seems likely indefinitely to remain, 2 per cent of the amount of the bond. There are special rates, however, for lost life-insurance policies and for certain instruments bearing no interest, as shown on page 84 of the Manual. This 2 per cent or special rate is not an annual charge, but is a final premium covering the cost of the bond for all time. The bonds remain in force indefinitely so far as the obligee is concerned, and must be carried as an open liability on the surety company's books (unless terminated by unexpected developments), with a corresponding reserve, for at least seven years.

(c) UNDERWRITING CONSIDERATIONS. These bonds are written under modern conditions, as indicated above, in considerable volume, but it does not follow that they are written freely. On the contrary, they can be prudently issued only in behalf of certain kinds of principals, and even as to such principals only when certain conditions are fulfilled. The application blank develops the information needed by the underwriter; and that blank should be completed with scrupulous care and attention to details, because the acceptability of the business will depend to a large extent upon the condition of things disclosed by the application.

The underwriting of lost-instrument bonds may be said to hinge upon these three considerations: the character of the principal, the degree of negotiability of the missing security, and the financial responsibility of the principal. The character and general reputation for probity of the principal is of prime importance, because that determines the measure of dependence to be placed upon his or her explanation of the loss of the instrument. Under some conditions an underwriter may confidently accept at par a statement that the missing document was accidentally destroyed by fire, for instance, while the same statement under other conditions might be entitled to little credence.

The second point is likewise of obvious underwriting importance. A missing registered bond, for example, unendorsed by the owner of record, is a comparatively safe subject for a lost-instrument bond, because of the many safeguards thrown around a change in ownership of such documents. A lost certificate of stock, even though unendorsed, is not so readily bondable (notwithstanding the fact that certificates of stock are not, while bonds are, negotiable instruments), because shares of stock are more common and more freely handled on the exchanges and elsewhere. A lost coupon bond, on the other hand, is a highly dangerous instrument to have at large, as possession of such a document is almost universally, and with good legal reason, considered satisfactory evidence of ownership.

The third consideration, financial standing of the principal, is highly important, of course; but this will rarely be a controlling factor in the underwriting of lost-instrument bonds, because the surety company's responsibility for the missing document continues indefinitely, while principals die or lose their fortunes. Sometimes collateral security is required as a condition precedent to the issuance of these bonds. It cannot be held forever, of course, but if the surety is so protected for a few years, the chance of trouble thereafter is thought to be slight.

CHAPTER XVIII

AUTOMOBILE-CONVERSION BONDS

241. Two Classes of Principals

This chapter has to do with the bonds required from partial-payment buyers of motor vehicles. The arrangements, of which there is a considerable variety, under which cars are handled and sold often subject the manufacturer, distributer, or dealer, or some outside person (usually a finance company) concerned with the matter, to risk of loss due to dishonesty on the part of buyers entrusted with cars not fully paid for.

There are two classes of such buyers—the persons who buy the cars to operate themselves, and the persons who buy them for purposes of resale. While the risk in the two cases is of the same general nature, the incidental underwriting factors are so different that it seems logical and advantageous to discuss separately the two classes of bonds covering the two classes of buyers.

242. Security Required from a User Buyer

When an automobile manufacturer, distributer, or dealer sells a car on an installment basis to one who buys the car to use, a conditional contract of sale, chattel mortgage, lease, or trust receipt (whichever is required by the law of the state in which the car is to be kept) is executed by the parties, the object of the instrument being to secure to the seller title to or interest in the car until all payments have been made by the purchaser. The buyer, however, gets immediate possession of the car, and may abscond with it if he likes or otherwise unlawfully dispose of it. The seller protects himself by requiring the buyer to furnish a bond covering this contingency of theft of the car.

Sometimes this bond given by the user buyer of a car runs in favor, not of the dealer seller of the car, but of some third person or concern that finances the sale, or of such third person and dealer jointly. Few automobile dealers have sufficient capital of their own to enable them to settle promptly with the manufacturer or wholesaler for the car and wait for reimbursement and profit until the buyer completes his installment payments. If the dealer cannot finance the matter himself, he applies to a bank or a finance company, which advances the price of the car and thus enables the dealer to obtain his profit at once. As security for the advance the banker receives from the dealer an assignment of the dealer's claim against the buyer for the unpaid part of the purchase price of the car. This claim is evidenced by the notes of the buyer (usually maturing at monthly intervals), secured by a chattel mortgage or like instrument; and these notes, with or without the endorsement of the dealer, together with the mortgage deed, are turned over to the banker. The car having been delivered to the buyer, the banker protects himself further by a bond indemnifying him against loss from the theft or conversion of the car by the buyer while the latter's notes remain unpaid.

243. Security Required from a Dealer

Manufacturers and distributers are often willing to enter into an arrangement with a dealer whereby the latter is enabled to get possession of a car and place it upon his floor for the purpose of ready sale and delivery, although he is unable to pay for it until he has actually sold it to a user buyer. This general arrangement takes various specific forms such as one of the following:

(a) Sometimes a car is sold to a dealer by a manufacturer on an installment basis, the dealer buying it for his own account and giving the manufacturer a chattel mortgage or other instrument evidencing the interest of the manufacturer in the car. The dealer obtains immediate possession of the car, and the manufacturer requires a bond indemnifying him against conversion of the car by the dealer, who cannot lawfully dispose of it until the manufacturer's lien has been satisfied. The situation here so far as the bond is concerned is really the same as that described in the preceding section.

(b) A dealer may obtain from a manufacturer possession of a car for the purpose of selling it, an appropriate receipt being given by the dealer, who becomes warehouseman or bailee of the car, and who may have an option to buy it at a price agreed upon. The manufacturer requires indemnity against the conversion of the car by the dealer.

(c) The situation described in the preceding paragraph may be modified by the fact that a banker may have advanced the price demanded by the manufacturer or wholesaler, thus enabling the dealer to get the car into his premises subject to the rights of the banker and to whatever restrictions the banker has placed on the ultimate disposal of the car. The banker may require in such cases insurance against the conversion of the car by the dealer.

244. Nature of Hazards Covered

It is clear from the foregoing general description of the automobile-conversion risk that the hazards covered are numerous and in some cases complex. They may be specifically indicated as follows:

(a) A user principal may make off with a car before

all the notes are paid, or sell it to someone else and disappear with the proceeds, or in some other way practice fraud upon the obligee to the latter's pecuniary damage.

(b) A dealer principal may practice fraud in numerous ways, including the following:

(1) He may steal a car bodily, decamping with it for parts unknown.

(2) He may sell a car and similarly make off with the proceeds of the sale.

(3) He may sell a car, and instead of leaving town may continue business at the old stand, meanwhile making no report of the sale and using the proceeds thereof for his own purpose.

(4) He may sell a car for cash and pocket the cash, reporting the transaction to his own seller or banker as a credit sale and giving the seller or banker corresponding forged notes.

(5) He may not sell a given car at all, but may set it aside for his own subsequent profit, and meanwhile may tell his seller or banker that he has sold the car to John Jones on a partial-payment plan, and may take up his own notes held by his seller or banker against the car with notes bearing the forged signature of John Jones.

245. Form of Automobile-Conversion Bond

Many different forms of bonds have been used to fit the foregoing conditions, but most of the few companies now writing the business do so upon two forms, one for user principals and the other for dealer principals, that have been virtually standardized—that is, the companies are using identical forms of bonds and are declining to change them under any conditions. These forms are regarded as sufficiently broad to cover all the numerous variations in the general plan of operations described above. Insurance as to specified cars only, and not blanket protection, is provided—no claim can ever accrue under either form of bond except in connection with some particular car that has been identified by number and otherwise in the schedule attached to the bond. The companies are not prepared to issue a bond providing blanket insurance—that is, a fidelity bond of the usual type issued in a fixed amount and covering within that limit any and all cars, without description or notification to the surety company, that may be delivered to the principal. The standard forms, however, will afford protection of the kind indicated, if the obligee will send to the surety company the necessary notifications.

The amount of the bond required from a partial-payment purchaser is the amount of the purchase price remaining unpaid after the stipulated initial payment has been made. The amount of the bond required from a deferred-payment purchaser or an optional buyer is the purchase price of the car.

In the case of partial-payment transactions the bond remains in force until the expiration of one year, when liability is automatically extinguished, or until the buyer pays for the car, if final payment is made within one year. In the case of dealers' bonds liability continues as long as the car remains in the possession of the dealer.

Since the users' and dealers' notes are accepted by the obligee in reliance upon the protection of the bond, and since that protection would be uncertain if the bond were subject to cancellation, the surety may cancel the bond only as to *subsequent additions* to the schedule.

246. User-Principal Underwriting Considerations

This would seem to be a simple fidelity risk. The bond is concerned only with the acts of the principal as regards a specified piece of property (the car), the amount of liability is continually reduced, and the risk in general seems normal and safe. The following suggestions, however, may be made.

(a) THE OBLIGEE. Whether a dealer or a finance company, the obligee must be of unquestioned business and personal standing, entirely above suspicion of becoming a party to any fraudulent transaction. The reliability of a manufacturer or large distributer is easily established, and may usually indeed be assumed; but the reliability of a retail dealer is a different matter, and it is clear that an unscrupulous dealer might easily cause loss to the surety. He could, for example, get equally unscrupulous persons to pose as buyers and execute the necessary papers, including an application for a bond, on the strength of which he could secure cars from a wholesaler and dispose of them as he liked; or, if he were dealing with a finance company, he could sell to the lender his confederates' worthless agreements to pay future installments.

(b) THE PRINCIPAL. The buyer of the car should be a person well known in his community, of excellent repute, with a good-salaried position or in business for himself, or, if not engaged in business, otherwise of some financial responsibility. No elaborate investigation of the principal seems necessary in most cases, because the foregoing simple requirements can ordinarily be satisfied without much research. In many cases this business originates with distributors or bankers whose transactions are extensive, and who make investigation of buyers through their credit department before any papers are signed; and these papers will ordinarily be shown to the surety company upon request.

(c) BINDING BY AGENTS. Since from the nature of the case dealers and bankers will need to know promptly whether or not a bond is procurable, it seems necessary to allow local agents to bind surety companies on these risks when they are satisfied that the foregoing underwriting requirements are fulfilled. In practice, unfortunately, it is often exceedingly difficult to get agents to make even the slight investigation described in paragraph (b) above; and yet in no other way, it is thought, can the business be safely written.

247. Dealer-Principal Underwriting Considerations

Dealer bonds have proved to be extremely difficult to underwrite successfully. The following suggestions seem to be warranted by the experience so far developed.

(a) MORE THAN A FIDELITY RISK. While a dealer bond, like the corresponding user bond, involves, theoretically at least, nothing more than a fidelity hazard, the risk is deemed far greater than that incident to user bonds; because the dealer will be constantly receiving cars as he disposes of others, so that the liability will be continuous and perhaps cumulative, and because the dealer, if he gets into a tight place, is strongly tempted to use improperly the proceeds of a sale. As a practical underwriting problem, therefore, the underwriter must consider, in dealing with these bonds, not only the character of the principal, but also his record, his financial condition, and his general business prospects.

(b) MONTHLY INSPECTIONS ESSENTIAL. It seems necessary to require that the obligee shall verify at least monthly the cars supposed to be in the dealers' hands. This verification should be effected through an actual inspection made by some competent and reliable representative of the obligee, and preferably through one of the commercial agencies that now make it a business to render service of this kind for motor manufacturers and bankers. Most companies deem this verification of so much importance that they will not issue bonds for dealer principals unless the verification precaution is arranged in advance. The companies do not make the inspections themselves, ordinarily, nor bear any part of the expense of making them.

(c) COMPLETE INFORMATION ESSENTIAL. It is highly desirable that the underwriter be fully advised as to the plan of operation between the dealer and the manufacturer or the banker as the case may be. He should have copies of the essential papers, including the contract signed by the dealer, the trust receipt or similar instrument, and whatever paper evidences release from ownership or control of the car by the obligee.

248. Coinsurance Requirement

For several years the companies writing these automobile-conversion bonds gave complete indemnity for losses due to dishonest acts of user principals and dealer principals. The experience of the companies was far from favorable, and many of them discontinued the business entirely. Several companies, however, believing that suretyship of this nature was a legitimate and even a necessary adjunct to present-day automobile financing, felt that it should continue to be furnished by bonding companies; but they sought to avoid abnormal losses by requiring obligees to coinsure a part of each risk as follows:

(a) Dealers have repeatedly sold cars, because a bond providing complete indemnity has been obtainable, to persons whom even a superficial investigation would have shown to be unsafe user principals. The standard form of bond provides, therefore, that dealers shall bear 20 per cent of any loss.

(b) Finance companies and others protected by bonds

have not infrequently allowed the dealers to go unchecked
for long periods, and have extended large amounts of
credit without exercising ordinary safeguards and supervision, relying upon their bond in the event of trouble.
Moreover, the substantial initial deposit required of the
dealer has, with complete indemnity as respects the
balance, enabled the holder of the bond to retain his
profit in cases where a default has occurred, even though
a loss has been sustained by the surety. For these
reasons, and also because dealer bonds have been shown
by experience to be extra-hazardous, a higher percentage
of co-insurance, 33⅓ per cent, is required in the case of
dealers.

249. Inclusion-of-All-Cars Requirement

It seems clear that isolated automobile-conversion
risks cannot safely be accepted. Obviously the selection would be against the surety company and the business would be abnormally hazardous, if a dealer should
bond only such users as he deemed untrustworthy, or if a
manufacturer should bond only such dealers as he
deemed irresponsible. All companies, therefore, it is
thought, take the position that they will not issue bonds
in behalf of dealers or manufacturers who offer them only
a small, and presumably the most doubtful, part of their
risks.

250. The Whole Situation Unsatisfactory

While the experience of the companies with user bonds
has not been so bad, heavy losses have been sustained
even in that quarter; and I suppose it to be true that no
company has thus far made any money on its dealer
bonds. No doubt the experience would have been distinctly
better, and perhaps satisfactory on the whole, if the

existing rates and underwriting requirements, including the coinsurance feature of the present bonds, had been effective from the beginning. Even now, however, notwithstanding the high rates and the unusual conditions imposed upon the insured, few companies deem it prudent to provide this suretyship.

When all the essential elements of an underwriting problem are known in advance, so that what seem to be adequate safeguards can be set up and made to cover every point of excessive exposure, it is baffling and discouraging to find that heavy losses none the less result. Sometimes part of the protective machinery fails to function in the way contemplated; and sometimes (this is particularly maddening), although every safeguarding semaphore goes to danger automatically and instantly as it ought, yet the derailing safety switch fails to work, and the fated bond rushes on to crash into a heavy loss ahead. The dealers' bonds particularly bear a certain sinister resemblance to assigned-accounts bonds (cf. section 47) as to both the internal and external features of the risk, and here, as in that other ill-starred case, something more than ordinary underwriting foresight seems necessary, if one would visualize the situation completely and take in all the dangerous features lurking in the background.

CHAPTER XIX

A DIFFIDENT WORD TO HOME-OFFICE EXECUTIVES

251. A Lesson from the Scientists

In writing this book I have visualized my reader as the average agent of a surety or casualty company, not expertly familiar with the bonding business, but interested in the subject and glad to learn more though from a source of dubious reliability. Even such an attitude on my part betrays sufficient assurance; and I do not know what will be thought of me for venturing to presume that my views may be of interest to the "best minds" of the business. However, in surety underwriting we learn to take chances; and some people rush in where angels fear to tread.

It was my good fortune, aeons ago, to hear James Russell Lowell deliver an address to Harvard undergraduates. I was seated in the bald-headed row only a few feet from Mr. Lowell, and he looked at me hard at one point in his address, when he remarked how little some students had to show for their college training. Mr. Lowell seemed to think that he would give point and force to his observation by fixing an eagle eye upon me when he made it. The implication was fairly obvious—imperative, I may say; in fact, it would be no violent breach of language to call it absolutely obligatory. All the fellows around me seemed to see the point. They made the necessary inference, the inevitable, irresistible, inescapable inference. Then Mr. Lowell, having established that point and illustrated it so convincingly, went on to say that, even so, every student, however careless he might be of his golden opportunities, could hardly fail to derive some benefit from his alma mater. He said, I remember, that if a man did no more than merely browse around the library, and stumble now and then into a lecture-room, by regrettable error, he was bound, nevertheless, to absorb, through his shoulder-blades perhaps and almost against his will, more or less wisdom and culture from the glorious superabundance in the Harvard atmosphere. Mr. Lowell, by the way, did not think it necessary to glance in my direction when he added this qualifying endorsement to his original proposition; and I have always thought it was pretty small of him not to let me in on this extenuating addendum after exploiting me so brazenly in the first instance; but I suppose he saw no reason why he should ruin his entire argument.

However, there is one good thing that even I was able to salvage from my four misspent years in Cambridge—namely, the idea of co-operation. I saw exemplified by the professors there and by their colleagues in other institutions of learning a spirit of co-operation and helpfulness as to the subject of their common researches. They had their private ambitions, and they strove for individual honors, but they opened up their records to each other, divulged their aims, published promptly the results of their experiments, and did everything possible otherwise to help along the common cause. Their work as regards each other was contributive rather than competitive.

The work of surety executives as regards each other is necessarily competitive in a high degree, but I like to think of it as also contributive and co-operative in the manner of the scientists. For there is a science of surety underwriting, which the home-offices particularly, and the field as well to a large extent, are all the time studying and developing and understanding better. We are all attacking in some way the problems of this science of surety underwriting, the home-office executives trying to discover and formulate its laws and principles, and the fieldmen trying to apply those principles with the best results for all concerned. We have common difficulties to overcome, common problems to master; and it is surely desirable on all accounts that we join forces and contribute, each of us what each of us can, to the common fund of knowledge and experience, so that all may go forward together on the highway to safety and success.

252. An Arduous Calling

Experienced bonding executives need not be told that they should welcome assistance from any source, even from competitive quarters, in their large task of keeping their companies solvent and prosperous. Most people perhaps regard their particular callings as exceptionally exacting, but surety underwriters, as I have tried to show elsewhere, may be pardoned for holding such views. The excessive mortality of surety companies—fewer than half of them, I suppose, have survived—confirms the conclusions of general reasoning regarding the difficult nature of the business.

After the event it is easy to see why a surety loss might reasonably have been deemed a possibility, if not a probability. It is good for the soul, though not a fascinating pastime, to analyze one's failures; and when an underwriter does this by going over the papers on which he decided to assume a risk that caused a loss, he can usually see that more thoroughness here or wider knowledge there or greater alertness somewhere else would have put him on his guard and perhaps averted the loss. The worst of it (or perhaps the best of it, from the disciplinary point of view) is that swift retribution overtakes the surety man who makes a mistake. If a surgeon errs, his blunder, as somebody points out, may be buried with his patient, just as a lawyer's error may be entombed in musty law books that nobody reads; but if a bonding underwriter nods ever so little, his lapse from perfection is blazoned in dollars and cents and red-inked on the ledger where he who runs may read.

253. Are Some Underwriting Problems Unsolvable?

Nevertheless, it is all, as I view it, a matter of methods and mentality—of patience and thoroughness in assembling and testing all pertinent underwriting information; of experience and foresight in prescribing the conditions under which risks may be assumed; of judgment in weighing the chances of loss and fixing a commensurate premium; and of efficiency in handling claims and making recoveries. Upon this theory almost any bond reasonably required in volume in the normal course of business should be writable at a profit, under conditions not impracticable, and at a premium that the traffic will bear. I confess that this pleasing and convenient theory is not supported by the experience of the surety companies so far in certain lines. In the case of assigned-accounts bonds, for example (cf. section 47), and automobile-conversion bonds (cf. section 250), both of which are called for in large volume, seem to be a legitimate incident of the given situations, and may be subjected to rigid safeguarding conditions by the underwriters, no company, if I mistake not, has yet written the business without loss. In my hesitant opinion, nevertheless, the reason does not lie in the absolute unsolvability of the problems involved, but rather in our failure to explore the situation to its ultimate reaches and provide an adequate safeguard at every danger point.   Exploring expeditions, however, are costly, and some of us may have done our part in these two fields!

254. Standardized Forms and Practices

About twenty years ago a friend of mine in Detroit was importuned by a young inventor to buy some stock in a motor-car company that the inventor was struggling to put upon its feet.   My friend turned a deaf ear to this entreaty, but he did buy some stock in another automobile company similarly beginning its career.   Afterward he had to pay heavy assessments on his stock, whereas if he had made the former investment, it would now represent (with its aqueous accretions) a large fortune.

Various factors account for the opposite results of the two ventures, but it is commonly believed that the marvelous success of the former company was due primarily to its policy of manufacturing only one or two models of automobiles and to its insistence upon standardizing all parts and practices.   As a result of consummate organization along these lines, motor cars are turned out by the company with the regularity of newspapers from a modern press.   An inclined plane running from the factory to an area outside is used to remove cars as fast as they are built; and a completed car glides down this plane every seven seconds.

When a fastidious customer insisted upon having his car painted a certain irregular color, and the salesman in turn urged this demand upon Mr. Ford, the latter replied, "You may offer your customers any color of car they prefer, provided they select the precise shade of black that we are now using at the factory."

Our business is not that of building motor cars—there

are a few trifling differences; and absolute standardization upon one product is hopelessly out of the question in our extremely detailed and complicated business. We can, however, and we do, apply the same principle in numerous ways; and what I have in mind, in bestowing this wealth of information and of wisdom upon my readers, is to urge them to make further use of this prime requisite of efficiency. Already, indeed, notable progress along this line has been made by the companies through the Surety Association. What would they have done, for example, with the unprecedentedly complex and difficult blanket-bond situation without the standardization of bond and rider forms, brokerage, and other uniform practices adopted by the Association? How in the world could the companies, without this form of co-operation, ever have handled their enormous commitments in this line with anything like the comparative efficiency and ease that have in fact characterized their conduct of the business? In a few other special fields likewise standard bond and application forms have been used with successful results.

255. An Example and a Vision

The standard form of reinsurance agreement is a striking case in point. In the old days there were as many forms of reinsurance agreements as there were companies operating, and every time a piece of business was reinsured both sides were forced to scrutinize the resultant agreement with minute care (or should have done so), lest some provisions be found therein, as frequently happened, requiring modification or explanation. For about seven years now, however, the companies have avoided all that danger and saved all that time, since they have known that every point affecting the interests of both the reinsured and the reinsurer was considered at great length and disposed of with justice to all concerned in the standard form of reinsurance agreement prepared by a Surety Association committee and adopted by the Association on May 12, 1915. About all the companies have used the form exclusively since that date, and it has served its highly important purpose, as I suppose, with complete satisfaction to all concerned.

What the companies have thus far done in this matter of standardized forms and practices is a mere bagatelle compared with the expanse of opportunity open to them. We should have standard forms of bonds for all important classes of suretyship; standard forms of applications for all bonds; standard forms of indemnity agreements; standard forms of receipts for collateral security; standard agency contracts, accounting records and practices, statistical cards, reinsurance submission blanks, and any number of other underwriting and administrative instruments now serving for the companies the same general purpose in a variety of ways. Some of these instruments are doubtless better than others. Competent committees, with the help of all the interested companies, could prepare forms better perhaps than any now in use and surely better than the average form in use. The fine thing about it, moreover, is that any form or rule or practice so standardized and adopted by the companies after research and consideration is infinitely perfectible. It will be good at the start; but it should ultimately become, with the aid of experience and of additional study, the one way in which best to accomplish the given purpose. It would not be practicable, of course, to carry out this ambitious program in a day or a month or a year; but a start could be made in a day, and continual progress could be made thereafter. Ultimately a vast and scientific system of forms and rules and underwriting principles and practices could be built up and rounded out and all the time improved until the whole business of corporate suretyship could be conducted upon a plane of ease and efficiency and economy and safety far above the standards of today.

256. Reinsurance Submissions

So many large bonds are written nowadays that the reinsurance feature of the surety business has become highly important, and more uniform and systematic methods of handling it seem desirable. As it is now, tenders of reinsurance are made in a variety of ways not all of which are satisfactory. Frequently, for example, a company will send its entire file to the proposed reinsurer, and put up to the latter the job of extracting therefrom the salient facts of the case. That trustful procedure is, of course, rather desirable, if not quite necessary, under some conditions (where a fidelity risk, for example, is more or less off color), but in general the reinsured's liberal commission allowance for acquisition and administrative costs should include a brief and logical presentation of the essential facts for the convenience of the reinsurer. Sometimes, on the other hand, the reinsured errs just as far the other way, and asks the reinsurer to accept the business upon a totally inadequate statement of the case. Something like this, for example, is likely to come in, about two minutes before closing time, on a crowded wire:

"Say, Old Top, want to let you in on a choice piece of reinsurance. Bill Jones—you know Bill, the big contractor down in Skowhegan, Maine—is going to build a sea-wall from Bar Harbor to Halifax, a $100,000,000 job, to be completed in twenty years. We're putting you

down for half the $10,000,000 bond.   All right?   Got to
know two hours ago."

In some cases (a big, long-term, joint-control, trustee's bond, for example) many underwriters would almost rather reinsure than write the bond, since they thus
save themselves an immense amount of costly detail—
just as the unhappy man who was being ridden out of town
on a rail remarked that except for the honor of the thing
he would just as soon have walked.

Some companies anyway, and perhaps most, subject
their important and complicated underwriting propositions to a sifting process from which only the essential
facts emerge, boiled down and logically segregated, upon a
single sheet of paper, for the use of the person or persons
who must decide whether or not to issue the given bond.
Some such system seems necessary to the prompt dispatch
of business, and will presumably be adopted ultimately
by all companies.   Wherever these underwriting-data
sheets are in use they afford an easy means of acquaint-
ing prospective reinsurers with the merits of a case.

Certain companies offer the same piece of reinsurance
simultaneously to a number of other companies, on the
chance that some of the offerees will decline the business
and with a view to making sure of the reinsurance anyway.   After an underwriter has contracted an oculist's
bill in deciphering a carbon copy about thirteen removes
from the original draft, and has exercised his gray matter
over a knotty problem, he does not like to be told that
his participation is not desired because another company
accepted first.   Overlapping reinsurance offerings are
to be deprecated, it seems to me, unless the bond is so
big that room can be made for every offeree who desires
to participate, though not perhaps in some cases in the
amount originally proposed.

257. Opportunity for Important Constructive Action

Some of the numerous Napoleonic intellects in the surety business should get to work upon an all-round, inter-company, self-winding reinsurance plan, whereby a company, contemplating the issuance of a bond of larger amount than it is willing to carry alone, will know in advance that it can place the excess with a group of automatic reinsurers by merely filling out a small allotment slip and sending it to a central office. Such a system seems to me highly desirable and entirely practicable. Abundant operating material is ready to hand, the convenience and safety and other advantages of the system are obvious, every element of the problem is known and well understood, and nothing is lacking except a well-conceived and thoroughly-worked-out plan of operation. Certain objections are manifest; but none of them, it seems to me, are insuperable or begin to outweigh the favorable features. A few classes of bonds (uncancellable, long-term obligations, for example) would perhaps need to be excluded, at first anyway, because of the objection that some reinsurers might not be in existence when a distant loss occurred. All such contingencies, few and comparatively unimportant, could be cared for, and enough of the plan would be left, the great bulk of it in fact, to make it very much worth while.

258. A Plea for Conservative Practices

Most underwriters perhaps deem themselves conservative, and think the other fellow rather too liberal for his own good and that of his competitors; and there is no doubt, generally speaking, that some bonds, rejected by underwriter A as extra-hazardous, will be accepted by underwriter B, while other bonds, turned down for the same reason by B, will be written by A.   It is a difference of opinion that makes horse-races, they say; and surely it is a difference of underwriting opinion that gives the surety brokers their chance.   The explanation in some of these cases is, not that A is inclined to take greater chances than B (or vice versa), but that A (or B) understands the given situation more thoroughly than the other man, and more expertly appraises the risk.

It is true, nevertheless, that *all* underwriters know certain practices to be more conservative than others are, and that they resort to these other more or less riskful ways only because they fear the loss of valued agents or patrons, or think that some competitor will take the chance and thereby gain an advantage if they do not, or for some other reason of business expediency.   The undesirable practices referred to are of various kinds and degrees of gravity, and I shall venture to mention only three, all of which seem to me important and largely controllable by home-office executives.

(a) UNDERWRITING AUTHORITY FOR FIELDMEN.   While we must all give our agents a certain measure of underwriting authority, I suppose it to be true that none of us would give them as much as we do unless we feared that a more conservative course in that respect would cause some good producers to transfer their business to companies willing to give them a freer hand in the underwriting of their bonds.   In suggesting the possibility that some companies go too far in that direction, I am anxious not to be misunderstood by agents who may be good enough to read this book.   I know that fieldmen use their best judgment, and are conscientious in their exercise of underwriting discretion, and do not put their companies upon risks unless they suppose the business to be good; but I know, also, that the problems of surety

underwriting are many and baffling, and that comparatively few fieldmen have mastered them; and I know, too,
that the bonding companies are all the time paying
losses upon bonds executed by agents that they would
not have to pay if the given risks had been put up to the
home-office. It has happened repeatedly with me, as it
must have happened with all home-office executives,
that a bond executed by an agent has been seen to be
dangerous and undesirable as soon as it was reported,
and that afterward a claim has resulted. The agent
meant well in every case, and thought that he was doing
the company as well as himself a good turn in writing
the bond; but, in fact, he was merely dipping into the
surplus of his company, and making a draft upon his
own standing with the company, and showing it that his
experience and judgment and general underwriting
capacity had been unequal to the strain put upon them
in the given case.

(b) COLLATERAL SECURITY. In the matter of requiring security, home-office executives seem to me at
times not to evidence overmuch their possession of a
spinal column. Every little while I have an appeal bond,
say, or some similar instrument amounting to a pure
financial guarantee, all lined up for execution upon full
collateral security, when some other company with a
more trustful disposition or with better underwriting
judgment (perfectly absurd, of course, but it sounds well)
snatches the bond from my grasp with an offer to write it
without collateral; and the very next day perhaps I turn
the same neat trick upon some medieval, fog-bound underwriter who does not know a choice bit of "velvet" when
he sees it.

I confess that I do not know just what can be done
about it. New underwriters are coming into the busi-

ness all the time, some of whom at least will learn only through bitter experience the unwisdom of waiving collateral; and others perhaps, who are not new in the business and who ought to know better, will occasionally illustrate somebody's said observation that experience, like the stern lights of a vessel, throws light only upon what is past. All that we can do, I suppose, is to keep on trying to educate ourselves and our agents and the bond-buying public into the undeniable fact and eternal truth that suretyship is not insurance, that the premium charge for bonds of the kind in question represents a mere service fee and is utterly inadequate for even a small loss-payment fund, and that there is nothing illogical or unreasonable or in the smallest degree improper in requiring full cash-or-its-equivalent security as a condition precedent to the execution of any bond of this class.

(c) JOINT CONTROL. Some diversity of practice among the companies exists in the matter of declining to write probate bonds unless either sole control or joint control of the securities of the trust estate will be permitted. This difference is due, I suppose, not to any real variance of view among underwriters regarding the desirability of control, but because it is feared, by those who waive the safeguard, that their volume of business will suffer if they insist upon more conservative methods. Here again it is easier to diagnose the disease than to prescribe a remedy; and here again perhaps the only practicable cure for the trouble must be sought in the slow education of all the contributors thereto.

"Regenerative braking," a new phenomenon in mechanics incident to electrical railroading in the mountainous districts, suggests an analogy here. Steam has given way to electrical power, on the Chicago, Mil-

waukee and St. Paul Railway, for a distance of 209 miles
from Tacoma east and a further distance of 440 miles
through the Rocky Mountains, with extraordinarily
good results in all respects. When trains reach the top
of the divide, they coast for miles and miles down the
other side. No power, of course, is required, except for
holding back the train, and by the curious paradox of
regenerative braking the electric motor is made actually
to produce power, instead of consuming it, on these down
grades. When the crest of the grade has been reached
the helper locomotive, which has been pushing the train
from the rear all the way up the mountain, is switched
around the train and coupled with the forward locomotive. Both are then operated as a unit, and the train is
controlled by regenerative braking all the way down the
slope. The power so produced by gravity is turned
back into the trolley wire, thus helping other trains
toiling up the mountain at the same time and incidentally
cutting down the bill for electric current.

Let us recall this interesting by-product of electric
locomotion when we are tempted to waive joint control
in an undeserving case. By regenerative underwriting
we shall not only hold our risk in good control on the down
grade that otherwise leads to loss, but we shall also store
up and send back to our toiling competitors climbing the
grade on the other side a fund of moral energy which will
be highly welcome and which is much needed in their
business.

259. An Inspiring Profession

The Oxford Dictionary defines "profession" as a voca-
tion that "involves some branch of learning or science."
Surety underwriting thus falls well within the term, since
it involves all branches of learning and all sciences and

everything else under the sun. Those who follow this
profession may well felicitate themselves, it seems to me,
not only upon the absorbingly-interesting and intel-
lectually-stimulating nature of their calling, but also
upon the charming personnel of the profession as now
constituted. It was only the other day, so to speak,
that this new outlet for executive talent came into being;
but already a certain esprit de corps is taking beneficent
shape, wholesome traditions are forming, and similar
features of good omen incident to the older professions
are beginning to characterize this one. Not far off is the
day, if indeed it be not already at hand, when the business of corporate suretyship will be regarded by the
brightest young men as appropriate and promising for
their life-long careers, and when the high executive posts
therein will be prized as positions of dignity and distinction and grave responsibility second to none in the world
of commerce and finance.

CHAPTER XX

SUGGESTIONS TO AGENTS

260. Fieldmen Indispensable in Corporate Suretyship

While this book has been written primarily for the use of fieldmen, and while it is hoped that almost all of it will be found more or less appropriate and useful to such readers, it has nevertheless seemed worth while to include one chapter aimed directly at them (loaded with heavy buckshot). Everybody knows that insurance agents render a necessary and highly useful service to the assured, but they are not so important to the home-office in some lines of insurance—aside, of course, from the trifling fact that they produce the business: they are not so important, I mean, from the underwriter's point of view. That, however, is not at all the case as regards the bonding business. In that line the agent's service to the obligee or principal, while frequently marked, is sometimes not notably valuable. In many cases, for example, the form of the bond is fixed by law or practice, and the rate is not reducible by negotiation or competitive submissions, so that the agent is not in a position to procure for his client any greater protection or any lower rate than would be obtainable in any event. In a multitude of instances, however, the agent, if he knows the surety business and otherwise has the requisite equipment of character and education, can be of the utmost assistance to the underwriter. He must, indeed, in many cases do a certain part of the underwriting himself, and he *can* do a great deal of it, if he will, and if he knows how; that is to say, he must procure in any event a certain amount of information that the underwriter requires, and he *can* get almost all of it, and assemble it logically and effectively, and verify it, and make it fit, generally, for underwriting use.

261. Complete Information Essential

It would seem to go without saying that the underwriter should receive full information about the risks that he is expected to assume; but it happens every day, in all home-offices, that applications for important bonds come in, with requests (or demands) for immediate issuance, though information of vital importance is lacking. Sometimes, indeed, the underwriter cannot make out from the papers submitted precisely what kind of bond is wanted. They say that you can always tell a Harvard man—but that you cannot tell him much; these agents seem to regard all underwriters as Harvard men, and do not even try to tell them much. Not only, of course, must the information be complete, but it must be favorable. The surety company is always in sufficient danger, even when proceeding at half-speed in charted seas and under placid skies; but sometimes the underwriter is asked to go ahead at full speed in a dense fog, and with the roar of breakers knelling in his ear.

Agents, for example, occasionally send in application papers showing some fatally weak spot in the case— the fact that the business has been declined by another company, that the principal is rated by the mercantile agencies in a way indicating inadequate financial responsibility for the given undertaking, etc. Obviously in cases of that kind the very first thing for the agent to do, if he expects the application to be seriously considered, and if the facts warrant it, is to explain thoroughly and convincingly why the bond is acceptable notwithstanding the danger signals flashing from the papers. The underwriter must be governed by the evidence embodied in the material submitted, and if that is bad, no amount of hearsay or general-impression information to the contrary will make the business acceptable. The underwriter must believe what the papers tell him rather than what the applicant for the bond tells the agent. The home-office is as helpless in that respect as was the hen-pecked husband in court trying to bolster up some preposterous story told by his wife, who had preceded him on the witness stand. He was making bad weather of it, and finally the judge broke in, saying, "My good man, you are doing as well as you can, but this yarn of your wife's is beyond all reason. I don't believe a word of it." The poor man mournfully replied, "Judge, you may believe it or not as you please; but I've got to." The home-office is under a similar compulsion to believe the application papers.

There are all gradations of agents in this matter of the submission of acceptable papers. Many, alas, send to the home-office applications imperfectly completed, and accompany them with letters that rather confuse than clarify the issue; others procure applications, indeed, reasonably well filled out, but they submit with them no amplifying and confirmatory material such as the given situation obviously calls for; and a modest percentage of the whole endear themselves to the home-office underwriter by anticipating his requirements and presenting the case so clearly, fully, and dependably that all the grateful home-office man need do is to weigh the facts and evidence and make an easy and quick decision.

262. Losses Due to Inadequate Investigation

We people at the home-office sometimes amuse ourselves with a study of our surety losses, so as to see how it all happened. You have to go a long way to find better explainers than we are in cases of that kind. Analyzing one's failures is about as pleasant a pastime as would be the analogous process of conducting one's own post-mortem. We have not done the latter—yet; but we are quite capable of it, and often do much queerer things than that. There are numerous ways, each more saddening than all the others, in which surety losses may be viewed. The aspect of the matter that seems to me manifestly called for here is one showing how far fieldmen are responsible for such losses. I select that point of view, in order that at least one section of the chapter may prove interesting, informative, uplifting, and altogether delightful.

In the matter of contract bonds, for example, I should like to cite the experience of a large surety company that recently traced back to their sources in the application papers loss payments aggregating $500,000. It was found that the lamentable result indicated broke up under analysis into sixteen general causes. More than half of these causes originated in the fact that the company either did not take the trouble to make, or more probably was not permitted by the heartless agent to make, a proper and thorough investigation; that is to say, 65 per cent of the losses were found to have been preventable, and might have been wholly or largely avoided if the agent and the company—yes, that is the proper sequence—if the *agent* and the company had made a thoroughgoing investigation of the conditions before the bond was issued.

263. Have Something Definite to Propose

Home-office people receive letters in disheartening volume from agents and the public demanding bond

forms, quotations, and "complete information," in
connection with some half-baked proposition or shred of
a plan submitted by the correspondent; and when the
home-office tries to get somewhere by utilizing as best it
can the fragmentary data submitted, the whole plan is
abruptly and completely changed and a fresh start must
be made. Almost always, in these cases, no surety
company would write the bond that the proposer dimly
has in mind, except upon terms that would be deemed
unreasonable, though in fact they would be as sweetly
reasonable as anything that Matthew Arnold ever wrote.

The first thing for applicants to do in any such case is
to furnish a copy of the form of bond desired; and if they
cannot do that (as they rarely can), the least that they
can do is to state in plain language precisely what
insurance or suretyship they want. Almost always that
simple requirement completely blocks them, because they
do not know what they want. The schemers realize
vaguely that their plan lacks coherence or offers opportunity for leakage and loss in unpleasant ways, and
they have conceived the happy thought of putting it all
up to the surety company and permitting it, for a
trifling premium, after it has gratuitously spent considerable time and some money in giving the proposition
some sort of shape, to hold the bag and act as a general
clearing-house for any and all awkward balances on the
wrong side.

Whatever they finally evolve in the way of a bond
form usually amounts to a pure financial guarantee; and
whether or not a surety company will execute the
instrument depends, of course, upon the financial
responsibility of the principal. Rarely are the circumstances such that the thing is practicable at all, from the
standpoint of the surety company.

Not criticizable on the score of indefiniteness was an application for a bond recently received by me from the prospective heir of a man, a presumed bachelor, seventy-five years old, who had been "rather gay in his day." The gentleman desired a bond conditioned that no wife would turn up to contest his estate.

264. Be Not Too Persistent

It was said of Gladstone that he could persuade most men of most things and himself of anything. Similarly the average agent can persuade the average home-office underwriter of the acceptability of most risks, and himself of the acceptability of *any* risk. It is really not worth while, however, after a piece of business has been carefully considered and declined by the home-office, to go back and urge reconsideration while the conditions remain essentially what they were. Yet all the time it happens with every company that zealous and disappointed agents, on receiving word of the rejection of some delectable piece of business, wire for reconsideration without advancing a single additional reason warranting further study of the case. Under such conditions, all that the home-office can do, desirous as it may be of helping out the agent, is to reaffirm its position. I am not suggesting, of course, that an agent who is firmly convinced of the desirability of a given bond should invariably accept an adverse decision as absolutely final, and make no further effort to put the bond through. While initial rejections commonly stand, in practice, as we all know, they may sometimes be converted, through the agent's ardent alchemy, into acceptances, grudging, acquiescent, or even confident, as the case may be. In most such cases, however, the risk is improved in some way after the first submission—additional indemnity is

secured, perhaps, or part collateral is offered, or some
weak point in the principal's credentials is satisfactorily
cleared up, or additional testimony is secured of a highly
favorable nature. All that I have in mind, therefore, in
venturing to disparage overpersistence, is the futility of
wasting wires and letters over rejections when no *fresh*
considerations are advanced.

Recurring to the company that so enjoyed itself over
those $500,000 contract losses, I grieve to note that the
tickled-to-death analyzers ascribe 8 per cent of their
losses to bonds "forced upon the company by the re-
peated pleadings of agents."

265. Agents' Violations of Underwriting Authority

Although surety agents as a class are, as Pat puts it,
"aqual to nun" when it comes to loyalty and efficiency
and intelligent compliance with instructions, yet some of
them are not always careful, when about to issue a bond,
to make sure that the risk is one within their discretionary power. I referred above, for example, to contract-bond loss payments aggregating $500,000 that
were found analyzable into sixteen general causes; and
one of the important causes, accounting for a considerable
percentage of the losses, was the execution of bonds by
fieldmen without authority.

There are few transgressions on the part of fieldmen
that the home-office finds it harder to forgive than unauthorized executions of bonds. When the right of
suffrage was thrown open to the masses of people in
England a great statesman said, "Now we must teach
our masters." That is precisely the way the home-office
feels when it gives to agents a measure of underwriting
authority; and it would feel still more solicitous if it
were not confident, generally speaking, that this measure

would never be exceeded. Of course, the home-office means not to be unreasonable about this matter—it allows a certain tolerance. To illustrate: in a celebrated law-suit involving an alleged forged signature Professor Benjamin Pierce, the famous mathematician of Harvard University, was called upon to examine the forged signature with one known to be genuine, and give his opinion as to the probability that the signature in dispute, shown to be precisely identical with one known to be genuine, was in fact genuine. He testified that such an absolute and complete coincidence of strokes, from beginning to end, would occur, in accordance with the mathematical theory of chances, only once in the number of times expressed by the thirtieth power of five —nine hundred and thirty-one quintillions of times. Now, I am confident that home-offices would not be thought unduly punctilious in this matter of unauthorized executions of bonds; and I hereby magnanimously agree, in behalf of home-offices generally, that after an agent has executed 931,000,000,000,000,000,000 bonds, all within his authority, he may execute one more bond of an amount exceeding his authority by, say, one-quintillionth of 1 per cent.

266. Do Not Ask for Excessive Authority

Many agents, especially those whose experience has lain chiefly in casualty and fire fields, and with whom the surety business is a sort of side-line, ask their home-offices for liberal powers of attorney, so that they may bind their companies upon surety risks in the same free and easy manner in which they assume casualty and fire risks, upon request, and without prolonged investigation. They do not always realize that these latter lines of insurance differ markedly from suretyship in two important respects, both of which have a vital bearing upon this point.

In the first place, one elevator or boiler of a given type, one person falling within a given classification of accident or health insurance, and any similar unit risk in most of the miscellaneous lines of insurance, is a good deal like the other units in the same classification, and no special and minute investigation is necessary before accepting a piece of business; but that is not the case with most of the more important surety risks. Just as one star differeth from another in glory, so surety risks, even when they fall within the same general underwriting classification, differ acutely in desirability; and usually these differences do not appear upon the surface of things, but must be ascertained through painstaking investigation.

The second respect referred to in which surety risks are less prudently acceptable at sight than casualty risks lies in the uncancellability of the former. If an agent puts a company on a boiler, liability, or fire risk, in an excess of underwriting zeal or though a misapprehension of the conditions, and it afterwards seems desirable to get off, the company may terminate its liability by a simple cancellation notice; but that is not at all true in the case of most important kinds of surety bonds, as we have seen so frequently in the preceding chapters. The Arabs have a proverb, "While the word remains unspoken you are master of it, but as soon as it is spoken it is master of you." How often an underwriter thinks of that when hesitating over some borderline risk, knowing that as soon as he dispatches the telegram or initials the papers the resultant bond will be absolute master of him and of his company.

Fieldmen, therefore, should remember all this, and be correspondingly moderate and reasonable in their requisitions upon the home-office for underwriting powers; and even when they have authority to assume a given risk, if time permits (and it can often be made to permit), they would be well advised to put the decision up to the home-office nevertheless. Indeed, many successful agents who have a considerable measure of underwriting authority avail themselves of it as sparingly as possible, preferring to have the home-office pass upon business whenever that is practicable; and they are particularly desirous of following this course in the case of doubtful risks, partly because they thus evade responsiblility to a large extent for any subsequent misfortune, and partly because, if the bond is turned down, they stand better with their client by being able to point to their wicked partner at the home-office.

267. Get Together

More and more it is coming to be understood in all lines of business that even the keenest competition is compatible with cordial personal relations between the bloodthirsty competitors and with co-operative practices on their part of decided benefit to them and with no corresponding disadvantage to anybody. This is particularly true in the domain of insurance, and agents everywhere would do well to cultivate and sustain the get-together spirit. They should avail themselves of every opportunity to improve their relations with each other. Conferences of local representatives of competing companies should be arranged when new and troublesome questions arise, and everybody interested should participate actively in such conferences. Local associations should be formed, and luncheons should be arranged every month or so; and all members should attend such affairs and join heartily in their incidental features—

without, however, going so far as to land ultimately under the table.

Lady Randolph Churchill once gave in London what she called a "dinner of deadly enemies." She invited people known to be uncongenial in degrees ranging from mere instinctive aversion (such, for example, as a field-man naturally has at the start for a home-office personage) to violent abhorrence (such as he has after he really gets to know the man). Nevertheless, Lady Churchill's guests were all persons of tact and good manners. They recognized their obligation to their hostess. The humor of the situation was not lost upon them. Ancient grudges were allowed to slumber, animosities were subdued, asperities softened. The affair was a huge success. Insurance fieldmen would do well, if the conditions are anywhere so bad as that, to hold a dinner of deadly enemies, and to show diabolical ingenuity in seating next to each other (but with strong men near at hand) feudists of an extreme type.

Of course, all this is not to say that you should let up even a little bit in the strain for business. Go after it with a sportsman's ardor, but also with a sportsman's fairness. Look your competing neighbor in the eye, give him fair and sincere words—and then beat him to it!

This last bit of advice I know to be quite superfluous, and in giving it I remind myself of the lady on shipboard. She was a good sailor, but her husband was getting paler all the time, and he excused himself from going down to dinner, suggesting that she go with a friend near by. This friend was a very polite Frenchman, and when the lady asked him whether he had dined, he replied, "On the contrary, madame." "How distressing," she said, "I am afraid that my husband, too, is going to be seasick. Can you tell him something to do?" "It isn't necessary, madame, he'll do it anyway."

268. Insist upon Collateral in Proper Cases

One easy way in which agents may co-operate, with substantial benefit to themselves and to their companies, is by insisting upon the deposit of collateral security in 'the case of bonds that amount to pure financial guarantees. When the conditions are such that collateral security is known to be a reasonable requirement and essential to the safety of the surety company, agents should not try to play off one home-office against the other, but should get together and agree to compete for the business upon the equal and safe basis of collateral security. It is not always easy to do that, but it becomes easier with practice and it pays handsomely in the end. Just as some things, accordingly to Kipling, have to be proved to a man on his front teeth, so it seems necessary for surety underwriters, both in the field and at headquarters, to learn afresh, from time to time, upon the painful front pages of their red-ink records, the fact that financial-guarantee bonds cannot safely be written without collateral security. An agent, for example, sends in an application for an appeal bond from some local Croesus, with apologies for taking any application at all and with symptoms of apoplexy at the home-office suggestion of collateral. Indeed, the application bears out the agent, and shows a sinful condition of wealth; and the misguided home-office issues the bond without security, upon the agent's breathless insistence that a competitor has his pen lifted ready to sign the bond if the gift is foolishly cast aside. A year or two later the Carnefeller principal loses his case, and the surety company is commanded to pay the judgment at the earliest moment. The home-office notifies the agent, and watches the first mail for a check, and when it does not arrive, the financial statement is brought out for fresh examination. "Suffer-

ing Mike," says the underwriter, "no man could get
away with all this money in so short a time—no man,
nor even a woman." He bears up bravely while a few
more mails arrive in complete futility; and finally the
surety company pays out its good cash, and waits for
months and sometimes forever for Croesus to "come
across." That is no fairy tale—not in the least. Every
home-office has gone through such experiences more than
a few times.

I wish that when a bunch of agents are competing with
each other for one of these velvety, a-shame-to-take-the-
money propositions, they could all be blocked in the way
that the legislators of Kanbratexia had in mind when
they passed a certain law to prevent grade-crossing
accidents. Skeletonized, the precious statute read as
follows: "When two trains on different tracks approach
the same crossing, both trains shall come to a full stop,
and neither shall proceed until the other has passed by."
And that is what they call *progressive* legislation.

269. Importance of Diversifying One's Lines

The most successful insurance fieldmen have their
favorite lines of business (accident, liability, and so on),
and give them a disproportionate share of their time, but
they cast a sheet anchor to windward by placing on their
books at least some risks in various other departments.
They do this partly because they find that business of
any kind invariably breeds business of other kinds, and
partly because they wish to insure themselves against
temporary or permanent reverses in their specialties.
An example of the first advantage may be found in the
fact that the careful handling of a contract bond, say,
will often cause the grateful contractor to place his
liability or his accident insurance in the same office.

An example of the second benefit may be found in the experience of agents who have suffered through annihilating legislation a woeful and almost instantaneous loss of commissions, but who have been able to replace them within a moderate time with other lines of which a nucleus was already on their books.

I do not know of any better stabilizer of commission earnings than a large volume of bond business made up of items representing all the chief kinds of suretyship (fidelity, court, contract, depository, etc.), and distributed, as it naturally would be, over a broad field of clients. An agent with a backlog of business of this character will be successful under conditions that would overcome many less fortunate producers. Just as a large business enterprise finds it advantageous, if not quite essential, to integrate its operations—that is, to make itself independent of primary producers, and include among its own resources every kind of material and all processes embodied in the finished product—so the business of an insurance agent or broker must be similarly self-contained, and rest upon a broad base of underwriting equipment and capacity.

270. Co-operation between the Field and the Home-Office

The various kinds of co-operation on the part of fieldmen with each other advocated in preceding sections should be supplemented and reinforced by wholehearted team-work between fieldmen and their respective home-offices; and I am sure that home-office executives generally very earnestly desire to co-operate with the field. That is so, notwithstanding our frequent failures to get your point of view, our exasperating delays in caring for urgent matters, our rejection of business that seems to you good, and our unsatisfactory conduct generally. I still insist that we mean to back you up in all practicable ways. I realize that it takes a lot of faith on your part to believe that, but I hope that you have it. Anyway, you can hardly fail to believe in us a little when we come to you, or, better, when you come to the home-office. Lord Salisbury, you remember, was of the opinion that four men sitting around a table could settle any question; and you all know how often it has happened that you and the home-office have been able to get together and adjust quickly around a table questions that have been the subject of long and perhaps vexatious correspondence. The only trouble in such cases is that the parties get together because the home-office promptly walks around the table to the place where the fieldmen are sitting.

The way you gentlemen put things over on us innocent and unsuspecting home-office rubber stamps reminds me of Rufus Choate. That famous advocate is said never to have lost a case that he tried before a jury. Sometimes the lawyer on the other side would warn the jury in advance that they must not allow Mr. Choate to dethrone their reason with his eloquence; and they, knowing Choate's reputation, would take the advice in good part, and show by their self-satisfied manner that they intended not to let the wizard work his oratorical magic upon them. And then Mr. Choate would begin. Perhaps his client would have assaulted some peaceful old gentleman in broad daylight without provocation, or have forged a signature to a deed, or would otherwise seem to an ordinary man to have no case at all; but Mr. Choate would evolve some ingenious theory in accordance with which the assault or the forgery would be seen to be, when all the facts were developed and properly interpreted, only the natural and even the necessary acts of an upright and honorable citizen. It is said to have been better than a play or a ball game to watch those complacent jurymen as Mr. Choate would begin to operate upon them. First the smug expression of security would gradually fade away from one face after another. Then juror number four would begin to look anxious, and number seven to fidget uneasily, and number nine to cast appealing glances at the attorney, until finally every last one of the jurors would be swept away completely from his moorings of decision, and would be borne along helplessly upon the flood of the advocate's eloquence whithersoever the witchcraft voice listed.

271. A Typical "Piece of Velvet"

So, gentlemen, do you Rufus Choates of the field work your imperial will upon us home-office weaklings. How often has it happened with me that one of you has written in about some bond, describing the conditions briefly and saying that he would go into details orally upon his forthcoming visit to the home-office. Perhaps it would be some simply preposterous proposition—a lease bond, say, in the sum of $1,000,000 given jointly by a barber and a bootblack guaranteeing the payment of $100 a day rent for a thousand years—you needn't laugh; that isn't a circumstance to some that we get. I would say to myself upon receiving this letter, "Yes, Mr. Agent, you're a live wire and a good sport all right, but I'll see to it that you don't get by with this one." And then in a day or two Mr. Agent arrives, straight from Timbuktu, with all his ingratiating and disarming and seductive arts, and begins the Rufus Choate business. And pretty soon I begin to see a new light. He shows me with crystalline clearness that the tonsorial artist is another Carnegie, that the knight of the blacking

23

brush makes Rockefeller look like a pauper or even a
home-office surety man, that a thousand years is only a
clock tick, and that in short the whole proposition is one
of the most "velvety snaps" that ever fell in my way;
and at the end of the demonstration I can only gasp
feebly, "Of course, we'll write this million-dollar lease
bond, and without security, too—*that* would be absurd;
but would it be asking too much, do you think, if the
barber and the bootblack were to sign an application for
the bond?" He graciously assents to that, and the
incident is closed.

272. A Way to Wealth

After all the unkind remarks leveled at fieldmen in
this chapter, I feel called upon in this final section to
make amends. You have heard perhaps of the man who
proclaimed an infallible means of becoming a millionaire
at the age of thirty. "Be honest," he said. "Be
industrious. Be thorough. Be loyal. Never mis-
represent. Don't gamble. Don't drink. Save your
money. And then, when you arrive at the age of thirty
—find a woman with a million dollars and marry her."

I know a simpler formula than that, since I have
thought of a way in which all fieldmen can make a huge
fortune in thirty days only instead of thirty years.
The home-offices, also, will be benefited incidentally, as
is fitting in view of the brilliancy and extraordinary
intellectual resourcefulness shown by me in thinking up
the plan. Let me hasten to acquaint you with it, that
the thirty days may lapse the sooner, and Rockefellian
riches be yours forever.

I start out with the undeniable proposition that anybody can sell a bond on which the premium is $1. My
second equally obvious premise is that a $2, $4, or $8

bond may be sold with similar facility. In fact, expert agents know that it is often easier to sell big contracts of insurance to men of large affairs than it is to sell a small policy to a smaller man. This, then, is my world-beating and yet simple program—it flashed over me the other day as such things will with us geniuses. The first day you go out and secure a bond on which the premium is $1. The next day you get a $2 bond; the third day a $4 bond; the fourth day an $8 bond; and so on up to the thirtieth day. See? Simple as rolling off a log. Surely it is a small price to pay for the huge reward in plain sight—merely practicing, for thirty days only, the gentle and elevating art of procuring bond business.

When your minions have finished counting up your premiums at the end of thirty days, you will find that they amount to the tidy sum of one billion, seventy-three million, seven hundred and forty-one thousand, eight hundred and twenty-three dollars. That final figure of twenty-three rather mars my delirious joy over the thing. I am sorry it worked out that way—rather raises a question about the soundness of the entire proposition. I thought it all out so carefully, however, and every step in the reasoning process is so rigidly rooted in pure logic, that I cannot see how there can be any mistake. Indeed, it finally, as you saw, came down to a mere matter of mathematical computation, and if you doubt my figures, you can work it out for yourselves. I have given the problem all my spare time for the last month, getting a different answer and a headache every time, and I should enjoy seeing some other fellow tackle the job.

APPENDIX

TABULAR INDEX—FIRST AID TO AGENTS

273. Explanation of Table

The table comprising the next section lists about all the important kinds of bonds that commonly come up in the day's work, and provides at least a starting point in one's quest for information. The first column, entitled "Kind of Bond," gives the name by which the bond is commonly known ("administrator," "depository," etc.). A number occasionally appears in parentheses after the name, to identify the governmental form of bond in question. "Obl." in this column means *Obligee*, and "Prin.," *Principal*.

The second column, entitled "Classification," names the particular division of suretyship to which the bond belongs. The following abbreviations are used in this column: "Cus. H.," *Custom House;* "Fid.," *Fidelity;* "Fiduc.," *Fiduciary;* "Int. Rev.," *Internal Revenue;* "Lic. and Per.," *License and Permit;* "Misc. Sur.," *Miscellaneous Surety;* "Pub. Off.," *Public Official.*

The third column, entitled "Rate Manual Page," shows where the bond is treated in the General Manual published by the Towner Rating Bureau, or shows that it is treated only in the Public Official Manual of the Bureau. The column was correct when this book went to press, and presumably will remain correct or nearly so for an indefinite period, since the Rating Bureau means to maintain a permanent paging system. If, however, the rate should not be found at the place here indicated, the new page may be found at once by consulting the Manual Index.

The fourth column, entitled "Section Number in this Book," refers to the section where the bond is specifically treated, or where some other bond, resembling the given bond as to underwriting features, is so treated.

The final column, headed "Notes," guides the reader to the note following the table that contains general underwriting information about the given kind of bond. These notes are necessarily only rough generalizations. They are intended to show the fieldman how his home-office is likely to view the *class* of bonds to which his immediate risk belongs. His particular bond will always, of course, be far superior to the average risk of its class.

274. Tabular Index

Kind of Bond	Classifi-cation	Rate Manual Page	Section Number in this Book	Notes
Abatement (Deferred Tax)	Int. Rev.	113–1, 117	237	2
Abstractors..........	Lic. and Per.	88 etc.	220	4
Administrators.......	Fiduc.	38 etc.	173–174, 176–180	3
Admiralty............	Court	33 etc.	130	1
Advertising Signs.....	Lic. and Per.	88 etc.	220	4
Agents..............	Fid.	1, 6, 28	11–41	6
Agents, Real-Estate....	Lic. and Per.	88 etc.	220	14
Alcohol, Withdrawal of (1448)..............	Int. Rev.	118	217	12
Alien, Entry of (554 etc.)	Misc. Sur.	119	235	7
Almshouses..........	Fid.	11	11–41, 46	15
American Legion......	Fid.	11	43–45	24
Amusement Enterprises	Fid.	30	11–41	8
Annual Supply........	Contract	50–51, 66	148–149, 134–147	9
Appeal (Supersedeas)...	Court	32 etc.	128, 231	1, 29
Appearance (Bail).....	Court	33 etc.	117–118	1, 29
Armories (Use of)......	Misc. Sur.	78	223	11
Arrest................	Court	32 etc.	116	7
Assay Offices..........	Pub. Off.	107	87–106, 114	13
Assessors............	Pub. Off.	Pub.Off.Man'l	87–106	13
Assigned Accounts.....	Fid.	77b	11–41, 47	29, 30
Assignee for Benefit of Creditors..........	Fiduc.	36, 43 etc.	181	11
Asylums..............	Fid.	11	11–41, 46	15
Attachment, Plaintiff's	Court	32 etc.	121	9
Attachment,Defendant's	Court	32 etc.	122, 231	1, 29
Attorneys (Collections)	Fid.	14a	42	11
Automobile Conversion	Fid.	5a, 5b	241–250	21
Automobile Confiscation	Misc. Sur.	5b	275, Note 10	10
Automobile Companies	Fid.	5a	11–41	15
Auctioneers..........	Lic. and Per.	88 etc.	220	14
Awnings..............	Lic. and Per.	88 etc.	220	4
Bail.................	Court	33 etc.	117–118	1, 29
Bankers' Blanket......	Fid.	8a–10	70–86	17
Bankers' Trust Receipt	Misc. Sur.	61AA	239	27
Bankers, Private (Obl.)	Fid.	27a	11–41, 70–86	15
Bankers, Private (Prin.)	Fid.	27a, 27c	11–41, 226	7
Bankruptcy...........	Fiduc.	37	181–183	11
Banks (Obl.)..........	Fid.	6–10	11–41, 50, 70–86	15
Banks (Prin.).........	Depository	75–77	150–170	28
Beneficial Orders......	Fid.	17–20c	11–41, 43–45	16
Benevolent Associations	Fid.	11	11–41, 46	16
Bid..................	Contract	51 etc.	147, 134–146	29
Bill-board............	Lic. and Per.	88 etc.	220	4
Billiard-rooms.........	Lic. and Per.	88 etc.	220	4

TABULAR INDEX—*Continued*

Kind of Bond	Classification	Rate Manual Page	Section Number in this Book	Notes
Bill of Lading (Unavailable)	Misc. Sur.	82	236	17
Blanket Bonds	Fid.	8a–10	70–86	17
Blasting	Lic. and Per.	88 etc.	220	18
"Blue Sky"	Misc. Sur.	80	225	18
Board of Trade	Fid.	12	11–41	15
Bond and Stockbrokers	Fid.	9a, 30	11–41, 70–86	21
Bonded Warehouse (To Bd. of Trade, etc.)	Misc. Sur.	85–86	275, Note 19	19
Bonded Warehouse (3581)	Cus. H.	121	230	12
Bonded Warehouse (1435)	Int. Rev.	118	214	12
Bonded Warehouse (351)	Int. Rev.	113	214	12
Bookkeepers	Fid.	1	11–41	15
Boxing-Club Licenses	Lic. and Per.	88 etc.	223	11
Branch Managers	Fid.	1	11–41	8
Brewers (20)	Int. Rev.	117a–2	201	7
Brokers, Bond and Stock	Fid.	9a, 30	11–41, 70–86	21
Brokers' Blanket	Fid.	9–10	86, 70–85	21
Building and Loan Associations	Fid.	13	11–41	22
Building Permits	Lic. and Per.	88 etc.	220	4
Buyers	Fid.	2, 81	11–41	8
Canopies	Lic. and Per.	88 etc.	220	4
Canvassers	Fid.	6	11–41	5
Cartmen's License (3855)	Cus. H.	121 etc.	230	12
Cashiers	Fid.	1	11–41	15
Certiorari	Court	32 etc.	128, 231	1, 29
Chain Stores	Fid.	31	11–41	8
Chamber of Commerce	Fid.	12	11–41	15
Charitable Institutions	Fid.	11	11–41, 46	16
Charter Parties	Contract	60	134–146	7
Chattel-Loan Companies (Obl.)	Fid.	13	11–41, 46	8
Chattel-Loan Companies (Prin.)	Lic. and Per.	88 etc.	220	14
Cigar and Cigarette Manufacturers (71)	Int. Rev.	115	275, Note 20	20
Cigarette	Lic. and Per.	88 etc.	220, 228	4
Claimant of Seized Goods (4615)	Cus. H.	32	230	9
Clerk of Court	Pub. Off.	Pub. Off. Man'l	87–106, 113	13
Clubs	Fid.	29	11–41	8
Collateral-Trust Receipts	Misc. Sur.	61AA	239	27

TABULAR INDEX—*Continued*

Kind of Bond	Classifi-cation	Rate Manual Page	Section Number in this Book	Notes
Collection Agencies (Obl.)	Fid.	14a	42	11
Collection Agencies (Prin.)	Lic. and Per.	88	220	7
Collectors	Fid.	2	11–41	5
Collector's Indemnity (7581)	Cus. H.	121b	230	7
Collectors of Internal Revenue	Pub. Off.	108	87–106, 114	13
College Societies	Fid.	11	11–41	15
Commission Merchants	Misc. Sur.	81	220, 224	7
Commissioners, Sale of Real Estate	Court and Fiduc.	37, 43	184	11
Committees	Fiduc.	38 etc.	186, 189–192	3
Common Carriers (3587)	Cus. H.	121	230	11
Conservators	Fiduc.	38 etc.	186, 189–192	3
Consignees	Fid.	2	11–41	7
Constables	Pub. Off.	Pub.Off.Man'l	87–106, 111	21
Consumption Entry, Single (7551)	Cus. H.	121a	230	12
Consumption Entry, Term (7553)	Cus. H.	121a	230	12
Contract	Contract	47–74b	134–149	29
Convict Lease	Contract	60	134–146	2
Co-operative Companies	Fid.	15	11–41	6
Costs	Court	32 etc.	126	9
Cotton Compress	Fid.	15, 81	11–41, 224	21
Counter-Replevin	Court	32 etc.	124, 231	1, 29
County Treasurers	Pub. Off.	Pub.Off.Man'l	87–106, 107	13
County Clerks	Pub. Off.	Pub.Off.Man'l	87–106, 113	13
Curators (Guardians)	Fiduc.	38 etc.	186, 189–192	3
Cutting Timber	Contract	48, 70	134–149	2
Dealcoholizing Plants (1408)	Int. Rev.	117	203	7
Dealers in Leaf Tobacco (771)	Int. Rev.	115	275, Note 20	20
Debts and Legacies	Misc. Sur.	45	231, 233, 238	7
Decedents' Debts	Misc. Sur.	45	233	7
Denatured Alcohol (1462)	Int. Rev.	118	215	12
Denatured Alcohol (1480)	Int. Rev.	118	216	12
Department Stores	Fid.	16	11–41	15
Depository	Depository	75–77	150–170	28
Destroyed or Lost Securities	Misc. Sur.	84	240	7

Tabular Index—*Continued*

Kind of Bond	Classification	Rate Manual Page	Section Number in this Book	Notes
Detective License......	Lic. and Per.	88 etc.	220	14
Discharge of Attachment	Court	32 etc.	122, 231	1, 29
Discharge of Injunction	Court	32 etc.	120, 231	1, 29
Discharge of Lien......	Court	32 etc.	131, 231	1, 29
Discharge from Arrest..	Court	33 etc.	117–118	1, 29
Distillers (30 or 30½)....	Int. Rev.	117	201	12
Drain-Layers	Lic. and Per.	88 etc.	220	4
Druggists (1408).......	Int. Rev.	117	204	11
Electricians..........	Lic. and Per.	88 etc.	220	4
Elevators, Grain (Prin.)	Misc. Sur.	85–86	275, Note 19	19
Elevators, Grain (Obl.)	Fid.	21	11–41	6
Employment Agencies..	Lic. and Per.	88 etc.	220	14
Executive Officers.....	Fid.	1	11–41	16
Executors............	Fiduc.	38 etc.	175, 189–192	3
Explosives...........	Lic. and Per.	88 etc.	220	18
Exportation or Transportation, Single (7557).............	Cus. H.	121b	230	12
Exportation or Transportation, Term (7559)	Cus. H.	121b	230	12
Exporters (547–48 etc.)	Int. Rev.	114	205	9
Farmer's Co-operative Elevators..........	Fid.	21	11–41	6
Federal Reserve Banks.	Fid.	8a	11–41, 70–85	16
Fidelity Foreign Risks..	Fid.	3a	11–41, 66	21
Filled-Cheese Manufacturers (214).........	Int. Rev.	116	275, Note 32	21, 32
Financial Guarantees...	Misc. Sur.	62	231	1, 29
Flavoring Extracts (1408).............	Int. Rev.	117	212	9
Forthcoming..........	Court	32 etc.	122, 231	1, 29, 31
Franchise and Ordinance	Misc. Sur.	81	220	7
Fraternal Orders.......	Fid.	17–20c	43–45	24
Freight Charge........	Misc. Sur.	82	236	2
G. A. R. Posts.........	Fid.	11	43–45	24
Garnishment..........	Court	32 etc.	122, 231	1, 29, 31
Grain Elevators (Obl.)..	Fid.	21	11–41	6
Grain Elevators (Prin.).	Misc. Sur.	85–86	275, Note 19	19
Guarantee of Merchandise...............	Misc. Sur.	Not rated	234	7
Guardians...........	Fiduc.	38 etc.	186, 189–192	3
Hack-Drivers.........	Lic. and Per.	88 etc.	220	4
Hoisting.............	Lic. and Per.	88 etc.	220	4
Hospitals, Colleges, etc. (1448).............	Int. Rev.	118	207, 217	11
Hotels..............	Fid.	21	11–41	8

TABULAR INDEX—*Continued*

Kind of Bond	Classification	Rate Manual Page	Section Number in this Book	Notes
Hunters	Lic. and Per.	88 etc.	220	4
Immigrants (554 etc.)	Misc. Sur.	119	235	7
Importers' Warehousing (7555)	Cus. H.	121a	230	7
Income Tax (Deferred Payment)	Int. Rev.	113–1, 117	237	2
Industrial Alcohol (1432)	Int. Rev.	118	213	12
Injunction, Defendant's	Court	32 etc.	120, 231	1, 29
Injunction, Plaintiff's	Court	32 etc.	119	7
Insurance Companies (Bonded Staff)	Fid.	22–25	11–41, 50	33
Insurance Companies (Qualifying)	Misc. Sur.	83	227	29
Jewelers	Fid.	26	11–41	21
Jitney-Cars	Lic. and Per.	83a etc.	220–221	7
Junk Dealers	Lic. and Per.	88 etc.	220	4
Labor Unions	Fid.	26	11–41	8
Laundry Companies	Fid.	31	11–41	8
Law-List Companies	Fid.	14a	42	11
Leaf-Tobacco Dealers (771)	Int. Rev.	115	275, Note 20	20
Lease	Misc. Sur.	64	231	1, 29
Legatees (Refunding)	Misc. Sur.	45	238	7
Lenders' (Lien Bonds)	Misc. Sur.	65	232	7
Letter-Carriers	Pub. Off.	111	114	4
Libel, Release of	Admiralty	33	130, 231	1, 29
Lien, to Forestall One against Building or Improvement	Misc. Sur.	65	232	7
Lien, to Release Known Lien	Court	32 etc.	131, 231	1, 29
Lien on Plant (3)	Int. Rev.	113	219	7
Liquidators	Court	36	181–184	11
Loan Offices	Fid.	13	11–41, 46	6
Local Lodges	Fid.	17–20c	43–45	24
Lost Securities	Misc. Sur.	84	240	7
Lumber Companies	Fid.	26	11–41	8
Maintenance	Contract	54 etc.	134–149	29
Managers	Fid.	1	11–41	15
Managers, Warehouses	Fid.	90	11–41, 48	6
Manufacturers of Cider (1408)	Int. Rev.	117	202	7
Manufacturers of Wine (1408)	Int. Rev.	117	210	7
Marshals	Pub. Off.	110, 111	87–106, 111	21
Marshal's Indemnity	Court	33 etc.	127	9

TABULAR INDEX—*Continued*

Kind of Bond	Classifi-cation	Rate Manual Page	Section Number in this Book	Notes
Masters (to Sell Real Estate)............	Court	37, 43	184	11
Mechanics' Lien.......	Misc. Sur.	65	131, 231	7
Milk Dealers.........	Lic. and Per.	84a	220, 229	2
National Guard.......	Fid.	27	11–41	16
Non-Beverage Alcohol (1408).............	Int. Rev.	117–118 etc.	200, 202–204, 206–212	7
Notary Public........	Pub. Off.	Pub. Off. Man'l	113, 220	4
Oil and Gas Leases.....	Misc. Sur.	64	222	7
Oleomargarine Manu-facturers (214)......	Int. Rev.	116	275, Note 32	21, 32
Open Estates........	Misc. Sur.	45	233	7
Opening or Obstructing Streets.........	Lic. and Per.	88 etc.	220	4
Orders, Fraternal.....	Fid.	17–20c	43–45	24
Patent Infringements...	Misc. Sur.	66	231	18
Pawnbrokers.........	Lic. and Per.	13, 88 etc.	220	14
Peddlers, Tobacco (111)	Int. Rev.	115	275, Note 20	20
Permanent Exhibition (7565)............	Cus. H.	121b	230	18
Petitioning Creditors...	Court	32 etc.	132	11
Pistol-Toting.........	Lic. and Per.	88 etc.	220	11
Plumbers............	Lic. and Per.	88 etc.	220	4
Post Office Staff......	Pub. Off.	111	114	4
Private Bankers (Obl.).	Fid.	27a	11–41, 70–86	15
Private Bankers (Prin.).	Fid.	27a, 27c	11–41, 226	7
Proposal............	Contract	51 etc.	147, 134–146	29
Public Administrators..	Pub. Off.	46	87–106, 173–174	21
Public Buildings, Use of	Misc. Sur.	78	223	11
Public-Service Corpora-tions..............	Fid.	28	11–41	15
Purchasing Agents.....	Fid.	2, 81	11–41	8
Pure Food and Drugs Act	Court	33	117, 122	2, 29
Railroad and Steamship Lines.............	Fid.	151–159	11–41	26
Railway Mail Clerks...	Pub. Off.	111	87–106, 114	21
Real Estate Agents.....	Fid.	1, 6, 28	11–41	6
Real Estate Brokers....	Lic. and Per.	88 etc.	220	14
Receivers............	Fiduc.	36 etc.	182–183	11
Rectifiers (1408).......	Int. Rev.	117	208	7
Redelivery (Counter-replevin)...........	Court	32 etc.	124, 231	1, 29
Referee in Bankruptcy..	Fiduc.	110	181–184	11
Refunding...........	Misc. Sur.	45	238	7
Release of Libel.......	Admiralty	33 etc.	130, 231	1, 29
Reindemnifying.......	Pub. Off.	Pub. Off. Man'l	96–99	7

TABULAR INDEX—*Continued*

Kind of Bond	Classification	Rate Manual Page	Section Number in this Book	Notes
Removal of Cause.....	Court	33 etc.	125	9
Renovated-Butter Manufacturers (214).....	Int. Rev.	116	275, Note 32	31, 32
Replevin (Plaintiff's)...	Court	32 etc.	123	9
Return of Property....	Misc. Sur.	80	223	23
Safe-Deposit Companies	Fid.	6-10	11-41	15
Salary Loan Offices.....	Fid.	13	11-41, 46	8
Salesmen............	Fid.	2	11-41	5
Sanitariums (1408).....	Int. Rev.	117	207, 217	9
Screen-Wagons........	Contract	"74 U. S. Mail"	134-147	25
Second-Hand Dealers..	Lic. and Per.	88 etc.	220	14
Sewer-Tappers.......	Lic. and Per.	88 etc.	220	4
Sheriffs..............	Pub. Off.	Pub. Off. Man'l	87-106, 111	21
Sheriff's Indemnity....	Court	33 etc.	127	9
Sidewalks............	Contract	69 etc.	134-149	29
Signs................	Lic. and Per.	88 etc.	220	4
Six-Months (7563)......	Cus. H.	121b	230	18
Snuff Manufacturers (71)	Int. Rev.	115	275, Note 20	20
Social Clubs..........	Fid.	29	11-41	15
Specially Denatured Alcohol (1475).......	Int. Rev.	113, 118	215-216	12
Star-Route..........	Contract	"74 U. S. Mail"	134-147	25
Stay of Execution......	Court	32 etc.	128, 231	1, 29
Steamship and Railway Lines............	Fid.	151-159	11-41	26
Steamship Ticket-Agents	Fid.	29	11-41	6
Steamship Ticket-Agents and Bankers.......	Fid.	27a, 27c	11-41, 226	7
Stipulation for Costs...	Court	32 etc.	126	9
Stock and Bond Brokers..........	Fid.	9a, 30	11-41, 70-86	21
Storing Explosives.....	Lic. and Per.	88 etc.	220	18
Street-Opening or Obstruction..........	Lic. and Per.	88 etc.	220	4
Supersedeas..........	Court	32 etc.	128, 231	1, 29
Supply..............	Contract	50-51, 66	148-149, 134-147	9
Tax-Collectors.......	Pub. Off.	Pub. Off. Man'l	87-106, 109	21
Temporary Importation (7563).............	Cus. H.	121b	230	18
Theatre License	Lic. and Per.	88 etc.	220	4
Theatrical Companies..	Fid.	30	11-41	8
Ticket-Agents........	Fid.	29	11-41	6
Timber-Cutting.......	Contract	48, 70	134-149	2
Tobacco Manufacturers (40).............	Int. Rev.	115	275, Note 20	20
Tobacco Peddlers (111).	Int. Rev.	115	275, Note 20	20

TABULAR INDEX—*Concluded*

Kind of Bond	Classifi-cation	Rate Manual Page	Section Number in this Book	Notes
Trucks (1408)	Int. Rev.	117	209	7
Trustees	Fiduc.	36 etc.	188–192	3
Tutors	Fiduc.	38 etc.	186, 189–192	3
Vessel, Single (7567)	Cus. H.	121b	230	11
Vessel, Term (7569)	Cus. H.	121b	230	11
Warehouse Custodians .	Fid.	15, 21	11–41, 48	6
Warehouse (Prin. to Bd. of Trade, etc.)	Misc. Sur.	85–86	275, Note 19	19
Warehouse (3581, 3583)	Cus. H.	121	230	12
Warehouse (351)	Int. Rev.	113	214	12
Warehouse (1435)	Int. Rev.	118	214	12
Warehousing, Importers' (7555)	Cus. H.	121a	230	7
Wine Dealers (1408)	Int. Rev.	117	211	9
Wine Manufacturers (1408)	Int. Rev.	117	210	7
Withdrawal of Alcohol (1448)	Int. Rev.	118	217	12
Workmen's Compen-sation	Fid.	25a	11–41	15
Workmen's Compensa-tion and Employers' Liability	Misc. Sur.	72	227, 231	2
Writ of Error	Court	32 etc.	128, 231	1, 29
Writ of Prohibition	Court	32 etc.	119	7

275. Notes Accompanying Tabular Index

1. These bonds are deemed financial guarantees (section 231) and are commonly issued only in connection with collateral security (section 6).

2. These bonds are deemed financial guarantees (section 231) and are commonly written only in connection with collateral security (section 6) or otherwise only in behalf of exceptionally responsible principals.

3. These bonds are deemed desirable business when issued in behalf of principals of good character. Joint control (sections 189–192) is frequently necessary or desirable.

4. These bonds are written freely, and upon an insurance basis (section 3) for the most part.

5. Most surety companies prefer not to write under any conditions certain classes of bonds, and they make up accordingly what they call

their "Prohibited List"—a statement of these undesired and black-listed risks. Surety classifications are sometimes embodied in the lists, but the prohibition applies particularly to fidelity bonds, since almost any surety bond, however monstrous its condition, would be issuable for a responsible principal or with adequate collateral. There are some classes of fidelity bonds, however, with which it is hardly worth while to bother, because no premium that the traffic will bear would cover acquisition costs, losses, and claim expenses; that is, it is clear at the outset that the bonds cannot be prudently written without a thorough investigation, that a large proportion of rejections are inevitable from the nature of the case, and that the paltry premium obtainable will by no means justify the necessary expenditure. Sewing-machine agents, book-canvassers, and commission salesmen in general are examples of these impracticable fidelity risks. The only way to treat these cases is to charge a big premium, and especially to prescribe an adequate investigation fee in the case of each applicant, payable in any event, whether or not the applicant is bonded. Such an arrangement is fair to the surety company, which would otherwise more than exhaust its premium in futile investigation expenses before any loss fund could be accumulated; and it is fair to the employer, because he can well afford to pay a small investigation fee rather than take into his service somebody so untrustworthy as not to be bondable.

6. These bonds are deemed rather dangerous, but are writable, after thorough investigation, for principals of excellent standing.

7. These bonds call for thoroughgoing investigation and exceptionally careful underwriting. Collateral security is sometimes in order.

8. These bonds are not deemed particularly desirable, but are written by most companies when the investigation uncovers no specially adverse conditions.

9. These bonds are written rather freely in behalf of reputable and strong business concerns or individual principals.

10. These bonds would seem on general principles to constitute excellent business; and in some parts of the country (the Pacific Coast, for example) the experience has been good. Difficulties have arisen, however, over claim adjustments in cases where the illegal use of the bonded cars seems to have been contemplated by the obligee from the beginning and to have inspired the purchase of the protection.

11. These bonds are written rather freely, as they are commonly called for by reputable and responsible principals.

12. These bonds are written rather freely, without collateral security,

when required by business concerns of good standing. Otherwise collateral is in order.

13. These bonds are written rather freely, for principals of at least fair standing, in accordance with the principles of official underwriting outlined in Chapters VIII and IX.

14. Though these bonds are classified as "License Bonds," they are not on that account to be lightly regarded. Usually they run in favor of the public and virtually guarantee the right conduct of the principal. Claims are probable in the case of unscrupulous principals. Security is commonly unobtainable, and in its absence the suretyship should be provided only for principals of excellent business standing.

15. These bonds are written freely, for the most part, but in accordance with the principles of fidelity underwriting set out in Chapters II–IV.

16. These bonds are deemed exceptionally desirable, and are written freely, for the most part, in accordance with the principles of fidelity underwriting set out in Chapters II–IV.

17. These bonds are eagerly sought by the companies, generally speaking, notwithstanding the fact that the business thus far has not proved particularly profitable.

18. These bonds are deemed highly hazardous, and are commonly written only in connection with collateral security (section 6), or otherwise only in behalf of exceptionally responsible principals.

19. Warehouse bonds of several varieties, and similar grain-elevator bonds, virtually guarantee the validity of the documents evidencing the storage of the given merchandise. Theoretically such bonds would seem to be highly hazardous, and that is doubtless true in some cases. Frequently, however, the warehouses and elevators are operated under regulations refined to the last degree of efficiency and safety, so that error or fraud is well-nigh impossible. Moreover, the principals upon these bonds are likely to be concerns of the highest reputation and responsibility.

20. These bonds, conditioned for compliance with the law, are not deemed particularly hazardous, and they are written freely in behalf of principals supposed to be at least fairly reputable citizens and of a financial responsibility reasonably commensurate with the amount of the bond.

21. These bonds are deemed highly hazardous and are on the "Prohibited List" of some companies.

22. These bonds are highly acceptable as a class because they or-

dinarily concern small, local organizations, and because the persons bonded are likely to be well and favorably known, the money contributed is quickly paid out to borrowers, and only an honesty bond is expected. In two classes of cases, however, these bonds call for thorough investigation and expert underwriting—when a statutory form of bond is prescribed involving much more than a mere honesty hazard, and when the organization is not local and small in scope, but has thousands of shareholders and is run largely along banking lines, but without the safeguards incident to ordinary banking operations. In this latter case these associations sometimes become "one-man" institutions, and huge defalcations occur.

23. These bonds are written rather freely and without collateral when moderate in amount and required by reputable and responsible principals (e.g., arms, equipment, etc.); but the same bond is sometimes given under conditions necessitating collateral or unquestionable indemnity.

24. These bonds are written freely with little or no investigation except when the amounts are large, because the principals are likely, from the nature of the case, to be exceptionally trustworthy.

25. These bonds are on the "Prohibited List" of many companies. With what distrust they are regarded by underwriters is indicated by the fact that out of approximately 11,000 star-route and screen-wagon contracts in process of performance in March, 1922, only about one-quarter were bonded by corporate sureties. While the Post Office Department would doubtless have preferred to receive corporate bonds, it was forced to put up with personal sureties in the case of three-fourths of the contracts.

26. Competition for the fidelity bonds of the transportation companies has always been so keen that the business is no longer deemed particularly desirable, except perhaps for the sake of its incidental advertising and prestige benefits. In the case of strong lines, however, the judicial bonds required from the carrier in the course of its litigation sometimes make the business profitable as a whole. In the case of weak lines this latter incident of the arrangement is a liability and an embarrassment.

27. These bonds seem rather dubious to some underwriters, but they are written by a number of companies.

28. These bonds are eagerly sought by the companies, generally speaking. Difficult underwriting problems arise, however, in the case of small banks in many parts of the country and in the case of both large and small banks in some parts of the country.

24

29. These bonds are highly hazardous as a class and call for particularly careful underwriting.

30. These bonds are now written rarely, if ever. To underwriters experienced with them they look like the man described by Mr. George Ade as "a Cream Puff that should have been Served Day before Yesterday."

31. Forthcoming bonds are often the same as bonds to discharge an attachment; but the term is variously used in different jurisdictions. Garnishment bonds are required from plaintiffs who attach property in the hands of third parties.

32. Manufacturers of oleomargarine and similar products must file a bond conditioned that the principal will not defraud the government of any taxes, will render true inventories and returns, will affix caution notices to his products before removal from the place of manufacture, and will otherwise comply with the law. These bonds are deemed abnormally hazardous. Oleomargarine may be made to look like butter, consistently with the law, but a tax of 10 cents a pound is imposed on such a product. Uncolored oleomargarine, however, is taxed only a quarter of a cent a pound. Many losses have been sustained on these bonds because principals have sold the colored product as butter rather than as oleomargarine, paying no tax and omitting from the package the prescribed labels and caution marks.

33. Ordinary fidelity bonds are commonly desired by insurance companies covering their home-office staffs, field managers, traveling representatives, and local agents. These bonds vary in value with the nature of the insurance business conducted, with the size and general organization of the company, and with other conditions. Certain states have enacted laws requiring the officers of insurance companies to give bonds conditioned for the faithful performance of their official duties. These bonds are more hazardous than ordinary instruments because the insuring clause must embody, without qualification or condition, the broad words of the statute (they will be read into the bond if a foolish attempt is made to keep them out), and because all sorts of unexpected opportunities for loss may thus develop (cf. section 50). ✓

CPSIA information can be obtained
at www.ICGtesting.com
Printed in the USA
BVHW030925021118
R9314600001B/R93146PG531298BVX1B/1/P